GOOD INTENTIONS
CORRUPTED

GOOD INTENTIONS CORRUPTED

THE OIL-FOR-FOOD PROGRAM AND THE THREAT TO THE U.N.

JEFFREY A. MEYER

AND

MARK G. CALIFANO

WITH AN INTRODUCTION BY

Paul A. Volcker

PUBLICAFFAIRS

New York

Published in the United States by PublicAffairs™, a member of the Perseus Books Group.

Library of Congress Cataloging-in-Publication Data
Good intentions corrupted : the Oil-for-Food Program and the threat to the U.N. / edited
by Jeffrey A. Meyer and Mark G. Califano ; introduction by Paul A. Volcker.
p. cm.
Includes index.
ISBN–13: 978–1–58648–472–9
ISBN–10: (invalid) 1–58648–472–9
1. United Nations. Oil-for-Food Program. 2. United Nations. Oil-for-Food Program—
Corrupt practices. 3. Humanitarian assistance—Iraq. 4. Food relief—Iraq. 5. Economic
sanctions—Iraq. 6. Petroleum industry and trade—Iraq. I. Meyer, Jeffrey A.. II. Califano,
Mark G.
JZ6373.G66 2006
956.7044'3—dc22
2006049379

FIRST EDITION

10 9 8 7 6 5 4 3 2 1

CONTENTS

Introduction by Paul A. Volcker:

The United Nations at Risk

I was a student full of idealism when the United Nations was founded. Its foremost member, the United States, had emerged victorious and unchallenged as leader of a war-shattered world. Like so many of my generation of Americans, I knew that we must reject a return to isolationism and avoid the temptation of unilateral interventionism. Instead, our vision was one of *collective* security with our allies (and soon with former enemies). There would be a shared responsibility to settle peacefully disputes among nations large and small and to help build the economic and social foundation for democracy and human rights. Those would be the ideals of the United Nations Organization.

Now, a half century and more later, these ideals have led to practical success. At crucial points, the UN has acted to turn back naked aggression. It has helped resist nuclear proliferation. It has averted famines and ameliorated the plight of millions of refugees.

But reality has intruded on the idealistic vision. After more than fifty years in and out of public service, I've had plenty of opportunity to observe first-hand the frustration of good intentions—seemingly endless debate among UN member states, too much narrow self-interest, missed opportunities, corruption, and grand vision lost amid political impasse and administrative ineptitude.

I believe that the UN today is stranded at a critical crossroad.

The path ahead inexorably leads to large responsibilities for global security. Yet the Organization lacks the ways and means to travel that path with confidence and necessary support. Certainly, as I consider the UN's record, three conclusions seem inescapable.

First, the challenges foreseen by the UN's founders may shift in emphasis but persist in full force. They are, in fact, intensified by the revolution in technology and globalization:

- The threat of nuclear proliferation, for all the past efforts to limit the spread of nuclear weapons, is now more acute than ever;

- Terrorism, now increasingly international in scale, has become a central fact of life;

- Monstrous genocidal acts, far from receding into history, still occur, as in the Darfur region of the Sudan;

- The great Indian Ocean tsunami and the alarming rise in global warming signify the enormous and not fully anticipated challenges posed by irresistible forces of nature.

Secondly, in response to those and other challenges, the UN has become, of necessity, more operational rather than simply a forum for discussions among member states. It spends billions of dollars and manages complex enterprises. There are peacekeeping forces in eighteen countries today, large programs to promote economic development, permanent organizations to address disaster relief and refugees, specialized programs to deal with health, food, environment, and other areas that, by their nature, demand coordinated, multilateral responses.

Finally, as the responsibilities assumed by—or forced upon— the UN have increased, grievous weaknesses in managerial and administrative capacity have become evident. As a result, the whole enterprise lies at risk.

We, in the United States or wherever, simply cannot have it both ways: calling upon the UN to respond to large challenges while failing to insist upon the management capacity and integrity to meet those responsibilities.

All these factors—historic humanitarian challenges, unprecedented operational burdens, and abysmal administrative failures— were all reflected and revealed in the Oil-for-Food Program.

This small volume brings the evidence and the lessons from that Program to a broader public. It has been prepared in the conviction that the challenges cited—and others sure to come—demand a response from the international community. But if the UN is to be a useful, indeed an essential part of that response, then there can be no escape from the need for thorough administrative reform of the Organization.

WHY THE UNITED NATIONS?

The United States is strong, standing alone in the world in military force, first in economic performance and innovation, and convinced of the validity and relevance for all of principles of democracy, freedom, and human rights to which we aspire. Those are words that could have been written as easily in 1945. But now, as then, words alone—even the United States alone—cannot meet challenges that are intrinsically international. Matters of mutual security, the peaceful settlement of disputes, economic development, respect for human rights and international law by nature extend beyond the competence and capacity of any one country. And if that is true, the response also requires that relevant institutions be ready and able to act effectively.

That is the logic of the UN and its affiliated agencies. That Organization, founded at the end of a devastating war, now encompasses all sovereign nations that, by their membership, are committed to cooperation in a common cause. It confers legitimacy to action unique in world affairs.

For that concept to bear fruit, there is a further requirement. Willing cooperation and a sense of legitimacy cannot be sustained without a strong sense that the Organization has both competence and integrity. It is precisely those qualities that have been called into question by the UN's administration of the Oil-for-Food Program.

As things stand, critics have cast corrosive doubt on the honesty and effectiveness of the Organization, undermining its public support, its ability to maintain funding, and its capacity to react promptly and forcefully to new global challenges. That is why the lessons of the Oil-for-Food Program remain so relevant for all those that, like me, hope to see the UN able to meet the responsibilities thrust upon it.

THE INVESTIGATION OF
THE OIL-FOR-FOOD PROGRAM

The Oil-for-Food Program, launched with the best of intentions, was an ingenious effort to reconcile strong sanctions against the regime of Saddam Hussein with maintaining minimum standards of health and nutrition for the Iraqi people. Conceived as a temporary project, the Program lasted seven years, from 1996 until the American-led invasion of Iraq in 2003. Ultimately, some $110 billion dollars of sales of Iraqi oil and purchases of "humanitarian goods" were involved, all under UN surveillance. It was, by far, the largest humanitarian program undertaken by the UN, with the largest administrative and financial responsibilities.

Almost from the start, questions arose about the design of the

Program and its administration. With the passage of time, reports of illicit "surcharges" and "kickbacks" spread, allegations of administrative failures surfaced, and strong charges of corruption within the UN itself were pressed by those long critical of the institution.

In the spring of 2004, those facts, rumors, and allegations finally led UN Secretary-General Kofi Annan to initiate a thorough review of the management of the Program, his personal responsibilities, and the performance of the many private contractors. That initiative, confirmed and supported by the Security Council, resulted in the appointment of the *Independent Inquiry Committee into the UN Oil-for-Food Program.* I served as Chairman, with two highly experienced and strong-minded colleagues.

The Committee analysis and conclusions have been detailed in five Committee Reports totaling well over two thousand pages. To the specialist, they make fascinating reading, with full documentation of findings. Those Reports, in all their detail and supporting notes, cannot, however, be easily digested by the general public. This volume, prepared by two of the experienced investigators participating in the Committee's work, is designed to deal with that problem by providing a concise, accurate, and readable summary of the reports and their conclusions.

I have welcomed this new publication for a simple reason. The findings, conclusions, and recommendations of the Committee Reports deserve the widest possible attention and understanding because the evidence set out, of the need for administrative reform of the UN Organization, is indisputable.

The Oil-for-Food Program in key respects was unique. It was undertaken not because of a natural disaster, a lack of national resources, or an economic breakdown. Rather, its purpose was to alleviate the effects on the Iraqi population of the former Iraqi regime's response to comprehensive sanctions imposed by the UN itself on the Saddam Hussein regime. Without precedent in its complexity, it turned out to be the largest effort to provide humanitarian relief in the history of the UN Organization—or perhaps of any organization. It involved in its administration not only the central Secretariat and the Security Council, but nine other UN-related agencies as well. Altogether thousands of employees—mostly newly hired—were based in Iraq, living under difficult conditions and reporting both to a newly-formed Secretariat office in New York and to various agency headquarters.

In the circumstances, it is perhaps not surprising that the investigation identified and disclosed serious lapses in administrative discipline, a confusion of responsibilities, and, sadly, even evidence of corruption within the UN. In the process, it became evident that something more is at stake.

The difficulties encountered—the managerial weaknesses, the failures to accept responsibility, the ethical lapses—are symptomatic of systemic problems running through the UN Organization. They are also symptomatic of the willingness of too many businesses engaged in international trade to accede to demands for illicit payments and of too many countries to turn a blind eye to those practices.

The Committee's main conclusions with respect to the UN itself are unambiguous. The Organization requires thorough administrative reform, stronger executive leadership, more effective controls, and auditing.

Almost without exception, similar conclusions have been reached by others reviewing UN operations. What the Committee's Reports have done is to provide the evidence—the hard facts and the detailed analysis—that underlie and support those conclusions.

What has been lacking, even now, is the will to act—to act forcefully and effectively not just to repair the more glaring lapses but to make more fundamental and lasting reform.

The Committee concluded its report on the management of the Program with a simple admonition: "What is at stake [in the reform effort] is the United Nations' ability to respond promptly and effectively to the responsibilities thrust upon it by the realities of a turbulent and often violent world. In the last analysis, that ability rests upon the Organization's credibility—on maintaining a widely-held perception among member states and their populations of its competence, honesty, and accountability. It is precisely those qualities that too often were absent in the administration of the Oil-for-Food Program."

Now, almost a year later, some useful internal administrative reforms have been made. However, other proposed reforms of more fundamental importance have been held in abeyance or shoved aside, a reflection of the chronic inability of the Organization to change entrenched behavior.

As a consequence, the administrative capacity of the UN remains weak—far too weak to meet the demands the international community may reasonably place upon it. In the end, it is its member states and the world community that have been placed at risk.

THE ORGANIZATION OF THE INQUIRY

In March 2004 the Secretary-General of the United Nations, Kofi Annan, asked me to chair the three-person committee established to fully review the UN's management of the Oil-for-Food Program. The invasion and occupation of Iraq had ended the need for the Program, but charges were being widely aired in the media that raised serious questions about the internal operations of the UN, including the possibility of corruption as well as maladministration, touching upon the Secretary-General himself.

I was well aware that important issues bearing on the integrity and effectiveness of the UN had been raised in increasingly shrill tones in some U.S. Congressional quarters as well as in the press. However, the rationale for my involvement in any investigation was not obvious.

Certainly I was, and am, among those who believe that the United Nations has a unique and potentially constructive role to play in world affairs. However, my personal involvement had been limited, as was my experience in investigations.

A decade earlier, at the request of the then Secretary-General, Mr. Boutros Boutros-Ghali, I had co-chaired an international advisory group of financial experts to review methods of UN funding, then under heavy pressure particularly from the United States. Looking back, I recalled that group, while focusing on finance, had expressed substantial doubts about the management practices and effectiveness of the UN. In its conclusion, it emphasized the need for the UN Organization to instill greater confidence in its administrative capacity and discipline if member states were to provide adequate funding.

When the Secretary-General persisted in his efforts to recruit me, I thus had an instinctive understanding of the issues and emphasized several key points to him. A thorough investigation of the Oil-for-Food Program would require a sizable professional staff. It would take at least a year. It would be costly, both in terms of money and in highly intrusive demands for official records and communications, including his own.

Success, in any event, would be dependent on the perception and reality of absolute independence in staffing and investigative approaches. Committee conclusions and analysis would need to be made public in their entirety. Adequate financing would need to be assured "up front."

Beyond the Secretary-General's personal reassurance in those respects, I thought it crucially important that the Security Council itself provide authority for the "Inquiry" and call upon all member states, as well as all UN staff and organizations, for their full cooperation and support. The need for a formal resolution was a matter of some controversy, but agreement was reached in the Security Council rather promptly on a satisfactory language explicitly calling upon all member states and their agencies to cooperate with the inquiry.

In the meantime, I had discussed these arrangements with two other members of the Committee proposed by the Secretary-General. One, Richard Goldstone, was a recently retired justice of the highest court of South Africa. Ten years earlier, Justice Goldstone had led an investigation, under most difficult circumstances, of charges of corruption and brutality by the South African police and army as the apartheid regime ended. Given his subsequent responsibilities as Chief Prosecutor of the International Criminal Tribunals for the former Yugoslavia and in Rwanda, and his high standing in the international law and human rights community, there could be no doubt that Justice Goldstone brought both relevant experience and personal strength to the proposed Committee.

The third potential Committee member, Mark Pieth, was unknown to me, but I soon learned of his uniquely relevant and valuable background. Professor Pieth, from his base at the University of Basel, had a well-established reputation as one of the world's leading experts on money laundering and corporate corruption; he has, in fact, been the driving force in developing and overseeing the work of the Organization for Economic Cooperation and Development (OECD) in encouraging its members to adopt legislation and other means of cooperation to curb bribery and other corrupt practices in international business. He was well known to Swiss authorities with whom he had long worked in various capacities, helping greatly in facilitating cooperation with those officials as the investigation proceeded.

Reassured by the strong qualifications of the proposed Committee members, with an adequate Security Council Resolution, and with transitional funding in hand, I agreed to chair the newly established *Independent Inquiry Committee into the United Nations Oil-for-Food Program*. The clear understanding was that we would have full independence, operate with our own professional staff outside UN offices, and be free to make whatever recommendations we felt appropriate. For his part, the Secretary-General emphasized the need that the Inquiry be truly international in form and spirit, a point with which the Committee was in full agreement.

The Inquiry came to occupy increasing amounts of my time over the next eighteen months. The first organizational efforts were assisted by a few old "comrades in arms" who, among other things, were willing to reconnoiter in Baghdad and establish contact with both Iraqi and occupation authorities. A highly experienced investigator, Stephen Zimmermann, was borrowed for a few weeks from the InterAmerican Development Bank to help recruit staff and plan the investigation. A respected senior forensic accountant, Frank Hydoski, was lured out of retirement all the way from San Diego and provided invaluable judgment as well as great professional skill throughout the investigation.

It was not so easy to find a capable, widely respected, and experienced chief of staff ready to accept the professional risks as well as the challenge. With the Committee decision to stay broadly within UN salary scales, there could be little salary incentive. Fortunately, a bit of serendipity intervened. A Canadian friend proposed a different tack—not a professional investigator but a person with broad administrative, diplomatic, and governmental experience, someone who might be intrigued by the challenge. Mr. Reid Morden had long been one of Canada's most senior and respected civil servants, serving in succession as Director of the Canadian Security Intelligence Service, as Deputy Foreign Minister, and as President and CEO of Atomic Energy of Canada Limited. After leaving government, he had been associated with private security and intelligence organizations. As Executive Director, he clearly brought to the Inquiry relevant experience, a really unique combination of skills, and a sense of authority that was invaluable.

With those key positions in place, the top investigative positions could be quickly filled, drawing on experienced prosecuting attorneys, investigators, and forensic accountants from around the world. In the end, the Inquiry had a professional staff of more than seventy people, drawn from twenty-eight countries, with more than half citizens of countries other than the United States. It was a remarkable, diverse, and international group working long hours, united in the conviction that they were doing important work.

THE DESIGN OF THE PROGRAM

The Oil-for-Food Program was developed and designed in response to a recurrent dilemma in collective efforts to discipline an "outlaw" state. Diplomatic and political approaches can be brought to bear, but may, and often do, lack sufficient force. At the other extreme, military force carries the potential of wide-spread destruction, enormous uncertainties, and unintended consequences. Given those realities, sanctions, in the form of restraints on trade, are seized upon as a means of bridging the gap between diplomacy and force. However, broadly applied, such sanctions may result in great damage to an innocent population before they succeed in changing the policies of the governing regime.

That is precisely what happened in the case of the comprehensive sanctions placed on Iraq at the time of its invasion of Kuwait in 1990 and maintained after the Gulf War. Those sanctions were to continue pending firm evidence, which was not forthcoming at that time, of the absence of weapons of mass destruction and facilities to produce them. Without oil sales and the consequent scarcity of foreign exchange for food and medical supplies, reports of increasing malnutrition, rising infant mortality, and other health problems in Iraq became a source of humanitarian concern within the UN and among its member states.

In undertaking its investigation, the Committee engaged some of the world's leading experts to review the available evidence with respect to the nutrition and health of the Iraqi population during the period the sanctions were in effect. Their report essentially concluded that by the mid–1990s, nutritional standards were indeed approaching a point of crisis and that public health had seriously deteriorated.

The Oil-for-Food Program, in principle, would ease the dilemma. Limited amounts of oil exports would be permitted under UN surveillance, with the proceeds deposited in escrow accounts. Those funds would be available only for approved humanitarian purposes—initially food and medical supplies—again under UN surveillance.

For years, Saddam had resisted proposals for such a program. He had hopes that the inability of UN inspectors to find weapons of mass destruction and the concerns about the worsening condition of the Iraqi population would lead to elimination, or at least a broad relaxation, of the sanctions. When he did finally agree in principle in 1996, negotiation of specific terms and conditions were both extensive and contentious.

The Committee's inquiry revealed the extent to which Saddam Hussein sought to influence that negotiating process by means both fair and foul. They included an effort through intermediaries to offer very substantial bribes to the then-Secretary-General, Dr. Boutros Boutros-Ghali, himself. No evidence has been found that the Secretary-General ever benefited from such bribes, potentially amounting to millions of dollars, or even knew of the Iraqi efforts in that respect.

It is true, however, that Iraq did manage, in the name of its sovereign rights, to retain some important initiatives. In particular, Iraq would be consulted on the choice of an escrow bank and, subject to minimal UN review, Iraq could determine the buyers of oil and sellers of goods and the prices to be paid. Through negotiation, Iraq limited the observation and inspection procedures meant to assure the delivery and proper use of humanitarian aid.

There is ample evidence of how Saddam Hussein, personally, and his "Command Council" exploited those initiatives, rewarding perceived friends with financially advantageous contracts and later demanding bribes and other payments that illicitly siphoned off money from the escrow accounts. In its design, the Program had established checkpoints, surveillance procedures, and approval processes by UN officials or contractors. In practice, those controls simply were not adequate, or adequately enforced, to maintain discipline and control.

"Gaming" the Program

Some of the most fascinating reading in the Reports of the investigation is the ways and means by which Saddam Hussein "gamed" the Program.

Beginning in 1996 and early 1997, both the oil sales and the purchases of food and medicine proceeded much as planned. Saddam Hussein, in exercising his ability to designate both buyers and sellers, did favor companies registered with those permanent members of the Security Council most reluctant to maintain strong sanctions—specifically Russia, France, and China. Conversely, there was strong bias against potential U.S. or U.K. contractors.

As time passed, "allocations" of oil—that is, the right to designate actual purchasers—were increasingly made to influential individuals felt to be sympathetic to Iraqi interests. In addition to the names of Russian, French, Italian, and U.K. political figures, Mr. Benon Sevan, the UN Secretariat official mainly responsible for Program administration, appeared on Iraqi allocation lists. (Some of these individuals have forcibly denied knowledge or involvement.) The contracting companies "lifting" the oil, (i.e., actually taking delivery) or providing the humanitarian goods came to benefit from favorable pricing, sharing the "excess profits" with individuals receiving allocations. However, profit margins on oil sales were for a time effectively limited by the requirement for review of pricing by UN appointed experts.

By the turn of the century, and with several years of experience, Iraq adopted much more aggressive tactics, and UN surveillance proved weak. Contrary to program rules, those buying oil were required to make "surcharge" payments back to Iraq, ranging over time between 10 and 50 cents a barrel. Much larger amounts were involved in "kickbacks" demanded from sellers of humanitarian goods. Those payments were typically disguised as fees for "inland transportation" and "after-sales service," neither of which were valid charges. The illicit payments took circuitous routes back to Baghdad, sometimes in bags of $100 bills delivered through Iraqi embassies, more typically through a chain of front companies or complicit or captive banks.

Like those of other authoritarian regimes, Iraqi records were meticulously made and kept and were uniformly consistent with records collected from other sources. They indicate these illicit "surcharges" and "kickbacks"—in effect corrupt bribes—amounted to $1.8 billion over the life of the Program. No doubt, the Iraqi people were deprived of further billions by systematic underpricing of oil exports and excessively high prices of imports as the UN surveillance arrangements were circumvented or ineffective.

These were not, however, the largest sources of illicit income to Iraq. Beginning even before the Oil-for-Food Program started, Iraqi oil was sold directly to Jordan in substantial volume, and later to Turkey and Syria, in contravention of the explicit terms of the embargo. The value of that "smuggled" oil from 1991 to 2003 has been estimated at $10 billion. Moved mainly by truck to Jordan and Turkey and by pipeline to Syria, those shipments could hardly have been hidden from surveillance by U.S. or other intelligence services, and the evidence was not reported by UN inspectors at the border as this task was deemed outside their specific responsibility.

WHAT WENT WRONG

In the face of all the concerns about cutting off the flow of funds to Iraq, the elaborate checkpoints and safeguards established in the Oil-for-Food Program, and the degree of public scrutiny, how could so much go wrong? To what degree were the failures inherent in the nature and complexities of the Oil-for-Food Program—or in the nature and organization of the UN itself? Most significantly, what are the implications for the future, for the role of the UN in the world today?

These are basic questions that the findings of the Committee, with dozens of experienced investigators, and with a panoply of forensic and investigative tools, go a long way toward answering. What the full Reports so clearly demonstrate, and what this book amply reflects, is that it is a complicated story. There is no single villain, no arm or agency of the UN Organization that is alone at fault. There is no escaping a conclusion that the failures were collective. These failures essentially reflected an unwillingness to discharge administrative responsibilities in the face of political pressures, other national priorities, and the absence of effective internal controls.

Take, at the start, the role of the Security Council. There were clear differences of approach toward Iraq, particularly among the five permanent members with veto power. When agreement was finally reached on the Oil-for-Food Program, the Council was reluctant to, and did not, clearly delegate full administrative authority to the Secretariat. Yet, ensnared by its own need for consensus in decision-making and absence of expert staffing, decisions were repeatedly deferred and avoided when difficulties arose.

Diligent and aggressive measures were taken by the United States and Britain, in particular, to make sure that the ban on imports of military or "dual use" materials was enforced. Right from the start, however, the known "smuggling" of Iraqi oil to Jordan was simply "noted," and exports from Jordan to Iraq were not subject to UN inspection. In effect, the United States and others willingly closed their eyes to special arrangements violating the sanctions, presumably to avoid inadvertent damage to a "friendly" state. Later, the similar Turkish arrangements became known, but were never even acknowledged by the Security Council on the same grounds. Smuggling by pipeline into Syria, hardly a friendly state, was simply ignored.

The failure of the Security Council to act—neither openly acknowledging nor prohibiting—against such large breaches of the sanctions may well have colored attitudes toward other, individually less important but cumulatively corrosive, violations of Program rules.

At any rate, the weakness of Secretariat administrative discipline was revealed from the outset of the Program. Contracts needed to be negotiated with private firms responsible for managing the escrow accounts and for border inspection. Established procurement rules were simply overridden in an unacknowledged search for political balance. Internal auditors and inspectors were not consulted at that point, nor were those functions ever adequately staffed and supported as the Program continued. Senior level oversight was either weak or compromised.

The official directly assigned to manage the Program, Mr. Benon Sevan, was found, according to Iraqi records and other evidence, to have been designated for several oil allocations. There is strong evidence of illicit payments to him from those designated to "lift" the oil. The fact that such a grievous conflict of interest took place and continued over time is itself one symptom of the absence of reasonable administrative safeguards.

The single most sensitive and difficult question for the Committee was the accusation that the Secretary-General, Kofi Annan, was himself subject to an apparent conflict of interest because of the employment of his son by a UN contractor. No evidence has been found that the Secretary-General in any way was involved in, or attempted to influence, the contract at issue. It is not clear that, despite close contact with his son, he even knew of the contractor's interest in bidding. What did become evident, and a matter of great concern to the Committee, was his apparent willingness to accept quick (and later proved false) reassurances of his son's lack of involvement. At the time that the potential conflict was made public, there was simply no substantial investigation by appropriate authorities, within the UN or otherwise.

UN-related agencies—UNICEF, UNDP, WFP, WHO, and others —operate in varying degrees of independence from the Secretariat and the Security Council. Nine of them were called upon to cooperate in the Oil-for-Food Program. Basically, they were primarily responsible for the field operations, managing or overseeing the distribution of humanitarian goods on the ground in northern Iraq. In administering the Program, those very sizable agency operations, unlike usual practice, were all funded from a central source, essentially drawing upon the proceeds of Iraqi oil sales. Yet, Secretariat oversight and arrangements to coordinate operations among the agencies were weak and ineffective. In a number of instances, the agencies were called upon to undertake engineering and other projects that went beyond their core competence, and they yielded to political pressures. Altogether, too much of their performance fell below acceptable standards.

THE ROOT OF THE PROBLEM

The size and inherent complexity of the Oil-for-Food Program, the need to rapidly build staff on the ground in Iraq, the initial assumption that the Program might be short-lived, and the UN's absence of an existing administrative infrastructure for "command and control" all contributed to the administrative failures. As its investigation proceeded, the Committee came to appreciate that those failures were not uniquely characteristic of one complicated UN program. Rather, they were symptomatic of deep-seated and chronic administrative failings of the institution, failings that call for thorough change and reform.

In addressing these questions with a committee of the U.S. Congress, I was pressed to agree with allegations that had been made that the UN had a "culture of corruption." It is a sad fact that in two instances we did find evidence of corruption—by Mr. Sevan, as mentioned earlier, and in a quantitatively more significant way, in the purchasing department (now under a separate UN-sponsored investigation).

However, I did not, and do not today, believe the evidence developed by the Committee justifies a sweeping allegation that financial corruption is or was characteristic of the institution as a whole. Rather, as I suggested then and believe now, there is a "culture of inaction," of a strong tendency to evade administrative responsibility. That culture is rooted both in the character of the UN Organization and in broadly political considerations.

The UN is inescapably, and necessarily, a political institution. It is a meeting place of countries—192 member states of widely varying size and influence. Each has a single vote in the General Assembly, which carries the final responsibility for administrative affairs. It is the Security Council that carries primary responsibility for efforts to maintain peace and security, including the authorization of intervention by armed forces. But it has limited operational staff or expertise.

Supporting those political bodies sits the Secretary-General, designated by the UN Charter as Chief Administrative Officer, and his sizable Secretariat.

Presumably, the UN founders had in mind the clear need for an administrative staff to arrange appropriate facilities, to support meetings of the General Assembly and Security Council, to carry out their decisions, and to maintain liaison with other agencies.

But, of course, the role of the Secretary-General, *any* Secretary-General, has grown beyond purely ministerial responsibilities. He is, in practice, the chief diplomatic and political officer. He is perceived as able and willing in certain circumstance to take an initiative in international affairs of the most sensitive kind and to negotiate on behalf of the Security Council itself.

Those are the matters that are at the center of a Secretary-General's attention. Kofi Annan himself has described the problem to the General Assembly:

> As Chief Administrative Officer of the Organization, I have managerial responsibilities which have grown far more demanding with the extraordinary increase in the number and complexity of field missions and other operational activities. Yet at the same time the direct and active involvement of the United Nations in a far wider range of issues than in the past has placed enormous calls on my time and capacity in my role as a political instrument of the Security Council, the General Assembly, and other United Nations organs. In short, I am expected to be the world's chief diplomat and at the same time to run a large and complex Organization, as it were, in my spare time.

Quite apart from lack of time and focus, the Secretary-General will almost inevitably be called upon to temper administrative decisions by political and negotiating considerations. That was transparently the case with Boutros Boutros-Ghali in the design and organization of the Oil-for-Food Program. Considerations of administrative efficiency and effectiveness were overridden with the active influence or implicit consent of the permanent members of the Security Council. In more insidious ways, those same pressures have infected personnel decisions, influenced the staffing and authority of the auditing and control functions, and undercut the authority of administrators.

COMBATING CORRUPTION

While my comments—and the Committee conclusions—concentrate on the need for reforms within the UN Organization, there is another important implication of the Committee findings against which the need for reform of the UN must be considered. During the program Iraq took advantage of the contracting companies' willingness to make illicit payments in order to acquire and retain business. That willingness was pervasive enough to subvert an internationally supported sanctions regime.

Some 4,500 companies, registered in scores of countries, participated in the purchase of Iraqi oil or sales of goods to Iraq. All those transactions were notionally under UN surveillance of the terms and conditions. As detailed in the final Committee Report, during the period in which illicit payments were required by the Iraqi government, almost all the companies appear to have, directly or indirectly, made those payments to the Iraqi government through so-called "surcharges" or "kickbacks." Quite aside from the lapses in UN surveillance, the willingness of so many companies to make such payments portrays a disturbing picture of the extent of bribery and corruption in international trade.

Much attention is now being directed by the World Bank, the OECD, some governments, and many economists to the destructive impact of corruption on economic growth and stability in the emerging world. The effect is to limit the value of official assistance and to inhibit private investment where it is most needed.

The responsibility must be broadly shared. It lies with importers and exporters, with those making and those receiving investment, and not least with the governments of rich nations and poor who are sometimes complicit and have otherwise failed to act to detect and stop this behavior.

In that context, the varied response of governments to particular instances of alleged (and sometimes admitted) illicit payments under the Oil-for-Food Program is interesting. The Swiss government was particularly helpful in assisting Committee staff to identify some of the illicit financial flows, a reflection of that nation's concern that its own institutions not be corrupted. French and Italian prosecutors and investigators provided invaluable assistance and have rigorously pursued some of those involved. In two countries, Australia and India, intensive public commissions of inquiry were promptly launched in the face of political sensitivities. In the United States, there have been indictments of middlemen involved in attempted bribery or illicit payments. Law enforcement authorities in more than twenty countries have contacted Committee staff for specific information, and the Committee has provided information on scores of matters involving illegal and corrupt activity.

In sharp contrast, there has been no apparent concern by governments of countries where a large number of companies engaged in Iraqi trade were registered, including Russia or China. No requests for assistance have been made of the Committee, nor are there indications of legal action.

All of this emphasizes the relevance of existing efforts to reinforce international action to identify and ban bribery and corrupt practices in international trade. The United States has long had relatively strong laws and policies, and few U.S. companies were involved in illicit activity in the Oil-for-Food program. The World Bank, in its own operations and area of responsibility, is moving more aggressively. The OECD is encouraging appropriate legislation among its members and helping to coordinate national approaches. Many of the national authorities who worked with the Committee have used that opportunity to engage in unprecedented coordination of their investigations and prosecutions.

Clearly, the investigation of the Oil-for-Food Program has rung alarm bells and encouraged better international cooperation in dealing with corruption in trade. It has also revealed how much needs to be done and the large gaps existing among the efforts of individual countries.

WHERE DO THINGS STAND?

Since the Reports of the Committee were completed, a great deal of effort—spearheaded by a new Under Secretary for Administration—has taken place to improve administrative policies and procedures. In general, these efforts closely parallel recommendations of the Committee—recommendations that themselves echo conclusions of other commissions and experienced commentators.

In areas directly subject to control by the Secretary-General:

- There is for the first time a UN Ethics Office, a whistleblower protection policy, and a strong financial disclosure policy;

- Additional inspection and auditing positions are being authorized;

- Procurement irregularities are being investigated and adequacy of controls reviewed.

These are useful measures, in some respects "state of the art," drawing on principles of corporate governance as well as experience in public organizations. They are presumably being reinforced by the appointment of a new and forceful Deputy Secretary-General, with a mandate to implement administrative reform.

These steps, however, are limited by their nature and dependent on forceful implementation over time. There are other developments signifying that chronic resistance to reform remains strong.

One symptom, as of this writing, has been the tepid response of the General Assembly to a series of proposals by the Secretary-General that would enhance his administrative authority, partly out of the General Assembly's fear of attenuating its own prerogatives. The apparent consensus on the conceptual need for stronger auditing and oversight functions has not been reflected in needed funding or adequate assurances of independence. Little or no attention has been paid to the need for better coordination among the various arms and agencies of the UN.

WHAT NEEDS TO BE DONE?

As things stand, there is a clear danger that the reform effort will stall in the face of bureaucratic inertia and resistance of many member states.

At the end of the day, the responsibility lies with the General Assembly, the governing body of the UN Organization. The General Assembly, at best, is an unwieldy body. There are widely varying interests among its disparate members. It is seemingly frustrated by its apparent inability to reconcile administrative effectiveness with the particular (and political) concerns of its 192 members.

Too often, the reform effort is bogged down by suspicions that the authority of the General Assembly will not be respected, or that the influence by one group of members or another will be diluted or enhanced. Those perceptions miss a larger point. What is at stake is nothing less than the relevance and effectiveness of the UN itself, and its ability to command respect for its policies and practices. If the UN loses confidence and credibility, then how can the General Assembly, in which every member state, however small, has a voice and a vote, be of value to those members?

The basic interest of the Organization—of the Security Council, of the Secretariat, and of the General Assembly in particular—must be to make its operations competent and respected. As an essential part of that process, the natural and important role for the General Assembly is effective oversight of administration.

Clearly, that cannot be done by detached micro-management by so large and disparate a body. There need to be ways and means to focus attention on key points, of both organization and personnel.

The Committee came to two strong recommendations on those central points. We were reinforced in our conviction by the degree to which other investigators had come to very similar conclusions.

First: the United Nations Organization needs a strong *Independent Oversight Board*, with adequate staff support. Serving essentially as an arm of the General Assembly, that Board needs to go beyond financial audits to a full review of the staffing and budgeting of accounting, auditing, and inspection services. Those responsible for each of these functions should have direct access to the Board, and review with the Board its auditing and investigatory plans. The conclusions and recommendations of the Board should be regularly available to the General Assembly, and as appropriate to the public.

Second: there should be a *Chief Operating Officer*, with clear responsibility for implementing administrative programs and procedures. While reporting to the Secretary-General on broad policy matters, the COO should have the authority conveyed by appointment by the General Assembly upon the recommendation of the Security Council and direct access to the General Assembly with respect to administrative practices.

The purpose of those two proposals is clear. Political decisions will and should determine the substantive policies of the Organization, including when and where particular programs should be implemented. Once decided, the responsibility and the authority for carrying out those programs should be clarified. The focus must be on organizational, planning and personnel practices that emphasize the need for professional and administrative skills.

Without such basic organizational changes, the other reforms underway, valuable as they may appear to be, could all too easily atrophy and be swept away by political pressures and lack of attention. That is the lesson of the Oil-for-Food Program. More broadly, it is the lesson of the past.

THE RESPONSIBILITIES OF MEMBER STATES

In the end, the UN is accountable to its member states and to the general public. It is an unhappy fact that recent events have eroded the instinctive support for the UN among some countries. That is especially true in the United States, where growing disenchantment with the UN is reflected both in Congress and in polling of the citizenry. And it is the United States that inevitably carries particular weight in providing financial resources, diplomatic support, and, when necessary and agreed, military capacity.

There also remains a broad recognition that the UN is uniquely important, that it has a role no other organization can perform.

Those two strands of opinion can be reconciled only by reform—reform sufficiently convincing in concept and detail to justify a renewed sense of confidence in the Organization's competence and integrity.

The challenge is to broaden the understanding of that need, to secure the necessary leadership, and to find the means of overcoming entrenched resistance. Too much is at stake to let the field of reform lie fallow.

Recognition of that point has been manifested in the insistence by a sizable group of member states, including those that carry a large part of the UN's financing requirements, that funding will be withheld if reform benchmarks are not met.

Clearly, withholding funding is a blunt instrument. Threatened arbitrarily and capriciously by a single state, the result will be destructive and counterproductive. But, in the last analysis, it is the budget that is a legitimate and sometimes necessary instrument for controlling governments and institutions.

The UN cannot escape that reality. What it can do—what I think it must do—is recognize that failure to adopt reasonable and effective administrative reforms will inevitably risk consequences.

If those consequences reflect the concern of a broad coalition of nations—nations concerned about the reform and relevance of the institution—then budgetary restraints are reasonable and legitimate. Established programs will be squeezed, the good with the weak.

But the inverse should also be true. With confidence in the competence and integrity of the Organization, funding will be better assured. Needed new initiatives can then be financed. That is surely in the interest of the Organization and all member states, large or small, those that contribute large amounts and those that benefit from the programs and operations.

A new General Assembly is meeting. There is much on its agenda, including the choice of a new Secretary-General. I trust that, among the criteria for that choice, the need for leadership in the effort for administrative reform ranks high.

The point has rightly been made that the Oil-for-Food program was a reasonable and needed response to a very large challenge. In broad terms, it helped to maintain minimum standards of nutrition and health among the Iraqi population while the sanctions were kept in place.

But those successes were accompanied by increasing charges of administrative failures—failures amply confirmed by the Committee investigations of the Program.

A broad consensus has developed among those familiar with what has happened that reform—thorough and complete reform—is necessary if the UN is to be able to meet the responsibilities thrust upon it.

That need is not new. Past efforts to achieve reform have been long debated. Resistance has been strong, both within the bureaucracy and by member states.

Now with the facts at hand, a new opportunity is here. That opportunity must not be missed—not missed in the interest of the United Nations and all the member states ranging from the United States to the smallest, each of which shares in the common benefit of respected and enforceable international law and practice.

Patience is limited. The time for action is now.

PREFACE

This is a book about what went wrong with the Oil-for-Food Program in Iraq—the UN's largest humanitarian relief operation. Born out of the best of intentions, the program succeeded in meeting the basic food and medical needs of the Iraqi people, who suffered severely under UN sanctions. But the program ultimately mired in corruption and mismanagement, as Saddam Hussein figured out how to manipulate its workings for his political and pecuniary gain. The program's problems have left a stain on the prestige of the UN and undermined public confidence in its capacity to advance programs for peace and humanitarian relief in an ever-hostile and needy world.

The Oil-for-Food Program was conceived as a temporary, limited exception to the UN's economic sanctions against Iraq—to let Iraq sell some of its oil in order to buy essential civilian goods, like food and medical supplies. In theory, the program would not allow Iraq to buy military goods, much less luxury goods for the creature comforts of Saddam and his inner circle. Nor in theory was the program supposed to allow the Iraqi government any access to currency or cash that it could use to fund the purchase of forbidden weapons or goods. Instead, all the money from the sale of Iraqi oil was to be channeled to an escrow bank account that was controlled by the UN outside Iraq, and this account would be used to pay companies that supplied humanitarian goods to Iraq.

But practice departed from theory. The Iraqi regime skimmed about $1.8 billion of illegal surcharge and kickback payments that it solicited from its buyers of oil and its suppliers of humanitarian goods. The UN responded slowly and with limited effect; little was done in response to Iraqi manipulation of the program. Meanwhile, outside of the program, the Iraqi regime smuggled about $8.4 billion in oil to neighboring countries during the life of the program, and the UN rejected measures to bring this trade under the program, much less put a stop to it altogether. Part of what went wrong with the program was corruption. Another part was political partisanship, bureaucratic bungling, and the abject absence of safeguards to constrain Iraq from subverting the program for improper purposes.

Aside from the machinations of Saddam and his Iraqi regime, there is plenty of blame to go around—from the professional staff of the UN Secretariat, to the member country diplomats of the UN Security Council, to the administrators of various UN-related humanitarian agencies, to assorted politicians and diplomats who secretly accepted Iraqi oil allocations, to the bankers who ran the program's escrow account, to the inspection companies that monitored the imports and exports from Iraq, and to the officials of thousands of companies that illegally paid off the Iraqi regime to secure business for themselves under the program.

The story of what went wrong with the Oil-for-Food Program has been chronicled across thousands of pages in a series of reports issued by the Independent Inquiry Committee (IIC). But the story has yet to be told in one place, and here the story unfolds in the following seven chapters of this book.

Chapter 1 describes the start and structure of the program. It was more than five years after UN sanctions were first imposed that Saddam would even agree to the program and to furnish its relief for his suffering people. His apathy resulted in a superior bargaining position for Iraq to shape the terms of the program in a way that would allow it to manipulate transactions for Saddam's political and economic advantage. But this advantage was gained at the expense of a suffering population and the threat of serious malnutrition and disease. Iraq even tried, unsuccessfully, to bribe then Secretary-General Boutros Boutros-Ghali to make him more "flexible" about the initial terms and later administration of the program.

Chapter 2 describes the UN's initial selection in 1996 of three companies that would be indispensable to executing transactions under the Oil-for-Food Program—a bank to manage the UN-controlled escrow account, an oil inspection company to monitor the oil that Iraq exported under the program, and a trade inspection company to monitor the humanitarian goods that Iraq bought under the program. In accordance with well-established UN rules for procuring goods and services, these companies were supposed to be chosen by means of a competitive bidding process and award of the contract to the lowest qualified bidder. But politics preempted the principles of the procurement process, as each of the companies was selected for reasons of political preference dictated by certain members of the UN's Security Council.

Chapter 3 describes the UN's selection in 1998 of a new company to inspect humanitarian goods entering Iraq. This selection was marred by a concealed potential conflict of interest—the company that won the contract employed Kojo Annan, the son of Secretary-General Kofi Annan. The company was also under criminal investigation for payments it had allegedly made to the prime minister of Pakistan. The evidence indicated that the Secretary-General did not try to steer the contract to the company that employed Kojo. But Kojo himself ostensibly tried to help his company get the contract by calling on his insider contacts at the UN's procurement department.

When it became publicly known that the UN had awarded the contract to Kojo's company, the UN did little to investigate the situation. In the meantime, Kojo and his company falsely proclaimed that he no longer worked for the company, while in fact the company continued to make secret payments to Kojo for the rest of the time that the company held the UN inspection contract in Iraq.

Chapter 4 describes Iraq's manipulation of oil sales under the program. Iraq steered nearly half of its oil sales to companies from three permanent members of the UN Security Council—Russia, China, and France—that it believed were most sympathetic to lifting the sanctions against it. Iraq also allocated large amounts of its oil for the benefit of various foreign politicians, diplomats, and other opinion makers who it believed would help its effort to lift the sanctions. Beginning in late 2000, the Iraqi regime began enriching itself by extracting more than $200 million of illegal surcharge payments from its oil buyers. Scores of companies paid millions of dollars in cash to Iraqi embassies abroad or wired money to bank accounts in Jordan and Lebanon that were secretly controlled by the Iraqi government. The success of this scheme depended in part on the use of various front companies and other subterfuges to conceal the payments and the true identity of major oil traders that were controlling oil bought from Iraq. The UN's own escrow bank assisted major oil traders in keeping their identities concealed as the true parties in interest to Iraqi oil transactions.

Chapter 5 describes Iraq's manipulation of humanitarian goods transactions under the program. Beginning in late 1999, Iraq extracted illegal kickbacks from its suppliers, and by the end of 2000, it was requiring all of its suppliers to pay at least 10 percent of the contract price as a kickback. As with the oil surcharges, these humanitarian kickbacks were channeled through front companies and often to bank accounts secretly controlled by Iraq in Jordan and Lebanon. Even major Western companies such as DaimlerChrysler, Siemens, and Volvo Construction Group paid kickbacks, and the single largest payer of kickbacks was Australia's national wheat exporting company. More than 2,200 companies paid more than $1.5 billion in kickbacks through the end of the program.

Iraq's manipulation of the program did not go undetected. It was generally known to both the Security Council and the UN Secretariat. The remaining chapters of the book focus on the role of the Security Council and the UN Secretariat, with emphasis on their general failure to redress Iraq's abuse of the program.

Chapter 6 describes the UN Security Council's failure to respond to and redress the many reports of Iraq's exploitation of the program. The Security Council knew Iraq was extracting oil surcharges and humanitarian kickbacks but took little or limited action to put an end to these practices. Perhaps more surprising, the Security Council was also aware of massive oil smuggling by Iraq during the same years that the program was in operation yet did little to stop the smuggling over land to Iraq's neighboring countries.

Chapter 7 assesses the maladministration and corruption that infected the implementation of the program by the UN Secretariat and various UN-related agencies that took part in the monitoring and distribution of aid to the Iraqi people. The UN's principal officer in charge of administering the program, Under-Secretary-General Benon Sevan, was secretly designated as a beneficiary of oil allocations from the Iraqi regime, and he apparently profited by tens of thousands of dollars in cash from these allocations. In the meantime, Sevan did little to stop Iraq's broader exploitation of the program. Although Sevan's superiors at the UN were not aware of his illicit activities, Secretary-General Kofi Annan and Deputy Secretary-General Louise Fréchette failed to exercise meaningful oversight, as Sevan mismanaged the administration of the program and concealed significant information from the Security Council about Iraq's abuse of the program.

The various UN-related agencies that participated in the program were mostly successful in assisting the distribution of aid to people in Iraq's northern governorates, but they notably failed to complete several infrastructure projects that were beyond their core competency. The Iraqi escrow account was overcharged by at least $50 million for administrative expenses paid to the UN-related agencies.

Finally, the auditing and oversight functions of the UN were wholly inadequate. The number of auditors that were responsible for reviewing the program was a fraction of what was needed. Audits, when performed, were few and far between and did not cover many of the riskier areas of operation. And investigative oversight was virtually nonexistent.

The appendix to this book includes the IIC's recommendations for UN reform and more information about the IIC. As Paul Volcker's introduction makes clear, the threat to the UN is real in the absence of top-to-bottom reform of the world's foremost forum and force for peace and humanitarian welfare.

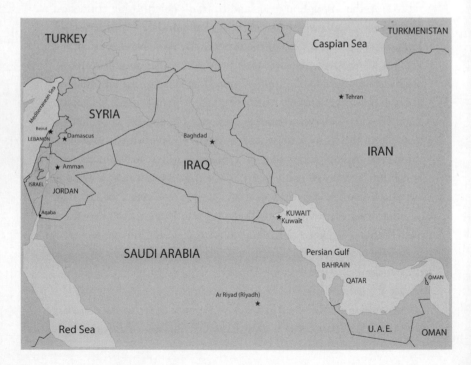

GOOD INTENTIONS CORRUPTED

1

DESTINED FOR CORRUPTION:

THE CREATION OF

THE U.N. OIL-FOR-FOOD PROGRAM

Among the people of Iraq, Saddam Hussein is known simply as "Saddam"—that is, "one who confronts" or "one who clashes." He rose to be Iraq's vice president at the age of only thirty-two and then took power barely more than ten years later as president and dictator in 1979. With his power soon came war, as the Iraqi army invaded Iran in 1980. Eight years of bloodshed followed, and the loss of as many as one million lives before the war ended without a victor in 1988. During the war, Saddam deployed poison gas on the enemy in Iran and on his perceived enemies at home among the Kurdish peoples of northern Iraq.[1]

By the summer of 1990, Iraq was at peace again with its neighbors. But Kuwait—the tiny-yet-oil-rich neighbor to the south—presented another tempting target. On the pretext of a dispute about rights to oil, Saddam amassed more than 100,000 troops on his southern border with Kuwait. Then, in the early morning hours of August 2, Iraqi forces stormed across the desert sands to take control of Kuwait by nightfall.[2]

The world roundly condemned the invasion. In New York, the UN Security Council responded with a landmark measure—Resolution 661—to prohibit most forms of trade and financial transactions with Iraq. These multilateral sanctions were among the most comprehensive and severe ever imposed against one nation, and they would endure more than twelve years, until the downfall of Saddam in 2003.*

Within months of Iraq's invasion of Kuwait, a worldwide military force, authorized by the UN and led by the United States, deployed to the Persian Gulf and liberated Kuwait from Iraq in February 1991. The United States, however, decided at the time not to invade Baghdad and topple Saddam's regime. Instead, the Security Council renewed its economic sanctions in order to compel Iraq to disarm. Security Council Resolution 687, passed in April 1991, required Iraq to destroy weapons or facilities relating to chemical, biological, and nuclear weapons, and to submit to intensive inspections by weapons experts from the United Nations Commission (UNSCOM) and the International Atomic Energy Agency (IAEA).

Saddam did not comply with Resolution 687. Year after year he stonewalled the weapons inspectors, and the sanctions continued. But the war and continuing sanctions meant a steady decline in the standard of living for most of Iraq's 18 million people. Iraq could not legally sell its oil, which previously had accounted for about 60 percent of the country's gross domestic product. One UN fact-finding mission in 1991 reported "near-apocalyptic results" and that "Iraq has for some time to come been relegated to a pre-industrial age" of development.

With no end to sanctions in immediate sight, the Security Council passed two resolutions in late summer of 1991 to allow Iraq to engage in an oil-for-food exchange program. Iraq would have been

---

*Unless otherwise noted, the facts set forth in the remaining narrative of this chapter are drawn from the following sources: Independent Inquiry Committee, *The Management of the Oil-for-Food Programme,* vol. 2, September 7, 2005, chapter 1 ("Programme Background and Manipulation by Iraq") and chapter 2 ("Negotiation and Establishment of the Oil-for-Food Programme"); and Independent Working Group established by the Independent Inquiry Committee, *The Impact of the Oil-for-Food Programme on the Iraqi People,* September 7, 2005.

allowed to sell up to $1.6 billion of oil on the world market for a period of six months, provided that it agreed to have the oil sales proceeds deposited to a UN-controlled escrow account and to be used to finance humanitarian supplies. The program was intended in theory to prevent any money from the sale of oil going to Saddam or to feed his military ambitions.

Iraq refused to go along with an oil-for-food plan, denouncing it as an infringement of its sovereignty, while also wary that such a plan could make sanctions seem more palatable to members of the Security Council and delay the lifting of sanctions in their entirety. In the meantime, the weapons inspections process dragged on from 1991 to 1995, and the weapons inspectors were unable to certify Iraq's compliance and to allow sanctions to be lifted.

As the plight of the Iraqi people worsened and support dwindled in the Security Council for continuing the comprehensive sanctions, Madeleine Albright, who was then the U.S. ambassador to the UN, pushed for reenacting an oil-for-food plan. The United States hoped that the plan would allow the sanctions to stay in place but provide more relief for the people of Iraq. Anticipating Iraq's excuses for rejecting the prior oil-for-food proposals, U.S. officials floated a plan that Albright thought "Iraq would have no reason to reject." The new plan would not only allow Iraq to sell more oil than previously proposed but also grant more power and discretion over implementation of the program to Secretary-General Boutros Boutros-Ghali, rather than to the Security Council. The new plan also would not propose any new in-country monitoring mechanisms, an innovation that UN officials observed was "far less intrusive" than had been previously proposed.

The result, Resolution 986, was passed by the Security Council in April 1995 and eventually led to the Oil-for-Food Program. But, despite the hopes of the Security Council, Iraq refused Resolution 986. The Foreign Minister of Iraq insisted to Boutros-Ghali that the program would allow "spies" to wander Iraq, as Iraq believed UN-

SCOM inspectors did in performing arms inspections. More significantly, he voiced concern that Iraq's acceptance of the plan would delay the Security Council's decision to lift the sanctions entirely.

Indeed, by the summer of 1995, Iraq had good reason to hope that the sanctions were nearing their end. It had stepped up its cooperation with UNSCOM inspectors, and it disclosed for the first time the location of significant chemical weapons material. Rolf Ekeus, the Executive Chairman of UNSCOM, briefed the Security Council in New York that Iraq had no capability to threaten its neighbors with missiles, chemical, or biological weapons. Ekeus further confirmed that Iraq was no longer acquiring weapons of mass destruction and that he was satisfied with progress achieved in the destruction and elimination of missiles and chemical weapons and with the ongoing monitoring and verification program. According to an UNSCOM report, Iraq had on the whole cooperated with UNSCOM in the ballistic missiles and chemical weapons areas, and UNSCOM had accounted for most prohibited weapons.

Although some questions remained about the extent of Iraq's disclosure of past weapons programs, these promising developments sparked discussion among some Security Council members about prospects for lifting sanctions soon. Iraq's Deputy Prime Minister Tariq Aziz ratcheted up the pressure by warning Ekeus on August 5, 1995, that Iraq would cease cooperation if no progress was made toward lifting the sanctions by the end of the month.

Iraq's hopes were suddenly dashed in mid-August 1995, when General Hussein Kamel Hassan Al-Majid—Saddam's son-in-law and a high-ranking military minister within Saddam's inner circle—defected to neighboring Jordan. The news was shocking not only because of Kamel's betrayal of family ties but also because Kamel was known to be a hard-liner who shared Saddam's abiding hatred of the United States and its policies. With Kamel's defection came exposure of the true status of Iraq's past weapons programs, particularly its biological weapons initiatives.

In light of Kamel's disappearance, Iraq decided to lead weapons inspectors to troves of new weapons-related documents stashed in a chicken house on a farm outside Baghdad. The Iraqi regime tried to blame the concealment of this information on Kamel, and it was immediately apparent that the sheer magnitude of the new weapons-related documents would take months for inspectors to inventory, translate, and review. Even assuming Iraq's full cooperation, the Security Council would be in no realistic position to consider lifting the sanctions in the near future.

The new political climate, coupled with the deterioration of the Iraqi economy, now created a willingness in Baghdad—even from Saddam—to enter into negotiations on implementing Resolution 986. In early October 1995, Boutros-Ghali met with Mohammed Said Al Sahaf, who was then Iraq's Minister of Foreign Affairs, and Nizar Hamdoon, who was then Iraq's ambassador to the UN, in order to urge Iraq to return to the negotiating table. During the meeting, the two Iraqi officials pointed out to the Secretary-General that, unlike earlier resolutions, Resolution 986 granted him more discretion in implementing the program. The Iraqi officials now sought a "point of view" of the Secretariat that would allow them to recommend restarting negotiations.

Later that month, Boutros-Ghali met with Iraq's vice president and Hamdoon to discuss the issue again. Echoing the words of Iraqi officials at the earlier meeting, Boutros-Ghali pointed out that, in contrast to the prior oil-for-food resolutions, Resolution 986 offered him "some latitude" about the way that the program would be implemented.

Two weeks later, Boutros-Ghali met privately at his request with Barzan Al-Tikriti, Saddam's half brother and Iraq's ambassador to the UN in Geneva. At this meeting he asked Al-Tikriti to convey to Baghdad his recommendation that Iraq accept Resolution 986. In response to Iraq's concern that the program would not allow Iraq to sell as much oil as it wanted to sell, Boutros-Ghali noted that the amount of oil could be subject to future negotiation. He warned, in view of the expiration of his term as Secretary-General at the end of the following year, that Iraq would "never get another Arab Secretary-General."

On December 10, 1995, Boutros-Ghali met with Aziz and pointed out that the negotiations on the implementation "should occur between Iraq and the Secretary-General, not the Security Council." Without stating that he would violate the strictures of Resolution 986, Boutros-Ghali emphasized that he would "show understanding" toward Iraq's concerns about how the program would be implemented. Aziz asked for a formal letter inviting Iraq to recommence negotiations.

Aziz in turn recommended to Saddam that Iraq agree to an oil-for-food program. He told Saddam that "the country was tired, the people were hungry, and things [with weapons inspections] will take time." Saddam agreed to go along, and Aziz advised Boutros-Ghali that Iraq was now prepared to negotiate on the terms of its participation in an oil-for-food program.

On the eve of negotiations, Boutros-Ghali gathered his senior staff to discuss strategy for the negotiation with Iraq. At that meeting he directed that the staff, including the UN's lead negotiator, Under-Secretary-General for Legal Affairs Hans Corell, take a "flexible approach" with Iraq. He also asked his senior staff to find "a face-saving device" to ensure the equitable distribution of aid within Iraq, especially in the northern Kurdish governorates, but without appearing to interfere with Iraqi sovereignty.

Four months and more than fifty negotiation meetings followed between high-level delegations from Iraq and from the UN Secretariat. The negotiations led to a formal memorandum of understanding (known simply as "the MOU") which was signed by the parties on May 20, 1996—nearly five years after an oil-for-food program had first been proposed.

While the UN negotiated with Iraq about the terms of an oil-for-food plan, General Kamel decided to return to Iraq in February 1996. He was soon murdered, along with several members of his family.

IRAQ'S ATTEMPT TO
BRIBE THE SECRETARY-GENERAL

The notion of an oil-for-food program in Iraq attracted the attention of many for reasons transcending sympathy toward the humanitarian predicament of the Iraqi people. For members of the Security Council, a program held implications for their respective political, security, and commercial interests. For the UN, an oil-for-food program was not just a way to feed people but also a potential source of funding to meet its Iraq-related initiatives, such as weapons inspections and reparations for the victims of the Gulf War. For the oil industry, a program would allow reentry into the market of one of the world's chief sources of oil. And for various politicians and businessmen, a program held the promise of lucrative gain.

One entrepreneur—Samir Vincent—managed at an early stage to insinuate himself into the plans and negotiations for starting an oil-for-food program. Vincent was an Iraqi-born citizen of the United States who lived in MacLean, Virginia—a suburban community outside Washington, D.C., that is home to the CIA. He had grown up in Baghdad and attended the same high school as high-level Iraqi officials such as Deputy Prime Minister Aziz and UN Ambassador Hamdoon. Among other matters, he had worked as a consultant for Coastal Corporation, a Houston oil company run by Texan Oscar Wyatt that had long-standing business interests in Iraq.

In early 1992, Vincent joined together with John Venners, then a public relations consultant, and William Timmons, a Washington lobbyist, to pursue the purchase and sale of Iraqi oil and the exploration by a consortium of companies of the Majnoon oil field in Iraq. To allow this project to go forward, Vincent hoped that sanctions against Iraq would be lifted and that Iraq might grant his venture a long-term concession.

At the same time that Vincent was pursuing possible oil deals in Iraq, he kept a close relationship with Hamdoon. Vincent frequently visited Iraq's UN "mission" office in New York and the ambassador's residence in New York. He was also known by Iraqi officials to have close ties to Iraqi intelligence officials and to Aziz, with whom he had been seen meeting in New York.

As early as 1992, Vincent sought access to UN officials to press for the establishment of an oil-for-food program that would be acceptable to Iraq. In November 1992, Vincent met at the direction of the Secretary-General with Ralph Zacklin, a senior UN attorney, to discuss several "talking points" based on informal discussions Vincent allegedly had had with U.S. officials and Iraqi officials, including Aziz. Vincent told Zacklin at the meeting that he was anxious for the UN's reaction to his talking points before he would meet the following week with Aziz and possibly with Saddam in Baghdad. After this meeting, Vincent traveled to Baghdad, where he met with at least some top Iraqi officials, including Aziz, Kamel, and Iraq's Oil Minister, Amer Rashid.

Two weeks later, on November 24, 1992, while Aziz was in New York to address the Security Council on sanctions, Vincent met with Aziz and Hamdoon at the Iraq mission. At this meeting, Vincent reviewed some of the contacts that he and Oscar Wyatt had made within the new presidential administration of Bill Clinton.

One week later, on December 1, 1992, Vincent met again with Zacklin at the UN. Claiming that Aziz took a great interest in his efforts, Vincent presented Zacklin with a diplomatic-style "nonpaper" and suggested that its points be adopted by the UN and sent to Iraq as the basis for further oil-for-food discussions. But Zacklin rebuffed Vincent's proposal, stating that the UN would deal directly with Iraq's government. As Zacklin would later recall, "This chap was obviously wheeling and dealing. . . . He came with his talking points, and I sent him packing."

Vincent, however, did not abandon his efforts at the UN. Instead, he drew upon his relationship with a Korean businessman named Tongsun Park, who had direct personal access to the Secretary-General. A native of South Korea, Park himself had a notoriously checkered past. In the late 1970s, he had been at the center of a Washington influence-peddling scandal known as "Koreagate," which led to his indictment by U.S. authorities in 1977 on charges of bribery, conspiracy, and racketeering. But these charges were eventually dismissed, and by the 1990s Park had established himself again within Washington's circles of political influence. He had owned a well-known Washington social institution, the Historic George Town Club, which was frequented by Washington political luminaries.

Park cultivated a friendship with Boutros-Ghali, who in turn viewed Park as a valuable source of information. When interviewed by the investigators of the Independent Inquiry Committee (IIC), Boutros-Ghali remarked that he did not have a formal intelligence service while heading the UN, and so he decided to supplement his knowledge through private sources and informal channels of communication. As Boutros-Ghali recalled, Park provided "first-class information" and was a valuable advisor because he "knew everybody" as "an integral part of the Washington *nomenclatura*."

Boutros-Ghali denied to the IIC that he had discussed an oil-for-food program with Park or even had met Vincent, and he specifically pointed out that as Secretary-General he could easily communicate directly with Iraqi officials without need of an intermediary. Accounts of other witnesses, however, reflect that Park introduced Vincent to Boutros-Ghali at the Secretary-General's residence in early 1993 and that they discussed oil-for-food prospects. Boutros-Ghali advised Vincent that Iraq would have to agree to export some of its oil through Turkey and otherwise to abide by any Security Council resolutions authorizing the program.

During the spring of 1993, Vincent turned for legal advice to Theodore Sorensen, a New York attorney and former special counsel and advisor to U.S. President John F. Kennedy. Sorensen's spouse served as a special adviser to Boutros-Ghali. Sorensen eventually prepared a draft letter for Vincent to present to Iraqi officials designating him as the "principle intermediary" to arrange for American suppliers to sell humanitarian goods to Iraq.

In June 1993, Park and Vincent met with Aziz, Hamdoon, and Al-Tikriti in Geneva, Switzerland. The Iraqis said they did not want the proposed oil-for-food program to undermine the lifting of sanctions and hoped Park could use his relationship with Boutros-Ghali to encourage an end to the sanctions. At about the same time, Aziz and Boutros-Ghali also met in Geneva, and a short time thereafter negotiations for an oil-for-food program resumed.

At least one Iraqi official familiar with the negotiations of 1993 noted that Iraq had won surprising concessions, among them a concession on the scope of intrusive "internal inspections" for the verification of the distribution of humanitarian aid within Iraq. Without specifically naming Vincent and Park, the official noted that Iraq's negotiations had "relied on several relationships we had arranged with the Secretary-General through common friends for whom financial interests were not far from the issue."

The hopes of Park and Vincent for an oil-for-food program languished through 1994 and the first half of 1995 until the defection of General Kamel. In the meantime, Park and Vincent pressed their efforts in Washington to persuade American officials to "rethink the Iraqi situation" and to urge the easing of sanctions.

In late 1995, as Iraq signaled its willingness to reconsider participation in an oil-for-food plan, the Iraqi leadership decided to smooth the way to an agreement by making payments to Vincent and Park, with the intent that some of the money be used as a bribe for Boutros-Ghali. The plan commenced at a time when Iraqi officials and the Secretary-General were emphasizing the considerable discretion Resolution 986 vested in the Secretary-General. The purpose of paying Boutros-Ghali, according to Iraq's Oil Minister, Amer Rashid, would be to ensure that he was "more flexible" and would take steps to "ease the conclusion" of oil-for-food negotiations.

In November 1995, Aziz instructed Rashid to give money to Vincent, and Rashid (as well as another Iraqi official interviewed by the IIC) understood that this money would be used for the benefit of Boutros-Ghali. For internal accounting purposes, Aziz advised Rashid to "create a debt" on the books of the Ministry of Oil to Vincent, and he assured Rashid that this instruction was given with the full consent and approval of Saddam. According to Rashid, he followed orders and entered in the books of the Ministry of Oil what was in effect an IOU for an aggregate amount of $13.5 million or $15 million to be paid in installments to a fictitious company.

Vincent picked up the first installment of money from Baghdad at some point in early 1996. The night before Vincent came to retrieve the money from the Ministry of Oil, two men from Saddam's Presidential Diwan delivered the cash in a briefcase to Rashid's office. The next morning Vincent came to Rashid's office and transferred the cash to his own suitcase. In accordance with Aziz's bookkeeping instructions, Rashid prepared and executed a number of documents in the presence of Vincent and other Oil Ministry officials. One of the documents included the IOU for a fictitious company—the name of which was suggested by Vincent and which Rashid would later recall was a Korean-sounding name.

According to Rashid, Vincent was paid either $350,000 or $500,000 in this initial installment. Another Iraqi official who witnessed the transaction remembered seeing a note for cash from the Presidential Diwan, which stated "to deliver $1,000,000 for the benefit of the Iraqi people." After Vincent received the cash, he immediately left the Ministry with his suitcase and departed in a car that was waiting to take him out of the country.

Travel records show that Vincent returned to the United States on February 21, 1996. After his return, Park went to Vincent's office in Virginia, where Vincent showed Park a copy of an agreement signed by Rashid providing that Iraq would pay Vincent $5 million if the Oil-for-Food Program was initiated. Vincent also gave Park a grocery shopping bag stuffed with at least $60,000 in cash in old U.S. dollar bills. Two weeks after his return to the United States, Vincent also met with Hamdoon at Iraq's UN mission in New York.

From January to April 1996, as revealed in Iraqi diplomatic cables, Vincent and Park served as "backchannel" conduits for communications between Boutros-Ghali and the Iraqi government during the course of the formal negotiations to start up an oil-for-food program. Park visited the Secretary-General's residence at least ten times from February to May 1996, including a visit on May 21, 1996—the day after the formal agreement between Iraq and the UN was signed. Although Boutros-Ghali acknowledged meeting with Park, he denied ever discussing the Oil-for-Food Program with him. Yet Hamdoon's calendar reflects three meetings with Vincent during this same time period, and phone records show at least forty-four phone calls to Vincent from Iraq's UN mission in New York. Vincent was observed waiting outside the negotiation conference room at the Secretariat building in New York in an apparent effort to learn of the progress in the negotiations.

After the MOU was signed on May 20, 1996, an Iraqi official wrote to Baghdad to note the usefulness of information furnished by Vincent and Park during the negotiations:

> I have no doubt that Samir Vincent through the Korean was in continuous contact with the Secretary-General during this period, as we checked what the Korean would transmit to us, and we found his information in accordance with our other channels of

communication with the Secretary-General either through your direct phone calls with him, my direct phone calls with him, or through his personal secretary Fayza Aboulnaga.

The official also stressed that Iraq would continue to need the cooperation of the UN Secretariat in the course of implementing and possibly expanding the program:

> Our need for the cooperation of the Secretariat continues in order to implement the resolution in a healthy/balanced manner. Therefore, it remains important to seek to execute/implement our previous agreement. Therefore, Samir [Vincent] will visit Baghdad shortly to discuss how to deal with the issue. In addition, the implementation of the previous agreement will be important not just to maintain our word but also to reinforce the possibilities of achieving other benefits such as the possibility of increasing the size of the deal upon renewal (keeping in mind the possibility of a complete lifting of sanctions based on circumstances) and the possibility of the Secretary-General adopting other steps such as lifting restrictions on the Iraqi Airways planes and others.

Travel records reveal that Vincent left the United States three days after the MOU was signed.

Iraq soon paid a second installment of cash to Vincent. Although witness accounts vary, it appears that $1 million in cash was released from the Presidential Diwan to the Ministry of Oil and then sent by diplomatic pouch to Hamdoon at the Iraqi mission in New York. Diplomatic pouches are exempt by law from national customs inspections, and the pouch was sent with an Iraqi Intelligence Service official on a Royal Jordanian airlines flight from Jordan.

Vincent picked up at least several hundred thousand dollars of this cash from the Iraqi mission in New York. Park later asked Wyatt Dickerson, a Washington, D.C., businessman and long-time acquaintance, to drive Park to Vincent's office in Virginia. Vincent then paid between $150,000 and $250,000 to Park at Vincent's office.

Even after completion of the MOU in May 1996, Vincent and Park stayed involved in discussions between Iraq and the UN, as there still remained many nuts-and-bolts issues of how the program would be implemented. The signing of the MOU led to many months of preparation activities before the first oil transactions eventually took place at the end of 1996.

In the meantime, Boutros-Ghali's term was due to expire at the end of the year, and he learned in the spring of 1996 that the United States would oppose his appointment to a second term. This was a bitter blow to Boutros-Ghali, and he became preoccupied with attempting to persuade the United States to change its position. Boutros-Ghali privately told a senior Iraqi official that his problems with the United States prevented him from being as effective a mediator between Iraq and the Security Council as he would have liked because of U.S. opposition to his reappointment.

By the fall of 1996, Iraq grew frustrated with delays in starting the program, especially when Boutros-Ghali postponed activity in the midst of a flare-up of military hostilities between the United States and Iraq in September 1996. After Iraq's Foreign Minister wrote to complain of the delay, Boutros-Ghali passed on an oral message through Vincent to an Iraqi official on September 16, 1996, in which he stressed his Arab loyalty, his resistance to U.S. pressure, and his urgent need for support in his bid to gain appointment to a second term as Secretary-General. An Iraqi official later described the Secretary-General's words:

> I am Iraq's most loyal friend and if there had been another Secretary-General under this tremendous pressure from the United States, he would not have been able to do what I did including signing the MOU. And this is the main reason that makes the United States oppose my reelection. I want to repeat my loyalty to my Arab friends

in Iraq and I will try by all my means to get the oil agreement back on track, and this time it will be achieved in a final manner. I call on my friends in Iraq to assist in my reelection campaign.

The next day Boutros-Ghali met with Iraqi officials to discuss expediting implementation of the program. Following this meeting, UN officials met with Iraqi officials three more times in October 1996 to discuss Iraq's lingering objections.

As the months passed, Iraq's positions—including its views concerning the number of in-country monitors of humanitarian aid distribution—became more flexible, but Iraq still worried about certain issues, including how the price of its oil would be set. On November 7, 1996, Park contacted Hamdoon on these issues and advised that Boutros-Ghali thought that he would be able to address them, except the matter of the oil pricing formula, which was outside his authority. Park's message was recounted in a cable from the Iraq mission to Baghdad. The cable, which used aliases to identify Park, Vincent, and Boutros-Ghali, also noted that Park asked about the fate of his "remaining payments" and the possibility of providing "them" quickly or "an important portion of them."

Shortly after the cable, Iraq made another payment under its agreement with Vincent and Park. Although witness accounts vary concerning precisely how this payment was made, Oil Minister Rashid recalled that some form of a third payment was made to Vincent. According to U.S. federal court papers, Iraq sent $1.55 million in cash by diplomatic pouch from Baghdad to the Iraq mission in New York. Vincent picked up money from the Iraqi mission and gave Park not more than $500,000 in cash—again, in old bills that fit into a single shopping bag. Financial records reflect that on December 22, 1996, shortly after 1:00 a.m., Park deposited $500,000 in cash at the MGM Grand Hotel in Las Vegas.

Ample evidence has established that Iraq paid money to Vincent and that Vincent in turn gave much of the money to Park. But no evidence was found that any of the money given by Iraq with the intention that it be paid to Boutros-Ghali was in fact given by Vincent or Park to Boutros-Ghali. Nor was any evidence found that Boutros-Ghali requested payment from Iraq, knew of Iraq's intention to pay him, or received money from Iraq. Boutros-Ghali has adamantly stated that he never received any money from Iraq, nor was he aware of such a scheme.

According to Rashid, Iraq decided after the third payment to Vincent that there should be no more payments for Boutros-Ghali as had been planned. The Iraqi regime was not pleased with his lack of progress in moving the program along. The Secretary-General was also a lame duck, having failed to persuade the United States to drop its opposition to his reappointment.

Iraq stopped giving cash to Vincent, but after the program started, it granted him a liberal supply of oil allocations—including the right to purchase nine million barrels of oil from 1997 to 2001 through his American company, Phoenix International, LLC. Vincent's company was one of the few U.S. companies granted contracts by Iraq under the program, and it netted more than $2 million from its sale of Iraqi oil.

In the meantime, by 1997, Park and Vincent appear to have stopped working together on oil-for-food issues. But Park had already aligned with a new partner: Maurice Strong of Canada. Strong had a long pedigree of high-profile UN positions, including heading up the UN Conference on the Human Environment from 1970 to 1972 and serving as the first Executive Director of the UN Environment Programme. In 1985 and 1986, Strong served concurrently as Executive Coordinator of the UN Office for Emergency Operations in Africa and as a member of the World Commission on Environment and Development. In 1992, Strong was Secretary-General of the renowned Rio de Janeiro Earth Summit.

More recently, in the latter half of 1996 and at Boutros-Ghali's request, Strong had returned to the UN to work on reform issues, and he would also support Boutros-Ghali's unsuccessful campaign for reappointment as Secretary-General. Indeed, Boutros-Ghali discussed with Strong the prospect of appointing him as Deputy Secretary-General and Strong's serving out Boutros-Ghali's remaining term if Boutros-Ghali left his position early; this was consistent with the terms contemplated by one of Boutros-Ghali's compromise proposals made to the United States in his effort to obtain U.S. approval for his appointment to another term. When interviewed by IIC investigators, Al Gore, who was U.S. Vice President in 1996, recalled discussing the Secretary-General position with Strong late in 1996. Gore asked Strong about names of potential candidates for Secretary-General who would be sensitive to global environmental issues, and he was surprised when Strong replied that he himself would be interested in the position.

Ultimately, however, Strong missed out on his ambition to be Secretary-General. When Kofi Annan took over as Secretary-General in January 1997, he asked Strong to continue working on reform issues, and he appointed Strong to the level of Under-Secretary-General as a senior advisor on reform, a part-time position held by Strong until 1998.

According to Strong, he had first met Park in Canada through a common acquaintance. Strong was wary of Park at first, but then when Strong moved to Washington to work with the World Bank, he learned that Park had acquired powerful friends, and Park and Strong developed a friendship. After Strong moved to New York in late 1996 to work on UN reform issues, he kept in contact with Park. In addition to their mutual interest in UN issues, Park and Strong aligned at least some of their business dealings. They traveled together through South Korea in October 1996 to promote interests of Canadian energy companies.

As to Park's ongoing relationship with the government of Iraq, it was in his interest to convey the impression that his services remained valuable despite the departure of Boutros-Ghali. This meant, at the least, that Park had a strong incentive to promote his ties to another high-level UN official such as Strong and to foreign governments willing to do business in Iraq, such as South Korea, to increase his worth in the eyes of the government of Iraq.

In late 1996, Park, Vincent, and Hamdoon met for lunch in a restaurant across the street from the United Nations offices. Earlier that day, Park had asked Strong to join them for the lunch. Strong ended up stopping by but not staying for long. While he was there, Hamdoon invited Strong to travel to Iraq. According to allegations filed in U.S. federal court, after Strong left the lunch, Park told Hamdoon that he had used Iraq's prior guarantee of money to be paid to him for the Oil-for-Food Program to fund his own business dealings with Strong. At that time, Park and Strong had spoken about Park's desire to purchase shares in an energy company, Cordex Petroleum, Inc., which was controlled by Strong through a family holding company.

By 1997, Park had also established an independent relationship with Hamdoon that no longer involved Vincent. Telephone records show frequent outgoing calls from Iraq's mission directly to Park starting in June 1997. Hamdoon encouraged Park to visit Iraq and made arrangements for him to travel there.

Although Strong did not have a formal "Iraq portfolio" within his UN job description, Iraq sought to cultivate his favor. Hamdoon met with Strong, as did Aziz; they both explained to Strong the detrimental effects that the sanctions were having on the Iraqi people, and again, as Hamdoon had done during the earlier lunch, they invited him to visit Iraq. Strong declined these invitations, and there was no evidence that Strong ever took action to advance Iraq's views at the UN.

Despite Strong's decision not to accept Iraq's invitation, he was ultimately the beneficiary of nearly $1 million from Iraq. The payment stemmed from a visit by Park to Baghdad in July 1997. Park invited Strong on this trip, but Strong declined. While in Baghdad, Park met with various Iraqi officials, including Aziz and Rashid, to promote potential business dealings between Iraq and Korea.

At the end of Park's trip, Aziz gave Park a cardboard box with $1 million in cash. Aziz also arranged for Park to be escorted with the money to the Jordanian border. When Park eventually arrived in Amman, Jordan, he got help from an expatriate Iraqi citizen to convert the cash to a bank cashier's check. They opened an account at an obscure bank in Amman, the Housing Bank of Jordan, and deposited the money. The bank in turn promptly issued a check for Park from the account in the amount of $988,885. The bank check was dated July 30, 1997, and made payable on its face to "Mr. M. Strong." According to one bank official, Park acknowledged that he had gotten the money in Iraq.

Park soon returned to New York and arrived on August 2, 1997. He was scheduled to have lunch with Strong on August 4, and he gave the check to Strong on that day. Strong, in turn, endorsed the check to a creditor to whom Strong had guaranteed that he would buy out shares that the creditor owned in his family-controlled Cordex Petroleum. The check was promptly deposited by the creditor on August 5. According to Strong, this payment was made to fulfill Park's previous agreement to invest funds in the company.

It was inconsistent with UN sanctions for Park to engage in an unauthorized financial transaction with the Iraqi government, such as his receipt of $1 million in cash. When questioned by IIC investigators about his receipt of the money from Park, Strong said he did not know that the money came from Iraq. He maintained this denial despite knowing at the time that Park had just traveled to Iraq and despite the printing on the face of the check reflecting that it was drawn from a bank in Jordan.

Park returned to Iraq later in 1997, when he received yet another box from Aziz with $700,000 in cash. He deposited this cash to a new account in his name at the same obscure bank in Jordan and then withdrew this money from the account with several bank checks. He used $500,000 of the funds to repurchase the Historic

George Town Club in Washington (which he had previously sold) and also obtained a $30,000 check made payable to Strong. When interviewed and asked about the reason for this second payment from Park, Strong stated that he could not remember the payment.

As a result of the various activities described above, Vincent has pleaded guilty in U.S. federal court to criminal counts charging him with conspiring to and acting as an unregistered agent of the government of Iraq, engaging in a prohibited financial transaction with Iraq, and making false statements on his U.S. income tax returns. He is cooperating with the U.S. government's ongoing criminal investigation. Park has been criminally indicted in U.S. federal court in New York on charges that include conspiring to act as an unregistered foreign agent and money laundering. No charges have been brought against Boutros-Ghali or Strong, and both have denied doing anything wrong. The IIC's review of the available financial records of Boutros-Ghali and his wife did not reveal evidence that he received any money from Vincent or Park.

Ultimately, Iraq's unsuccessful plan to bribe Boutros-Ghali had no effect on the program. But it foreshadowed Iraq's later successful efforts to pay off individuals it perceived to be friendly to its regime and to manipulate the program illegally for its own advantage.

OVERVIEW OF THE PROGRAM
AND THE KEY ACTORS

Although Resolution 986 described the Oil-for-Food Program as merely "a temporary measure" for the Iraqi people, the program endured for seven years, through the fall of Saddam's regime in 2003. Every six months from 1997 to 2003, the Security Council passed a resolution to reauthorize the program for another six-month phase. Thus, as one UN ambassador observed, "the most comprehensive coercive economic measures ever devised by the UN were tempered by the largest humanitarian relief operation in the UN's history."

The program was intended to furnish help for the Iraqi people and to do so without enriching Saddam or giving him access to unrestricted funds that could be put to military purposes. For this reason, the program did not allow Saddam to receive money directly from oil sales. Instead, it required all of the money from oil sales to go to an escrow account set up by the Secretary-General. This escrow money was available only for certain purposes. About two-thirds of the money (66 percent) was earmarked to buy medicine, health supplies, foodstuffs, and essential civilian needs for the Iraqi people. Of this, 53 percent was inititally designated for the population in central and southern Iraq and 13 percent for the Kurds in northern Iraq. The remaining one-third of the money was assigned

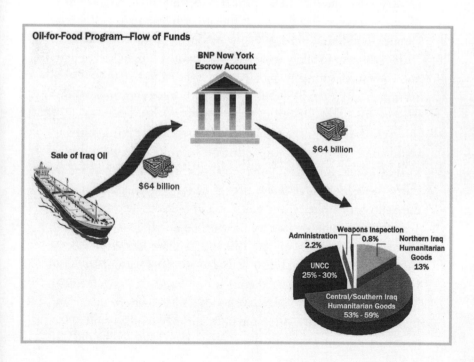

Oil-for-Food Program—Flow of Funds

BNP New York Escrow Account

Sale of Iraq Oil

$64 billion

$64 billion

Administration 2.2%

Weapons Inspection 0.8%

Northern Iraq Humanitarian Goods 13%

UNCC 25% - 30%

Central/Southern Iraq Humanitarian Goods 53% - 59%

to compensating victims of the Gulf War, paying for the costs of UN weapons inspections, and covering the UN's own costs to administer the program.

Oil was first "lifted" (i.e., loaded onto seagoing oil tankers) under the program in December 1996, and the first shipment of humanitarian goods arrived in Iraq in March 1997. Initially, Iraq could export $2 billion of oil per six-month phase. Then in February 1998, the Security Council more than doubled the amount to about $5 billion of oil per phase. In December 1999, the Security Council removed all limitations on the amount of oil Iraq could sell under the program.

Several years of sanctions had degraded Iraq's oil production and transport facilities into a general state of disrepair and deterioration. When the program started, however, the UN declined Iraq's request to use funds from the program to maintain and renovate its oil industry infrastructure. Yet as the program endured, the Security Council decided in June 1998 to authorize a limited "oil spare parts" program to allow Iraq to import up to $300 million of parts and equipment for maintenance and upgrades. In March 2000, the Security Council doubled the oil spare parts allowance to $600 million per six-month phase.

Over time, the range of humanitarian goods that Iraq could purchase under the program expanded well beyond essential food and medical goods. Iraq could purchase goods for many civilian and industrial sectors of its economy, including for construction, housing, mining, youth athletics, and cultural and religious activities.

From start to finish, Iraq sold more than $64 billion of oil to 248 companies under the program. About $32 billion of this oil income was spent on humanitarian goods for southern/central Iraq and nearly $5 billion for the northern Kurdish-controlled governorates. The funds were used to purchase goods and supplies from approximately 4,510 companies located in dozens of countries worldwide.

For each six-month phase of the program, the government of Iraq prepared a humanitarian goods distribution plan that was subject to the review and approval of the Secretary-General. While the government of Iraq administered and distributed humanitarian goods in central and southern Iraq, because of Saddam's mistreatment of and animosity toward the Kurds in northern Iraq, a separate administration, procurement, and distribution system existed for goods furnished to the northern governorates of Dohuk, Erbil, and Suleimaniyah. This system was administered in the name of the United Nations Inter-Agency Humanitarian Programme and involved the following nine entities: the Food and Agricultural Organization (FAO); the International Telecommunication Union (ITU); the United Nations Development Programme (UNDP); the United Nations Educational, Scientific and Cultural Organization (UNESCO); the United Nations Human Settlements Programme (UN-Habitat); the United Nations Children's Fund (UNICEF); the United Nations Office for Project Services (UNOPS); the World Food Programme (WFP); and the World Health Organization (WHO). In addition to their administrative responsibilities in northern Iraq, these agencies were tasked with monitoring and observing the Iraqi regime's distribution of humanitarian supplies in southern and central Iraq.

Apart from the requirement that all money from transactions under the program be channeled through an escrow account, the program had rules for the advance review and approval of each proposed sale of oil or purchase of humanitarian goods. This review was performed by a special sanctions committee of the Security Council and staff members of the UN Secretariat. The sanctions committee of the Security Council was known as the 661 Committee, after the name of the resolution—Resolution 661—that first instituted the sanctions against Iraq. The 661 Committee was one of the first of many sanctions committees that the Security Council has since established to monitor implementation of its sanctions regimes.

For the first several years of sanctions and before the Oil-for-Food Program started, the 661 Committee met sporadically to consider requests for ad hoc exceptions to the sanctions regime, such as notifications by donors of the shipment of humanitarian supplies to Iraq. The advent of the program fundamentally transformed and enlarged the 661 Committee's responsibilities, because the Security Council assigned the committee a key role: to review and approve billions of dollars of transactions that eventually would pass through the program. For oil sales transactions, the 661 Committee was in charge of reviewing and approving a monthly pricing mechanism proposed by Iraq and, in some cases, of reviewing and approving individual oil contracts. Various expert "oil overseers" were hired to assist the 661 Committee in performing these duties.

In similar fashion, for humanitarian goods transactions, the 661 Committee was responsible during the first three years of the program for reviewing all contracts and determining which ones to approve. It received input from UNSCOM and the IAEA, and approval was withheld for items that could potentially be used for military purposes. Several years into the program and because of the exponential growth in the numbers of contracts as the program expanded, the Security Council delegated more and more of the humanitarian contract review authority to staff of the UN Secretariat.

The 661 Committee's operations are best understood in light of the procedural obstacles and political realities that impeded its ability to make decisions on issues that came before it. Very soon after its creation in August 1990, the 661 Committee decided that it would make decisions only by means of unanimous consent among all fifteen of its members. Apart from the veto authority of the Security Council's so-called permanent five or P–5 members (China, France, Russia, the United Kingdom, and the United States), even the Security Council itself does not require consensus for its decisions. The result for the 661 Committee was procedural paralysis in the absence of agreement of all fifteen committee members.

The 661 Committee's chairmanship position was held by the permanent representative (ambassador) of the country chosen to head the committee. By contrast, the remaining representatives to the 661 Committee ordinarily were lower-level diplomats from the rest of the Security Council countries. In general, the Security Council selected a Western European country that did *not* have a permanent seat on the Council to chair the 661 Committee. Yet despite the "chairman" title and ambassador-level rank, a chairman of the 661 Committee wielded little real authority. One 661 Committee chairman described his role as "most miserable" because of the degree to which the committee was "polarized" and "dominated" in its discussions by the P–5 countries. Because of their permanency, the P–5 countries generally took a greater interest and had longer institutional memories and records of participation in the affairs of the 661 Committee. Another 661 Committee chairman wryly recalled that his duties were restricted to the point that "I could say yes to consensus" among the P–5 countries, and "my role was to bridge the gap among the [P–5] and not to break unanimity."

Perhaps the most significant aspect of the 661 Committee's rules and procedures was what they did *not* require. Although established as a sanctions and program monitoring body, the 661 Committee's rules did not explicitly require it to take action of any kind in response to a report of a violation of the sanctions regime or a violation of the program. With the exception of information indicating illegal arms trafficking, the 661 Committee rules stood silent on any obligation to inquire or investigate—much less to report or redress—evidence of illegal activity undermining the sanctions and the program.

All these characteristics of the 661 Committee—the blanket consensus rule, the lack of executive authority in its chairman, the domination by the P–5 countries, and the lack of requirement for action in response to allegations of violations—stifled the committee's effectiveness. These traits foreshadowed the committee's ultimate inability to counter Iraq's manipulation of the program for its political and economic gain.

Although the 661 Committee retained a central role in the review and approval of transactions occurring under the program, the Secretary-General and UN Secretariat were assigned significant administrative responsibilities affecting the day-to-day operations of the program. These powers included: (1) the authority to select a bank to manage the escrow account (along with accountants to audit the account); (2) the appointment of inspection companies to monitor oil exported from Iraq and goods entering Iraq under the program; (3) the review and approval of Iraq's distribution plan for goods imported under the program; (4) the preliminary review of goods contracts submitted for the 661 Committee's approval; (5) the in-country observation and monitoring of goods that entered Iraq under the program; and (6) reporting to the Security Council every 90 and 180 days as to the implementation of the program.

Within the first year of the program's creation, Secretary-General Kofi Annan established the Office of Iraq Programme (OIP), a special administrative unit to run all aspects of the program. OIP administered the program on behalf of the UN Secretariat and in coordination with the various UN-related humanitarian agencies. Annan appointed Benon Sevan, a veteran UN diplomat, as Executive Director of OIP, and Sevan served for the rest of the program until 2003.

In March 1998, the Secretary-General appointed Louise Fréchette —Canada's former ambassador to the UN—to the newly created position of Deputy Secretary-General. He delegated to her "overall supervision" of OIP. Thereafter, Sevan formally reported directly to Fréchette, who in turn reported to the Secretary-General. However, Sevan continued to meet with and advise the Secretary-General concerning developments in the program, directly and through S. Iqbal Riza, the Secretary-General's chef de cabinet (chief of staff).

DESTINED FOR CORRUPTION?

Was the Oil-for-Food Program destined from the start to be corrupted by Iraq? Arguably yes—because it was a basic premise of the program that Iraq was free to choose the companies with whom it did business. It could choose to whom it sold oil. It could choose from whom it bought its humanitarian supplies. Iraq's power to select its business partners meant it could channel its business for political reasons to contractors from certain countries in order to ingratiate itself with the governments of countries—such as China, France, and Russia—that were positioned to relax or remove the sanctions regime. These countries were similarly positioned to block efforts to reform the program in response to Iraq's manipulation.

Iraq's power to choose its business partners also meant more freedom and power for Iraq to extract secret kickback payments from the companies with whom it did business. Such under-the-table payments made to the Iraqi regime violated the sanctions and obstructed the very purpose of the program's rules to keep money out of Saddam's hands. Apart from a pro forma requirement that each company register with its home country's UN mission, the rules of the program did not require any prescreening of contractor participants or provide for any warning to contractor participants of the illegality of kickback payments to Iraq. No effective measures were in place to prevent Iraq from cheating the program with the assistance of companies eager to obtain and retain Iraq's business. As will be discussed in chapter 4, the decision to allow Iraq to choose its contracting partners unwittingly empowered Saddam with political and economic leverage to advance his paramount goal of overturning the sanctions regime and accumulating resources for his own purposes beyond the scope of UN control.

2

POLITICS AND PERFIDY IN PROCUREMENT:
THE U.N.'S SELECTION OF BANKING
AND INSPECTION CONTRACTORS

After Iraq formally agreed to the program in May 1996, the UN promptly set out to hire several contractors to provide essential services for transactions under the program. First, the UN needed a bank to manage the escrow account through which billions of dollars in program funds would flow. Second, the UN needed an oil inspection company to monitor the quantity and quality of oil that Iraq would export under the program. Finally, the UN needed a commercial goods inspection company to monitor and record the entry into Iraq of the humanitarian goods that were to be purchased under the program.*

Like other large organizations, the UN has so-called procurement rules that govern how it is supposed to acquire goods and services from third-party contractors. These rules are designed to ensure that the UN awards its contracts on the basis of fair cost and technical merit, rather than for political patronage or personal spoils. In 1996, the UN's rules generally required competitive bidding and the award of contracts to the lowest acceptable bidders.

*Unless otherwise noted, the narrative in chapter 2 is based on the Independent Inquiry Committee's *Interim Report*, February 3, 2005, 63–113 (describing initial selection of bank and inspection contractors in 1996).

Within days of Iraq's agreement to the MOU, Secretary-General Boutros-Ghali decided to create an Iraq Steering Committee of six high-level staff members of the UN Secretariat. According to Boutros-Ghali, the Committee's purpose was "to ensure the timely and effective implementation" of the Oil-for-Food Program across many UN departments, and the committee was to report directly to the Secretary-General "on a regular basis." Boutros-Ghali asked Under-Secretary-General Chinmaya Gharekhan of India to chair the committee, and among others he appointed as members the UN's top management officer (Joseph Connor of the United States), the UN's top legal officer (Hans Corell of Sweden), and the UN's Controller (Yukio Takasu of Japan).

Despite the power vested in the steering committee, its proceedings were far from a model of transparency or regularity. The committee had no written rules governing its meetings or decisions. It kept no official records or minutes of its proceedings and actions. Indeed, what little is known of the steering committee's activities surfaced quite by happenstance during the IIC's investigation—found within the personal files of two UN staff aides who took informal notes of meetings they attended. In stunningly candid terms, these notes reflected the willingness of UN officials to subordinate the principles of procurement to the perceived political preferences of the UN's Security Council members.

One of the first issues the Iraq Steering Committee discussed was whether it should adhere to the UN's standard competitive bidding rules. After the committee decided to ask for legal advice on this issue, an attorney from the UN's Office of Legal Affairs (OLA) advised that the UN's usual procurement rules should apply to the Oil-for-Food Program. The attorney's memorandum reminded the committee members that "numerous General Assembly resolutions have called for transparency in procurement and for the awarding of contracts on the basis of competitive bidding."

Ultimately, however, the steering committee decided to circumvent the UN's competitive bidding rules, while simultaneously fostering an appearance that proper procedures were followed. The UN ended up awarding each of the major banking and inspection contracts to a company that was not the lowest qualified bidder, in violation of the procurement rules and for reasons of political expediency.

Beyond politics, outright corruption also seeped into the procurement process. A key UN procurement officer—Alexander Yakovlev—tried to solicit a bribe from one of the oil inspection bidders. The IIC's subsequent discovery that Yakovlev had also received hundreds of thousands of dollars in bribes from other UN contractors (outside of the Oil-for-Food Program) ultimately landed him in U.S. federal court, where he has pleaded guilty to several criminal charges of conspiracy, wire fraud, and money laundering. The UN has suspended eight more of its employees pending its continuing investigation of more than two hundred allegations of fraud involving tens of millions of dollars relating to UN contracts outside of the Oil-for-Food Program.[1]

The problems with procurement for the Oil-for-Food Program are the focus of this chapter. The discussion first reviews the UN's selection of the escrow bank, then the oil inspection company, and finally the goods inspection company in 1996. These episodes reveal systemic problems with the procurement and oversight mechanisms and processes in the UN and a management culture that avoided self-examination and investigation. It painfully illustrates the ongoing need for fundamental reform of the UN's rules of procurement, oversight processes, and standards of ethical conduct.

SELECTING AN ESCROW BANK

The UN's first priority was to choose a bank to manage the escrow account and to confirm or issue letters of credit for the immense sums of money that would flow from the sale of Iraqi oil.

When the UN and Iraq negotiated the MOU, Iraq wanted the right to choose which bank would serve as the escrow bank, but the UN balked at giving Iraq this much control. Instead, it was agreed that the Secretary-General should select the bank but in consultation with Iraq about his choice.

Early efforts to select a bank revealed a preference for a French financial institution. On the day that the MOU was signed in May 1996, Secretary-General Boutros-Ghali's chef de cabinet contacted France's UN ambassador to ask if France could forward names of qualified banks. Two days later, Boutros-Ghali told the French ambassador that Iraq had proposed names of three French banks, including Banque Nationale de Paris (BNP)—the bank the Secretary-General would ultimately pick for the job.

In the meantime, the Secretary-General asked Yukio Takasu of Japan—the United Nations Controller and a member of the steering committee—to oversee the bank selection process, and the Treasury office developed a list of qualified banks, including various banks' capital and credit ratings as established by the industry standard measure of the International Bank Credit Agency (IBCA). An IBCA rating of "A" signified a bank of "impeccable financial condition," while a "B" rating signified a bank with a "sound credit profile and without significant problems." On the other hand, a "C" rating signified a "bank which has an adequate credit profile but possesses one or more troublesome aspects, giving rise to the modest possibility of risk developing, or which has generally failed to perform in line with its peers."

This process led to a list of sixteen possible banks. BNP did not make the list. Its capital and credit rating were not the equal of other major international banks. BNP had a credit rating of "B/C," and only one bank that made the list had as low as a "B/C" rating.

In keeping with the requirement of the MOU that Iraq be consulted about the choice of the escrow bank, Takasu forwarded his list of sixteen potential banks to Ambassador Hamdoon at the Iraqi mission. A few days later, the Iraqi mission replied with a list of its own of just four banks, all in France or Switzerland. BNP's name appeared as one of Iraq's four favored banks, despite the fact that it had not been on the list of sixteen banks sent for Iraq to consider.

Takasu advised the Iraqi mission that "the Secretary-General will make the selection on the basis of criteria such as credit quality, capital, operational capacities, services and pricing," and he added that "the bank to be selected should meet all those conditions." He then assembled a "short list" of six banks for consideration. The last of the banks on the short list was BNP—still with the lowest credit rating of "B/C" among other banks. Above BNP on the list were two Swiss banks (Union Bank of Switzerland and Credit Suisse), a German bank (Deutsche Bank), and two American banks (Citibank and Chase Manhattan). Noting that BNP's credit rating was not as high as the other banks, Takasu observed in a cover memo to his list that BNP was included only "because of the preference of the Iraq Government."

The UN then invited each of the six banks from the "short list" to submit within one week a proposal for services and pricing it would offer as the UN's escrow bank. During this period, Iraqi diplomats twice contacted Takasu to express Iraq's strong preference for one of the French or Swiss banks on the list, and Takasu so advised Boutros-Ghali.

Only four of the six "short list" banks submitted proposals: BNP, Chase Manhattan, Credit Suisse, and Union Bank of Switzerland. The UN Treasury office analyzed the service and cost aspects of each of the proposals and rated Credit Suisse highest in all categories. BNP ranked second-to-last on the technical merit of its proposal.

Just as it appeared that Credit Suisse could win the contract on the basis of its merit, the United States intervened to argue against the selection of a Swiss bank. Madeleine Albright, the future U.S. Secretary of State who was then the U.S. ambassador to the UN, met with steering committee chairman Gharekhan to state that it would be a "big mistake" to select any Swiss bank. First, she suggested that Swiss banking laws lacked transparency to maintain accurate oversight of the escrow account and letters of credit. Second, she noted that Switzerland was not then a member of the UN, which could make it difficult to enforce a Security Council resolution against a Swiss company. Finally, she suggested that Saddam and his family maintained their accounts in Switzerland and that a situation where their personal assets and the escrow account could overlap should be avoided.

The U.S.'s concerns did not appear to rest on any evidence that Credit Suisse held money belonging to Saddam's family. Nor did they account for the UN's ability to seek a contract that would allow it open access to and control of its records, as well as provisions for enforcement or penalties in the event of the bank's misconduct in violation of its service contract. In view of Iraq's stated preference for either a French or a Swiss bank, Albright's concerns tipped the commercial benefit of the escrow contract to a co-member of the Security Council (France).

On June 18, 1996, four days after the Albright meeting, the Secretary-General chose BNP for the escrow bank contract. At the time he did not explain why he chose BNP. Under the UN's financial rules, if the lowest acceptable bidder was not selected, there had to be an official certification that the "interests of the Organization" required an exemption from the competitive bidding process. But no such certification or other explanation was ever recorded by the Secretary-General or any other UN official.

When Boutros-Ghali was interviewed by IIC investigators about why he chose BNP, he said that the choice of a bank was a "third-class problem" and that he had "many other problems so Oil-for-Food was not the priority." Despite documentary evidence showing that he had contacted the French ambassador about proposing French bank candidates, Boutros-Ghali could not recall doing so. At first he claimed that he selected BNP because Iraq wanted him to do so, then he later stated that he chose BNP as a political compromise because of concerns raised by the United States. He said that he did not know which bank had been the lowest bidder for the contract and that cost was not important in relation to making sure there was political agreement about the selection of a bank.

The true reason for selecting BNP remained concealed even from the UN's legal office. Two weeks after BNP was chosen, Steven Katz, a senior UN lawyer assigned to assist in the negotiation of the terms of the contract with BNP, requested from Takasu formal documentation establishing that BNP had been selected as a result of a competitive bidding process in compliance with the UN's rules. Takasu replied that the proceedings of the Iraq Steering Committee were confidential and that he would have to provide a briefing on them at a later date. Takasu never did. Despite repeated inquiries, neither the briefing nor the documentation was ever provided to the UN's legal office.

Several months after the Secretary-General chose BNP for the contract, he issued an interim report about implementation of the Oil-for-Food Program. According to this report, he selected BNP from a list of banks with the "necessary credit quality ratings" and on the basis of a "careful consideration" of each bank's proposal. The report did not mention that BNP had the lowest credit rating among eligible banks and that it had the second-to-lowest rating for services offered. It did not acknowledge that political concerns preempted the procurement process leading to the choice of BNP.

SELECTING AN OIL INSPECTION COMPANY AND CORRUPTION IN THE UN PROCUREMENT OFFICE

After deciding upon an escrow bank, the next major step was to select a company to inspect the oil to be exported from Iraq. Resolution 986 limited Iraq to exporting its oil from only two places.

The first was Mina al Bakr—an oil loading platform fed by pipelines from Iraq's southern oil fields. Mina al Bakr, in the lower right-hand portion of the map below, lay several miles off the southern coast of Iraq in the Persian Gulf, where the water was deep enough to accommodate supersize oil tankers. Iraq's second export route was from a pipeline serving oil fields in northern Iraq that ran north from Iraq into Turkey and across to the Turkish port of Ceyhan on the Mediterranean Sea. This pipeline can be seen running to the upper left-hand corner of the map.

Oil is far cheaper to transport by water than over land. Buyers of Iraqi oil arranged for sea tankers to "lift" multimillion-barrel shipments of oil from the export points at Mina al Bakr and Ceyhan. The task for an oil inspection company would be to station in-

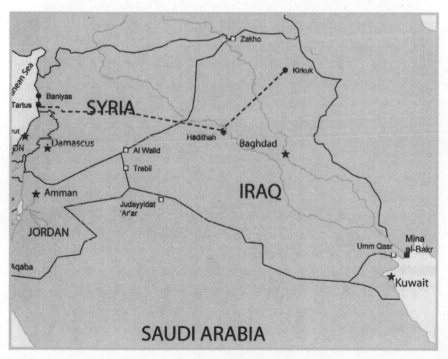

MAP OF IRAQ AND ENTRY POINTS

spectors at Iraq's export terminals to measure and monitor the out-flow of Iraqi oil. The inspectors would also confirm that each shipment of oil was in fact authorized by a UN-approved contract for the sale of oil under the program.

On June 11, 1996, the UN's procurement department issued a formal "request for proposal" to eight international oil inspection companies. The line officer in charge of this process was Alexander Yakovlev, a native of Russia with more than ten years' experience at the procurement department. Allan Robertson was chief of the procurement department.

Six companies submitted bids, including a Swiss company—Société Générale de Surveillance S.A. (SGS)—and a Dutch company—Saybolt Eastern Hemisphere BV (Saybolt). When the sealed bids were opened at the procurement department, SGS had submitted the lowest bid. Two days later, Yakovlev formally recommended to his supervisors that the contract be awarded to SGS as the lowest bidder.

Yakovlev, however, also saw an opportunity for personal gain. He knew a French businessman named Yves Pintore, with whom he had vacationed a summer or two before in the south of France. Now that SGS was well positioned as the lowest bidder, Yakovlev and Pintore arranged to approach SGS with an offer to help it win the contract. From France, Pintore called a vice president of SGS in Geneva. He told the SGS official that he "represented some influential people in the UN in New York" who could help if SGS was prepared to "work with" them to win the contract. Pintore gave some details about the contracting process to demonstrate his apparent knowledge of information from inside the UN's procurement department.

When SGS did not immediately respond to Pintore's offer, Pintore decided to demonstrate again his valuable access to inside information by faxing several pages to SGS of internal UN procurement department workpapers. His fax included Yakovlev's internal memo recommending that SGS be awarded the contract.

In the meantime, Robertson had balked at Yakovlev's recommendation of SGS. He decided the bidders should have an opportunity to
submit new bids to include the costs for oil quality testing and to ex-
clude other items that were no longer relevant to the UN's evolving
specifications. This change prompted an urgent fax from Yakovlev in
New York to Pintore's assistant in France to alert SGS about the new
request for an amended proposal that would come from the UN.
Yakovlev wrote in his fax that the matter was "very urgent" and that
Pintore "must contact SGS" to explain how the quality testing cost
should be added in SGS's response as an additional "lump sum" that
"should not exceed $150,000-$200,000 maximum." Yakovlev asked
to be alerted to the "action taken" by SGS, and he added that the
matter was so "urgent that I am sending [this] from the Office."
Though handwritten, Yakovlev's fax did not bear his name. Either
Pintore or his assistant sent the fax to SGS as a further demonstration
of Pintore's apparent access to inside information.

Both SGS and Saybolt responded to the procurement department's request for an amended bid, and again SGS remained the
low bidder by a wide margin. SGS proposed a contract price of
$1.9 million for an initial six-month service period—half a million
dollars less expensive than Saybolt's bid.

In view that SGS continued to be the lowest bidder, the procurement department recommended that the contract go to SGS. But it
met opposition from Joseph Stephanides, who was Chief of the
Sanctions Branch of the UN's Department of Political Affairs,
which acted as the procurement department's "client" for the purpose of this bidding process. Stephanides had concluded since before even the initial bids that a Dutch company would be a better
choice for the inspection work. Purportedly speaking on behalf of
the Iraq Steering Committee, he had previously complained that
SGS's proposal was defective because it included too many local inspectors who were from the Mideast region and who might, in his
view, be less independent than inspectors from outside the Mideast

region. Following this second round of bids, Stephanides again ar-
gued that Saybolt should be selected despite the fact that SGS remained the lowest bidder. In fact, the UN's request for proposal had
not identified the nationality of inspectors as a concern, and there
was little difference in the nationality distributions described in the
Saybolt and SGS bids.

Robertson decided to send out another request to SGS and Saybolt for the names of nonlocal inspectors and for the companies to
confirm that their bid prices would not change by reason of including the costs of inspectors who were not from the Mideast region.
SGS responded with the names of nonlocal inspectors and confirmed its original bid price. Saybolt, however, seized the opportunity not only to furnish names of nonlocal inspectors but also to
slash its overall contract price in a last-ditch effort to garner the contract. Saybolt not only reduced the man-per-day rate it would charge
for inspectors, but it also lowered the amount it would charge the
UN to conduct oil quality testing. With these reductions in charges,
Saybolt's amended bid price slid barely below—by about $38,000—
the bid of SGS.

Yakovlev protested Saybolt's move, complaining to Robertson
that Saybolt had been asked simply to provide inspector names, not
to submit a price reduction, and that this kind of unilateral price reduction was "a serious violation by Saybolt of bidding procedures
in the attempt to get an award of the contract." The cost of oil
quality testing—which comprised a large part of Saybolt's price reduction—had nothing to do with the geographical origin of the inspectors, about which the UN had asked the bidders for new
information.

It was indeed ironic that Yakovlev of all people was standing up
for enforcement of the procurement rules. It just happened here
that the rules now favored SGS, the company that Yakovlev was
hoping would pay him off to get the contract. Although Yakovlev's
hidden motive to favor SGS was surely improper, he had a valid

point that it was a violation of the procurement rules to allow one party unilaterally to reduce its contract bid when it had not been invited to do so. Nevertheless, Robertson ignored Yakovlev's complaint and refused to consult with the UN Office of Legal Affairs about the violation of bidding rules. Robertson now recommended award of the contract to Saybolt as the lowest contract bidder.

After Robertson recommended awarding the contract to Saybolt, the recommendation went to the UN's Headquarters Committee on Contracts for review. This review was generally required for all major contracts awarded by the UN. The Committee on Contracts discovered that the basis for Saybolt's reduction in oil testing costs was legally invalid because it rested on Saybolt's plan to sell the test results to private third parties. Saybolt could not sell this information, because the information legally belonged to the UN, which was paying for the cost of the testing. Accordingly, Saybolt was required to stipulate that it would not sell the test results. But despite the fact that the basis for Saybolt's winning price reduction was now known to be legally invalid, the UN still decided to award the contract to Saybolt rather than to SGS.

As for Yakovlev and Pintore, Robertson's improper decision to allow Saybolt to amend its bid had the ironic effect of thwarting their own plan to steer the contract to SGS. There was no evidence that SGS ever paid Yakovlev and Pintore. Indeed, perhaps Yakovlev's complicity might never have been discovered but for Pintore's ill-advised decision to send SGS a copy of Yakovlev's handwritten fax about the need for him to warn SGS how to pitch its amended bid. When IIC investigators queried SGS about the contract and received a copy of this fax, they were able to link the handwriting to Yakovlev through comparison of the note with known samples of his handwriting.

As the IIC was uncovering Yakovlev's corrupt role in the Saybolt-SGS bidding process, two investigative reporters—Claudia Rosett and George Russell—broke a story for Fox News about

Yakovlev keeping an offshore bank account in his wife's name and having suspect connections to another business that employed his son and was awarded business by the UN's procurement department (outside of the program). Following up on this information, the IIC soon acquired financial records showing that, since 2000, almost $1.3 million had been wired into an account controlled by Yakovlev in the name of "Moxyco Ltd." in Antigua. The records reflected that more than $950,000 of these payments came from various companies, or individuals affiliated with those companies, that had been awarded more than $79 million in UN contracts and purchase orders (from UN business not related to the Oil-for-Food Program). These records also showed transfers out of the Moxyco account to Yakovlev's UN credit union account and to an account in the name of Yakovlev's wife at a bank in Switzerland.

SELECTING A HUMANITARIAN GOODS INSPECTION COMPANY

The last of the major program contracts awarded in the summer of 1996 was for the inspection of humanitarian goods as they entered Iraq. The candidates for this contract were among a small group of global companies that specialize in private customs inspections—authenticating and certifying the shipment, arrival, quantity, and quality of goods and commodities in the course of international trade. For the program in Iraq, the UN sought to have inspectors stationed at the three border locations where goods imported under the program were allowed to enter Iraq. These locations included the southern Iraqi port of Umm Qasr on the Persian Gulf, the town of Trebil on Iraq's border with Jordan, and the town of Zakho on Iraq's border with Turkey. Later in the program, the UN authorized more entry points along the border with Syria and Saudi Arabia.

An early front-runner for the goods inspection job was Lloyd's

Register of the United Kingdom. Since 1994, seeking to assuage concerns that Jordan was a transit-way for illegal goods to enter Iraq, the government of Jordan had retained Lloyd's inspectors at Jordan's chief port in Aqaba to inspect arriving goods for the presence of any items bound for Iraq in violation of the UN's sanctions. Lloyd's periodically briefed the 661 Committee and officials of the UN Secretariat on the status of its inspection activities.[2]

In the spring of 1996, as Iraq and the UN were nearing agreement on the terms of the Oil-for-Food Program, Joseph Stephanides met with officials of Lloyd's to discuss extending the company's inspection activities to Iraq. The British government took an interest in promoting Lloyd's, and Stephanides assured a British diplomat in early April 1996 that, because he trusted Lloyd's, he would turn down other companies that were asking about a contract for the inspections in Iraq.

But the choice of inspection contractor was not up to Stephanides. As Stephanides later learned, the UN's financial rules required the inspection contract to be awarded by means of the competitive bidding process. On July 22, 1996, the procurement department issued a request for proposal to various humanitarian goods inspection companies, asking for a response in just eight days. Five of the companies responded with timely bids, and the lowest bidder—by far—was Bureau Veritas of France at a price of $4.3 million for an initial six-month term of inspection services. Lloyd's was the second lowest bidder, but its bid was still higher than that of Bureau Veritas by more than $1 million. The procurement department promptly recommended awarding the contract to Bureau Veritas as the lowest bidder.

Stephanides objected, voicing concern that—among other matters —Bureau Veritas had less trustworthy inspectors with links to the Mideast region, from countries such as Pakistan, Turkey, and Jordan. Because the procurement department did not share his concern, he went to the British mission, where he alerted a British diplomat that there was a "whopping" price difference between the bids of Lloyd's and Bureau Veritas. The British diplomat in turn advised Lloyd's that its bid was too high.

On the assumption that Lloyd's would lower its price to get the contract, Stephanides thought that there should be a letter sent to the procurement department advising of the willingness of Lloyd's to submit a lower bid. But Britain's UN ambassador decided instead to send a letter directly to the chairman of the steering committee advising that Lloyd's would now be willing to reduce its bid by $900,000 to a price of $4.5 million—just $200,000 more than the Bureau Veritas bid. The ambassador's letter expressed hope that this new information "will enable the Steering Committee to come to the right decision."

When the steering committee took up the matter on August 9, 1996, its concern was not so much the price offered by Lloyd's but the nationality of Bureau Veritas. As reflected in one staff aide's notes of this meeting, the fact that Bureau Veritas had submitted the lowest bid presented "significant political problems" because it would "be unacceptable to award the contract for goods inspection agents to a French company." This view was consistent with the position of at least some members of the Security Council that—in light of the selection of a French bank for the escrow account and a French citizen for one of the four "oil overseer" posts to assist the 661 Committee—a French company should not also receive the goods inspection contract.

The steering committee decided at another meeting three days later that it could not simply accept a lower bid from Lloyd's because, as the UN's legal counsel Hans Corell warned, "the rules were very strict in this regard" against allowing a company unilaterally to amend its bid during the competitive bidding process. The committee's chairman Gharekhan wondered aloud how Saybolt had been allowed to amend its bid for the oil inspection contract. There is no indication in the notes of the meeting that anyone pursued this discomforting question any further.

Corell discussed how the problem of awarding the contract to a French company could be avoided simply by terminating the competitive bidding process altogether. The UN's financial rules allowed for the suspension of competitive bidding requirements if it was deemed in the "interests of the Organization." This step would require a formal written certification of an Assistant Secretary-General. Corell suggested that authorization could then be "requested from the Headquarters Committee on Contracts to enter into negotiations with one firm—which obviously should be Lloyd's (although this could not explicitly be stated by the Steering Committee)."

The meeting ended without resolving the issue, and the steering committee took up the matter again the next day when it was joined by Joseph Connor, an American committee member who had been absent from the previous meetings and who served as the UN's Under-Secretary-General for Administration and Management. Connor was surprised that there was a problem with awarding the contract to Bureau Veritas, noting that he "had been unaware that nationality was an issue in awarding contracts." Chairman Gharekhan quickly corrected this misimpression. He explained to Connor that "everything about implementation of [Resolution] 986 was 'political,' and no aspect could be assessed purely on its merits." He added that Saybolt had gotten the oil inspection contract despite the fact that it had not been the lowest bidder. In reply, Connor said he would "go along with the formula."

And so politics won over principle in the award of the goods inspection contract—to allow the selection of Lloyd's over Bureau Veritas. The steering committee's instructions were relayed to Benon Sevan, who then served as the Assistant Secretary-General, who would be responsible for certifying the "interests of the Organization." Sevan drafted a memorandum with a heading of "Strictly Confidential" to the procurement department directing it to reject all bids for the goods inspection contract. The initial draft of the memo stated that the procurement department should enter into negotiations with the company that the procurement department "considers is best for the discharge of the duties." When the procurement department requested written clarification from Sevan that it should negotiate with Lloyd's rather than Bureau Veritas, Sevan responded with a revised memorandum proclaiming the "obvious conclusion" to be that Lloyd's should be chosen. Yet the reasons for this "obvious conclusion" were not stated in Sevan's memo.

As with the oil inspection contract, Yakovlev was also the line procurement officer in charge of the goods inspection contract. When he was instructed to award the contract to Lloyd's, he wrote a note to file protesting Sevan's failure to identify the "interests of the Organization" that justified selecting Lloyd's over the lower bid of Bureau Veritas. Yakovlev objected to presenting the Lloyd's bid for approval to the Headquarters Committee on Contracts in apparent violation of UN rules.

His protest was to no effect. The UN formally awarded the contract to Lloyd's without explanation.

Other suitors for the goods inspection contract were bitterly disappointed when the UN suddenly cut off the bidding process. One of the disappointed bidders was Cotecna Inspection SA of Switzerland. Its owner, Elie Massey, wrote to Corell in September 1996 that he was "astonished" to learn of the bidding cutoff and that the UN had given the contract to Lloyd's "without consultation and/or discussion with any other inspection company."

For Cotecna, the lesson must have been clear: political preferences and insider connections win UN contracts. As discussed in the next chapter, Cotecna would bide its time for another shot at the UN inspection contract and then at the next opportunity play the game by different rules.

3

SON OF THE SECRETARY-GENERAL:

FAMILY TIES AND A NEW INSPECTION COMPANY

Lloyd's didn't hold the UN contract for long. Not having been selected in the first place for its competitive pricing, Lloyd's increased its rates with each successive contract extension during 1997 and 1998. The UN acquiesced rather than taking the trouble to put the whole contract out for bid again. But by 1998 Lloyd's rates had spiked 45 percent higher than its original price, to a fee of $770 per inspector per day. This prompted the procurement department to recommend rebidding the contract in hopes of acquiring the necessary inspection services at a lower price.*

By this point in time, Lloyd's ally Joseph Stephanides was no longer a key player in the program. The program's administration had been consolidated as of October 1997 under Benon Sevan and within a newly created administrative unit known as the Office of Iraq Programme (OIP). OIP did not object to the procurement department's proposal to put the contract up for bid again.

The procurement department slated the rebidding process for

*Unless otherwise noted, the narrative in chapter 3 is drawn from the following reports of the Independent Inquiry Committee: *Second Interim Report*, March 29, 2005, 1–84 (describing selection of Cotecna Inspection in 1998 and conduct of S. Iqbal Riza), and *The Management of the United Nations Oil-for-Food Programme*, vol. 3, Chapter 7, September 7, 2005, 195–244 (describing new information concerning selection of Cotecna Inspection in 1998).

the fall of 1998. To allow time for this process to play itself out, the UN extended the Lloyd's contract one more time through the end of 1998 at a cost of $7.8 million—far more than the amount Lloyd's had charged for the initial six-month term when it won the contract in 1996.

Cotecna was a family-owned business based in Geneva. It was founded, owned, and controlled by Elie Massey, a native of Egypt and acquaintance of Boutros-Ghali. One of Massey's sons, Robert Massey, was Cotecna's chief executive officer. The Massey father-and-son team actively supervised Cotecna's worldwide operations.

Cotecna's interest in the Iraqi inspection contract traced back to the first negotiations for the Oil-for-Food Program in the early 1990s. In 1991, Cotecna wrote to Kofi Annan, who was then UN Controller and was involved in the initial program negotiations with Iraq, about its interest in the inspection contract. Annan passed the information on to the relevant UN department, which decided to give the inspection contract to Cotecna in 1992. But because the program did not then go forward, the UN did not enter into a contract with Cotecna at that time, and the UN reinitiated competitive bidding for the contract in 1996.

Despite losing the bid for the UN contract in 1996, the Masseys hoped to bid again, especially as the rest of Cotecna's business took a dramatic turn for the worse. In 1997, Cotecna lost two of its largest inspection contracts—one in Pakistan and one in Nigeria. The loss of the Nigerian contract hit especially hard, because Cotecna had held it since 1984, and Nigeria had been a cornerstone for the company's early growth. According to Robert Massey, by the end of 1998, Cotecna was "starving" and "losing money every month." If Cotecna could garner the Iraqi inspection contract, it stood to generate up to 20 percent of the company's revenue during what Robert Massey described as a "dark" time for the company's business.

It was a dark time for Robert Massey as well, because of an ongoing criminal investigation into his own activities on behalf of

Cotecna in Pakistan. In October 1997, the *Financial Times* of London published a story about a letter signed by Robert Massey agreeing on behalf of Cotecna to pay a 6 percent kickback to an offshore company that was controlled by the family of Benazir Bhutto, who was then the Prime Minister of Pakistan.[1]

The Harvard-educated Bhutto, whose ascendancy to power as a female prime minister had been celebrated as a political milestone in Pakistani politics, was now engulfed in a corruption scandal that eventually forced her from office. In January 1998, the *New York Times* published a front-page article describing "a widening corruption inquiry" involving Bhutto's "house of graft" and the discovery of more than $100 million in foreign bank accounts and properties controlled by Bhutto's family. The article discussed allegedly incriminating evidence acquired from the office of Bhutto's lawyer in Switzerland, who reportedly acted as a conduit and facilitator for illegal payments. Alleged payments by Cotecna, among other companies, featured prominently in the *New York Times* article.[2]

Six months later, in June 1998, the *Financial Times* reported that a Swiss magistrate judge had indicted Robert Massey for money laundering in connection with the Bhutto corruption scandal.[3] The Swiss investigation of Robert Massey would remain pending until mid–2001, when it was closed "on grounds of public interest" with no further explanation, and Robert Massey has denied any wrongdoing.

By the time the Iraq inspection contract came up for bid again in 1998, Cotecna had long employed Kojo Annan—the young son of Secretary-General Kofi Annan. Kojo applied to Cotecna for a job in September 1995, when he was twenty-two and shortly after graduating from university in England. Kojo knew of Cotecna through Michael Wilson, who was Cotecna's vice president for marketing operations in Africa and one of Kojo's boyhood friends from Ghana. Wilson's father had served as Ghana's Ambassador to Switzerland and was a long-standing friend of Kofi Annan. Wilson himself knew

Kofi Annan well and, in the Ghanaian tradition, considered him to be like an "uncle." Wilson spoke with Kofi Annan at some point in 1995 about the possibility of Kojo coming to work at the company.

Not surprisingly, Cotecna decided to hire Kojo in 1995 because of his connections and standing. Though not yet Secretary-General, Kofi Annan was already a prominent native of Ghana and serving as an Under-Secretary-General at the UN. Kojo Annan's mother came from a well-known Nigerian family. According to Robert Massey, Kojo's connections in both Nigeria and Ghana could prove useful to Cotecna's business in these countries.

Kojo shared the news of his job with his father and other family members in the fall of 1995. Kojo's parents had divorced when he was young, but over the years he remained close to his father, and through the years the two spoke by telephone as often as once every week. When interviewed by the IIC's investigators, the Secretary-General stated that he had repeatedly told Kojo not to mix his business activities with the UN because of the appearance of a conflict of interest that could result. He had warned all his children to be "very careful" in their business pursuits, because "I didn't want to have any conflict of interest—they shouldn't try to do business with the UN or get involved with the UN business."

After several weeks of training in the pre-shipment inspection business, Kojo officially started work for Cotecna in January 1996 as a Junior Liaison Officer in Lagos, Nigeria. This job involved Cotecna's inspection work in Nigeria and had nothing to do with the UN. Kojo received a modest monthly salary and the use of a company credit card for business expenses.

At the end of 1996, the Security Council voted for Kofi Annan's appointment as Secretary-General, and the General Assembly formally appointed him to the position. He started service as the seventh Secretary-General of the United Nations on January 1, 1997.

Kojo's job with Cotecna translated to access for Elie Massey to the new Secretary-General. In early February 1997, the Secretary-

General attended the World Economic Forum summit in Davos, Switzerland, where he and his spouse met socially for cocktails with Elie Massey and his spouse. There is no evidence that they discussed Cotecna's interest in bidding on a UN contract during this meeting.

Kojo remained with Cotecna in Lagos, Nigeria, during 1997. He won promotion to the post of Assistant Liaison Officer, then another promotion a few months later to Assistant Manager for the marketing of Cotecna's contract in Nigeria. But this position was short-lived because Cotecna lost its contract to another company in mid–1997. Lacking work for Kojo in Nigeria, Cotecna decided to transfer him to an office in the neighboring, desperately poor country of Niger. Rather than move to Niger, Kojo decided in December 1997 to quit his employment with Cotecna and start his own business.

But Robert Massey had other plans for Kojo—he sought to sign Kojo up for Cotecna as an independent consultant. Company records reflect that Kojo agreed to extend his contract for two more months during January and February 1998 to "provide assistance to Headquarters on a case by case basis upon direct request from R. M. Massey." In the months that followed, Kojo's work for Cotecna would apparently include assisting Cotecna's senior management in their successful efforts to win a contract with the UN.

On February 25, 1998, Elie and Robert Massey jointly wrote to the Secretary-General to congratulate him on a diplomatic breakthrough in Iraq. The occasion for this letter was the Secretary-General's defusing of the threat of military strikes against Iraq from the United States and an agreement with Iraq to allow weapons inspectors access to Saddam's presidential palaces.

One week later, Robert Massey wrote to Kojo's friend, Michael Wilson, to ask: "do we know when Kojo could come to Geneva to discuss his future with us?" Negotiations led to a formal consultancy agreement. Kojo signed up through the end of 1998 to "provide assistance to Cotecna in the research, development and designing of Pre-Shipment Inspection services and contracts with different West African countries." He would receive $2,500 per month for up to seven days of work, plus an additional $500 per day if agreed by both parties. Kojo kept an office in Lagos and did business using letterhead bearing Cotecna's name. Kojo told his father at the time that he had switched to a consulting relationship with Cotecna and hoped to branch out on his own to pursue other business interests.

But Kojo did not heed his father's warnings to avoid doing business involving the UN. Among Kojo's new projects for Cotecna in 1998 was to help Cotecna position itself to get the UN's inspection contract in Iraq. He was well positioned to help Cotecna because of his insider contacts at the UN's procurement department in New York. The procurement official best known to Kojo was Diana Mills-Aryee, whom he had known since boyhood. Following the divorce of Kojo's parents, Mills-Aryee had taken care of Kojo and his sister, Ama, for some period of time. Kojo called Mills-Aryee "aunty," a common term of familiarity in Ghana. Mills-Aryee acknowledged that Kojo came to visit her at the procurement department up to ten times between 1995 and late September 1998. She said that everyone in her office knew Kojo because he was friendly and good with computers, and he would help her colleagues with computer problems when he visited.

Mills-Aryee also introduced Kojo to Nora Dias, another procurement department employee. Dias was secretary to Sanjay Bahel, one of the chiefs of the procurement department. When Dias was interviewed by IIC investigators, she acknowledged that Kojo had visited the procurement department a few times between 1995 and 1997, but she denied seeing him or talking to him at any time in 1998.

At some point in February 1998, Kojo started working with Wilson to collect information from the UN for Cotecna's use. Wilson wrote in a fax to Kojo that "on Iraq, I am happy to note the progress you have made and I quite agree that we should position ourselves now." Wilson copied his fax to both Elie and Robert Massey.

That same month, the Security Council acted to double the amount of oil that Iraq was allowed to sell under the program, and this suggested a possibility that the UN would need more personnel to inspect a greater volume of humanitarian goods that would enter Iraq. Kojo contacted his father's secretary, Wagaye Assebe, to get information about the new Security Council resolution and also contact information both for Benon Sevan, who had become the UN's chief administrator of the program, and for the chairman of the Security Council's 661 Committee. With this information (which was otherwise publicly available), Robert Massey wrote to Sevan and the chairman of the 661 Committee, noting that the Security Council had passed the new expansion resolution, that "the future volume of humanitarian imports to Iraq will necessitate an increased number of inspection companies," and that Cotecna "would be happy to participate in any future tender for the provision of inspection services under the 'Oil for Food Agreement.'"

At the end of March 1998, Kojo contacted his "aunty" Diana Mills-Aryee in the procurement department to get more information about the UN's goods inspection process in Iraq. Kojo then wrote to Wilson on March 25, promising that "in the next few days I will furnish you with other points gathered by Aunty D." He asked Wilson to give him a list of questions and added that "I can then forward this to my people in New York and see what they can get for us."

In July 1998, Kojo took up with a new business associate in Africa—a Franco-Lebanese businessman named Pierre Mouselli. Kojo enlisted Mouselli's help in attempting to win back Cotecna's Nigerian contract, but they also explored plans of their own to set up companies to do business with Iraq under the Oil-for-Food Program. Mouselli had contacts among Iraqi government officials in Nigeria, and he and Kojo paid several visits to the Iraqi embassy in Nigeria. According to Mouselli, "the purpose [of these embassy visits] was Cotecna and what we could do in Iraq—the oil, the food, all." An Iraqi ambassador with whom they met asked Kojo if his father knew he wanted to do business with Iraq under the Oil-for-Food Program, and Kojo told him that his father did not know. It does not appear that the plans of Kojo and Mouselli to form their own companies to conduct business under the program ever came to fruition.

Later in the summer of 1998, Kojo and Mouselli traveled together to Durban, South Africa, where the Secretary-General and large numbers of diplomats had gathered for a summit meeting of leaders from the Non-Aligned Movement group of countries. Before the trip, Wilson sent Kojo several "country briefs," emphasizing on Cotecna's behalf the significance of making contacts with these countries at the "Presidential and political level."

While in South Africa, Kojo and Mouselli had lunch with the Secretary-General on September 4 in the Secretary-General's hotel room. When interviewed by the IIC's investigators, Mouselli recalled that the conversation touched on Kojo's activities for Cotecna in Nigeria and the interest of Kojo and Mouselli in forming their own oil and inspection companies. According to the Secretary-General, when interviewed by IIC investigators, the encounter with Kojo and Mouselli was "so brief I don't think we had much substantive discussion." He denied that they spoke about Cotecna's business interests or about Kojo's visiting the Iraqi embassy in Nigeria.

Upon returning to Nigeria after this trip, Kojo wrote to the Masseys and Wilson on September 14 that he had succeeded during the South Africa trip in making "many contacts," including at the "Presidential and political levels." He added that he and Mouselli had "put in place a 'machinery' which will be centered in New York [and] that will facilitate the continuation of contacts established and assist in developing new contacts for the future." His memo offered no further explanation of this new "machinery" in New York.

Kojo also contacted Assebe, his father's secretary, in early September to see if she could set up a meeting between the Secretary-General and Elie Massey in New York. By this time, it had already been agreed within the UN that the Iraq inspection contract would be put up for rebid, and the UN's procurement department was preparing the specifications for issuance of a formal request for proposals to various inspection companies—including Cotecna. There was no evidence that anyone within the UN, however, had advised the Secretary-General that the contract was about to be rebid, much less that Cotecna was on the list of companies to whom the procurement department would send a request for proposal.

A meeting between the Secretary-General and Elie Massey was eventually set for September 18, and UN records reflect that Elie Massey visited the Secretary-General's office for fifteen minutes from 12:02 p.m. to 12:17 p.m. In a busy day of meetings and appointments with high-level UN staff and advisers, it was the only meeting the Secretary-General had that day with a private citizen. It was also the only meeting marked "private" on the Secretary-General's appointment calendar, and so there are no staff notes or third-party witnesses to what they discussed.

According to both the Secretary-General and Elie Massey, they did not discuss Cotecna's interest in bidding on the UN's inspection contract in Iraq. Instead, both recalled that they discussed Elie Massey's proposal for the UN to raise money through a lottery-style fund-raising campaign and that the Secretary-General referred Massey to another senior UN official, Joseph Connor, to discuss this idea further.

When asked by the IIC about how the meeting with the Secretary-General was arranged, Elie Massey claimed that Kojo had nothing to do with it. According to Massey, he was already in New York City to move his possessions from an apartment he had owned there, and he

simply called the UN for an appointment after looking up the Secretary-General's telephone number in an "international information"
directory. Detailed records obtained from the Executive Office of the
Secretary-General, however, reveal that Kojo requested this meeting.
For his part, the Secretary-General advised the IIC's investigators that
he had agreed in advance to the meeting without knowing what Elie
Massey wanted to discuss.

In the meantime, having completed their travel to South Africa,
Kojo and Mouselli made plans to go to New York in late September 1998 to market Cotecna among diplomats gathered at the UN
for the annual General Assembly session. The scope of their marketing activities in New York is unclear during this timeframe. Kojo
stayed for most of his trip—from September 22 to October 10—at
his father's house, the official riverfront residence of the Secretary-
General on Sutton Place in New York City.

Near the end of Kojo's visit to New York, on October 9, 1998,
the UN's procurement department issued its formal "tender" or request for bid proposals to thirteen inspection companies—including
Cotecna. Ten days later, Kojo wrote to Elie Massey reporting the
UN's tender and that "Robert and Michael can brief you fully."

The deadline for submitting bids was November 5, 1998, and
only six companies submitted proposals. Cotecna's bid was by far
the lowest—about $1 million less than the next lowest bid. Cotecna
offered to charge a man-per-day rate of only $499, compared to
Lloyd's current rate of about $770.

But Cotecna's bid proposal was also significant for what information it did not include. First, there was no mention of Cotecna's
employment of the son of the Secretary-General and the appearance of impropriety that would be raised if the contract were
awarded to Cotecna. Nor did Cotecna disclose the fact that Robert
Massey remained under investigation for the allegedly corrupt payments he directed for the benefit of Pakistan's Benazir Bhutto.

Ironically, when Cotecna had first bid on the Iraq inspection contract in 1996, it filed a basic registration form with the procurement department listing the government of Pakistan as its primary business reference. By 1998, Pakistan was no longer a customer, and Cotecna was embroiled in the corruption scandal. But the UN's procurement department never contacted the government of Pakistan for a reference or took steps to have Cotecna update its registration form to reflect its current financial and legal status. The only background check conducted by the procurement department was to obtain a standard credit report from Dun & Bradstreet, which did not contain adverse information about the investigation of Robert Massey and the Pakistan bribery investigation.

It was not just the procurement department that was to blame. The Swiss mission to the UN also sent an endorsement letter for Cotecna but failed to note that Robert Massey was under formal criminal investigation by a Swiss magistrate for his business dealings in Pakistan. Remarkably enough, the Swiss mission acknowledged to the IIC that it does not perform background checks of companies that it endorses for UN business.

Although the procurement department did not learn of the Pakistani corruption allegations, the Secretary-General himself had spoken with Kojo about Cotecna's ongoing legal woes. Does this mean that the Secretary-General should have told the procurement department? The Secretary-General does not ordinarily have a role in the UN's procurement process, and he insisted when questioned by the IIC's investigators that at no time before Cotecna was awarded the inspection contract did he learn from Kojo or from other sources that Cotecna was bidding on the Iraq inspection contract.

Cotecna submitted its bid to the UN in early November 1998. According to Kojo's cell phone records, he started calling the UN's procurement department very soon after the sealed bids were opened. On the afternoon of November 6—the day after the opening of bids—Kojo made three calls for a total of eight minutes to the procurement department. These calls were interspersed with two calls to Robert Massey. All five of these calls took place within half an hour of each other. Kojo called the number for his acquaintance Nora Dias, who, conveniently enough, was secretary to Sanjay Bahel, the procurement department supervisor in charge of the bidding process for the Iraq inspection contract.

On November 11, Kojo placed another one-minute call to Dias's phone number. Within five minutes he called the number for Diana Mills-Aryee—"Aunty D"—who by that time had transferred from the procurement department in New York to a UN humanitarian aid office in Iraq. This call with Mills-Aryee lasted four minutes. Twenty-five minutes later, Kojo placed the first of two consecutive calls to Wilson, who was one of several Cotecna executives on a "task force" working to win the Iraq inspection contract. Kojo's two calls to Wilson lasted a total of thirty-seven minutes.

Nearly ten days later, on November 20, 1998, Robert Massey called the UN to inquire about Cotecna's prospects and to request a meeting. He ended up speaking to Stephani Scheer, who served as Chief of Office at OIP and was second at OIP only to Benon Sevan. Scheer told Robert Massey that contact with UN personnel during the bidding process was permitted only through the procurement department. Robert Massey then sent a memo summarizing this telephone conversation to Elie Massey, Wilson, and Kojo. That same night, Kojo called Robert Massey's number for six minutes, and then he called Wilson.

The fact that Robert Massey briefed Kojo on his contacts with the UN—in conjunction with Kojo's multiple phone calls to the procurement department—strongly suggests that Kojo was a full-fledged member of Cotecna's effort to win the UN contract. This severely undermines Robert Massey's sworn claim before a committee of the U.S. Congress that "Kojo Annan played no role in helping Cotecna obtain the U.N. contract."

By the end of November 1998, Cotecna had made the "short list" of the three finalist candidates for the UN contract, and the

UN invited all the finalists to New York for an interview about the details of their proposals. Robert Massey, joined by Wilson and two other Cotecna managers, met with staff of the procurement department and OIP late in the afternoon of December 1, 1998. Within two hours of this meeting, Kojo placed another one-minute phone call to Dias at the procurement department. Half an hour later, Kojo called Wilson for five minutes.

The next day, Kojo called Wilson again, and he also placed a one-minute call to Mills-Aryee in Iraq. Immediately after calling Mills-Aryee, he called the home telephone of Felix Downes-Thomas, a UN employee who had worked in 1996 on the UN's MOU negotiations with Iraq and who had also traveled to Baghdad for a few months to assist in opening the UN's humanitarian coordination office there. This conversation lasted twenty-four minutes and was followed by two more calls to Wilson and another call back to the home telephone of Downes-Thomas. Although Downes-Thomas no longer retained program-related responsibilities, the phone call from Kojo was consistent with Kojo's seeking to acquire more information about the program from an inside UN source. For his part, Downes-Thomas did not recall what they spoke about, but he denied to IIC investigators speaking to Kojo about the program. He stated that any conversations he or possibly his son may have had with Kojo were family-related, because his family had long known Kojo's family. Yet Downes-Thomas refused the IIC investigators' request for contact information to speak with his son.[4]

Cotecna's interview with the UN on December 1 went well, and OIP was impressed with the company's preparation and willingness to do the job. Curiously, however, even before the meeting at the UN on the afternoon of December 1, Cotecna seemed to know it would win the contract. Early that morning, Cotecna's vice president for operations, André Pruniaux, e-mailed a business associate that "we are about to be awarded the contract by the United Nations if we can start within a month."

On December 3, 1998, Scheer wrote to the procurement department to recommend Cotecna for the contract. That afternoon and again the next day, Kojo placed one-minute calls to Dias's number at the procurement department. Pruniaux e-mailed another associate in Lebanon, stating that "we now expect to be nominated by the UN before 10 December 1998." He then added: "This is of course extremely confidential." One week later, on December 10, the UN formally awarded the contract to Cotecna.

When asked by IIC investigators about his e-mails predicting the award of the contract to Cotecna, Pruniaux disclaimed any inside information from the UN. Robert Massey also claimed that he did not know in advance whom the UN favored for the contract. According to him, the UN's award of the contract to Cotecna came as a surprise.

Of course, the phone billing records alone do not say why Kojo called the procurement department or what he told Wilson and Robert Massey when he spoke with them during the contract bidding process. Kojo, Dias, and Mills-Aryee all denied speaking about the contract, yet none had satisfactory explanations for why Kojo kept calling during the contract bidding process. Indeed, for the five years of Kojo's cell phone records that were examined by the IIC, the only time Kojo ever called the UN's procurement department was during the fall of 1998, precisely when Cotecna's bid was before the procurement departments.[5]

Despite Kojo's evident efforts to contact the procurement department during the bidding process, no evidence surfaced that the Secretary-General himself did so or that he in any way attempted to favor or steer the contract to Cotecna. Nor did the IIC's review of the Secretary-General's financial records disclose any benefits received by the Secretary-General from Cotecna. The UN's procurement rules did not require the Secretary-General to review or approve the procurement department's decision to award the contract to Cotecna. Cotecna submitted the lowest contract bid by a very large margin, and it seems to have won the contract on the basis of technical merit, low cost, and its favorable presentation to OIP.

Did the Secretary-General know at the time that Kojo's company was bidding on the Iraq inspection contract? This question consumed large amounts of the IIC's investigative efforts, and the evidence ultimately proved inconclusive. On the one hand, the Secretary-General had many opportunities to learn from Kojo of Cotecna's bid during the frequent times he saw or spoke by telephone with him throughout the fall of 1998, a period in which Kojo was actively assisting Cotecna and contacting the UN procurement department. Yet both the Secretary-General and Kojo steadfastly denied any mention of the contract between themselves during the bidding process in 1998. The fact that a father and son often spoke with one another does not necessarily suggest that they spoke of the inspection contract, especially if Kojo was concerned that his father would be wary of an appearance of impropriety. Among millions of pages of UN records and e-mails examined by the IIC, no evidence showed that the Secretary-General was told that the Iraq inspection contract had been put up for rebid by the procurement department, much less that Cotecna was one of the bidders.

The most puzzling evidence before the IIC came from Michael Wilson. When Wilson was first interviewed by IIC investigators, he cryptically suggested that he had talked to the Secretary-General—presumably in the fall of 1998—about Cotecna's bid and the apparent conflict of interest engendered by Kojo's employment with Cotecna. But he quickly called back the IIC investigators to disclaim that he had spoken with the Secretary-General during the bidding process in 1998 about Kojo and a conflict of interest from Cotecna's bid on the UN inspection contract.

Wilson also wrote an e-mail to the Masseys and Pruniaux suggesting that the Secretary-General was apprised of Cotecna's contract bid during the Francophonie summit in Paris in November 1998. According to the e-mail, which was a kind of "trip report" sent from Wilson to the Masseys on December 4, 1998, to update them on his marketing work at the summit, Wilson said that "we had brief discussions with the SG and his entourage" about the contract and were advised that "we could count on their support."

When Wilson was asked by IIC investigators about this e-mail, he claimed that the e-mail was a fake or possibly a result of a dictation error. But this claim was plainly untrue. The e-mail was obviously authentic as confirmed by Cotecna personnel and from its appearance and format, as well as from the nature of its detailed recitation of other events occurring during the Francophonie summit.

Wilson also insisted to the IIC's investigators that he never spoke with the Secretary-General at the Francophonie summit. According to Wilson, he only briefly saw the Secretary-General pass by in a hotel lobby, while Wilson was waiting for Kojo to return from a visit to the Secretary-General's hotel room. According to Wilson, when he saw the Secretary-General in the hotel lobby, they waved but did not speak with one another.

Kojo and the Secretary-General acknowledged seeing each other at the Secretary-General's hotel during the Francophonie summit, but like Wilson they denied any discussion of Cotecna's bid for the Iraq inspection contract. All members of the Secretary-General's "entourage" referenced in Wilson's e-mail were interviewed by IIC investigators and did not recall any discussion of Cotecna's contract bid. Ultimately, it remained possible that Wilson's claim in his e-mail to have enlisted the support of the Secretary-General was no more than "puffery" in an effort by Wilson to make himself appear more important to his superiors at Cotecna.

When interviewed by the IIC investigators, the Secretary-General did not at first recall meeting with Elie Massey before the contract was awarded to Cotecna. He then remembered during a later interview his meetings of February 1997 and September 1998, but only recalled this after the IIC acquired evidence of these meetings from the UN's records. He initially did not recall speaking to Wilson after the contract was awarded to Cotecna about Kojo's employment there, but then later recalled doing so.

And so the evidence of the Secretary-General's knowledge was as confusing as it was inconclusive. But what was clear was that the Secretary-General did not act appropriately to redress the possible conflict of interest once he indisputably learned at a later time that the UN had awarded a contract to Cotecna. He learned this a few weeks after the contract had been awarded, when a British news reporter from the *Telegraph* in London queried the UN's press office on January 22, 1999 about the apparent conflict of interest and about why the contract had been awarded to Cotecna in the face of the ongoing Pakistani corruption scandal.

The *Telegraph* reporter also contacted Cotecna, and Kojo was evidently worried about the media fallout, as call logs at the Secretary-General's Sutton Place residence reflected Kojo's urgent efforts to reach the Secretary-General at 6:30 in the morning. The Secretary-General, who was then in Dublin, soon spoke to Kojo about the matter, and Kojo assured him that there was no ethical problem because he had stopped working for Cotecna. The Secretary-General also called Wilson to ask about Kojo's employment status. Wilson told the Secretary-General that Kojo was no longer with Cotecna. As discussed below, these claims of Kojo and Wilson were false.

In the meantime, Cotecna separately wrote to the British news reporter asserting that Kojo was no longer with the company and had resigned as of the date in October 1998 that the UN solicited bids on the contract "in order to avoid any direct or indirect possible conflict of interest" stemming from Cotecna's bid on the contract. Wilson sent a copy of Cotecna's letter to the UN's press office.

On January 24, 1999, the *Sunday Telegraph* ran a story headlined, "Fury at Annan's Son's Link to £6m UN Deal." In this story, Kojo Annan claimed that "I would never play any role in anything that involves the United Nations, for obvious reasons. I would appreciate if you would make that very clear. I never have done and I never will do." Similarly, a Cotecna representative stated that "Mr. Kojo Annan has never been, directly or indirectly, involved in any UN project and therefore could not, in any way, have provided an 'unfair advantage' to our company in this regard." It is apparent in light of the phone records and memos discussed above that these statements of Kojo's noninvolvement with the UN were false.

Despite the inquiry of the *Sunday Telegraph* reporter and the subsequent story, the UN conducted no more than a cursory investigation of these allegations and the propriety of the award of the contract to Cotecna. The Secretary-General asked Iqbal Riza, his chef de cabinet, to look into the matter. Riza in turn decided to have Joseph Connor, who served as Under-Secretary-General for Management with supervisory authority over the procurement department, to "urgently review the bidding and contract procedures as applied in this case to ascertain whether, in any way, the procedures were compromised or members of the Contracts Committee were aware of and possibly influenced by the fact that Mr. Kojo Annan had been employed by Cotecna."

Connor was annoyed at being tasked with this assignment, instead of having it handled either by attorneys at the Office of Legal Affairs (OLA) or by auditors and investigators at the Office of Internal Oversight Services (OIOS). He did not understand Riza to be requesting him to perform a full-scale investigation but just a search for background information to respond to any more media inquiries.

Connor asked someone, or perhaps several people, within the Department of Management to look into the matter and to gather information. Within the same day, he received a draft response memo for his signature. It reviewed the manner in which bids had been solicited, noting that Cotecna had submitted the lowest bid among several applicants and that Cotecna had been determined on the basis of a Dun & Bradstreet report to be free from pending administrative or criminal investigations. The final two paragraphs of the memo stated that based on a review of the procurement department recommendation and the minutes of the meeting of the Headquarters Committee on Contracts, as well as discussions with the line procurement officer (Alexander Yakovlev) and the chairman of the Contracts Committee, the relevant decision makers were not aware of or influenced by Kojo Annan's employment with Cotecna or Cotecna's involvement in the Pakistani bribery scandal.

An initial draft of the memo for Connor set forth the claim made in Cotecna's letter, that had been forwarded by Wilson to the UN press office, that Kojo had quit his employment with Cotecna in October 1998 in order to avoid a conflict of interest. The inclusion of this information in the memo indicates that the writer or the person who provided the information was in close contact with Cotecna representatives or Wilson during this short period, and that it was considered an important fact. For reasons that are unclear, this information was removed from the final draft of the memo.

Connor was surprised by the speed with which the memo had been prepared and the fact that all of the information relied upon in the memo had been "at hand." No supporting documents were presented to Connor with the draft memorandum, and Connor himself never saw any of the documents or spoke with Yakovlev or the Contracts Committee chairman. However, believing the memo to be reasonably "professional" and complete, he signed it and forwarded it to Riza.

When Riza was interviewed by IIC investigators and shown a copy of Connor's memo bearing the same date as Riza's request for an investigation, he responded, "That's hardly enough time." When asked if he considered this to be "adequate turnaround time" for Connor's review, he replied, "No, I think it came much earlier than I would have expected." And when asked if he and Connor discussed the findings of Connor's memo, Riza stated, "No, I don't think so. No."

One of the challenges for the IIC's investigation of the UN's handling of Cotecna's contract was locating records and documentation about who wrote or worked on the memo for Connor, including any collections of records within the Executive Office of the Secretary-General that might contain such information. One of the sources that held communications between the Secretary-General and the chef de cabinet had, however, been destroyed before the IIC could secure it. The IIC learned from Riza that he had authorized a request from his secretaries to shred several years of his personal "chron" files from 1997 to 1999, the period covering the Connor review. The timing of his shredding order was striking—coming just one day after the Security Council had formally endorsed the IIC's investigation and ten days after Riza himself had written to the heads of UN-related agencies requesting them to "take all necessary steps to collect, preserve and secure all files, records and documents . . . relating to the Oil-for-Food Program." Although there was no evidence to show that Riza intentionally sought to obstruct the IIC's investigation or that he was aware how long his secretaries continued to shred his documents, Riza's secretaries in fact continued to shred his "chron" documents over the next several months of the IIC's investigation, even after the Secretary-General issued a further order to all UN staff members directing them to preserve their documents relating to the Oil-for-Food Program.

Connor's final memo was promptly faxed to the Secretary-General in Geneva on the same day, January 25, 1999. Beyond this one-day inquiry, the UN took no further action to review the Cotecna contract. Although the heads of OLA (Hans Corell) and OIOS (Karl Paschke) were apprised of the issue, the Secretary-General did not ask them to conduct further investigation, and they did not decide on their own to conduct a further review. No disinterested person at the UN spoke to Cotecna or Kojo about the matter.

According to Corell, the Cotecna matter was a "red herring." But Corell believed (incorrectly, as described below) that Kojo was not employed by Cotecna at the time that the contract was awarded to Cotecna. Neither Corell nor Paschke took steps to verify the information in Connor's memo, and instead, following their discussions with other senior UN officials, they dismissed any need for further investigation. Others at the UN, including Riza and the Secretary-General's chief spokesman, thought the matter was simply a "press issue" that did not warrant a probing investigation into the circumstances of the contract award.

As to the allegations about Robert Massey's payments for Benazir Bhutto in Pakistan, the IIC's investigators asked the Secretary-General for his view of "what steps should have been taken where, as here, a company is awarded a contract with the UN and the UN learns that the CEO of that company is under an indictment for money laundering that stems from bribery monies paid to the head of a state in order to get contracts?" The Secretary-General replied, "I think the organization could have reconsidered its relationship with that company."

But the UN did not do so. Indeed, Connor's memorandum confirmed that the procurement department had *not* known about the Pakistani allegations at the time of the contract award. This should have been the starting point for further inquiry, not its conclusion. Instead, the UN renewed Cotecna's inspection contract several more times through the rest of the Oil-for-Food Program without further inquiry of Cotecna or others about the Pakistani corruption allegations of which it was now formally on notice.

The potential controversy passed quickly from the news in 1999. It did not come back to the fore until other questions about the administration of the Oil-for-Food Program surfaced in 2004. Cotecna again assured the UN in 2004 that Kojo had terminated his consultancy with the company in 1998, and that "since the end of his consultancy arrangement, he has not received any remuneration from Cotecna." Robert Massey told IIC investigators on June 1, 2004, that Cotecna had not had business or financial dealings with Kojo Annan since December 1998.

But all these assurances proved untrue. In late July 2004, Robert

Massey admitted to IIC investigators that Cotecna had maintained an ongoing financial relationship with Kojo since 1998, including payments of $2,500 per month to him for five more years through early 2004. According to Massey, these payments were part of a noncompetition agreement—an arrangement entered into between businesses and departing employees to discourage the employees from starting up a competing business or siding with existing competitors. Massey said that he had signed the agreement with Kojo in early January 1999, but he had forgotten about the agreement until he recently discovered it in one of his desk drawers.

Massey's assertion that Kojo simply received noncompetition payments was not true. Financial records showed that throughout 1999 and into early 2000 Cotecna continued to pay Kojo for his ongoing consulting services. These payments were above and beyond the stipulated amount of a monthly $2,500 noncompetition fee. Cotecna also paid certain credit card expenses for Kojo and for three flights from Lagos to Switzerland and London. Cotecna never produced records showing what, if anything, Kojo did in return for these consulting fee payments.

Cotecna and Kojo went to unusual lengths to conceal the fact of these continuing payments. Soon after the *Telegraph* story of January 1999, Cotecna started channeling its payments to Kojo through bank accounts in the name of two dormant companies named "Cofinter" and "Meteor" that were controlled by the Massey family. There was no legitimate economic purpose for channeling the money in this manner. The money was wired to one of Kojo's bank accounts in London.

Then, in approximately February 2000, Cotecna stopped using the dormant company accounts and started wiring the monthly payments instead to an account that was *not* in the name of Kojo Annan. Now the payment went to a Swiss bank account of another entity—Westexim Ltd.—that was designated by Kojo and controlled by Ralph Isenegger, a well-known criminal defense lawyer in

Geneva. According to Isenegger, Westexim was a shell company with a post office box in London and whose Swiss bank account was used for "tax purposes."

Kojo misled the IIC's investigators about his personal benefit from Cotecna's payments to Westexim. He claimed that the monies were used by Isenegger for a football (soccer) club with which he and Isenegger were involved and that he personally received only an "occasional payment" from the Westexim account. In fact, bank records revealed a standing order was entered with the bank for the transfer of funds from Westexim immediately to Kojo's personal account and that he personally received nearly $118,000 of the $122,000 that was wired by Cotecna to the Westexim account from 2000 to 2004.

Kojo stonewalled the IIC's request for banking and financial records that might shed light on what he received from Cotecna following the award of the UN contract. When pressured, Kojo's lawyers ultimately produced records from a single bank account that were so severely redacted that it was impossible to determine the source of funds and destination of disbursements from this account.

The IIC's analysis concluded that Kojo received at least $195,000 from Cotecna after the UN awarded Cotecna the contract in 1998. In addition, more than $130,000 of other suspect payments remained unexplained. This included one payment in 2001 from an offshore bank account of Cotecna in the Jersey Islands to a corporate account in Ghana in the name of a company that was controlled by Wilson and with which Kojo was also involved.

Kojo took some of the money he received from Cotecna to buy a new car—a Mercedes Benz ML 320 sport utility vehicle. He first saw the model at a car show in Geneva in early 1998, and he hoped to buy one for his personal use at home in Lagos, Nigeria. Kojo realized that UN employees could qualify for a 15 percent diplomatic discount, and so he set out to buy the car in his father's name. Wilson fronted a deposit of $3,000 for the car, and Kojo wrote in a memo to Wilson that he would need to "confirm with my Dad whether I can use his name" and that "I have to try and work out whose name we can use to get it shipped" to Africa.

On November 3, 1998—just two days before Cotecna submitted its bid on the UN contract—Kojo contacted a Mercedes Benz representative to describe the specifications for the car. He falsely told a sales representative that the car needed to arrive in Ghana in time for Christmas for the Secretary-General to use. In fact, the Secretary-General did not go to Ghana for Christmas in 1998. Presumably, Kojo intended to have the car shipped to Ghana and then drive it to Nigeria.

Ten days later, Kojo called Wagaye Assebe at his father's office to ask that someone from the UN sign a letter vouching for Mercedes Benz that the car was for the Secretary-General. Assebe prepared a note to the Secretary-General asking who in the office could sign the form for "the car [Kojo] is trying to purchase under your name." According to Assebe, she would have placed this note on the Secretary-General's desk, but she did not remember discussing the issue with the Secretary-General.

For his part, the Secretary-General told IIC investigators that he did not recall the note from Assebe and that he would not have approved a letter for his son to buy the car in his name. He acknowledged that he knew Kojo was planning to buy a car and that he gave $15,000 to Kojo for this reason. But he insisted that he did not know Kojo was buying a Mercedes Benz, much less that he was buying a Mercedes Benz in the Secretary-General's name. There was no indication that the Secretary-General signed any of the sales documents or spoke with any representatives of Mercedes Benz to authorize the use of his name.

Having persuaded Mercedes Benz to sell him the car in his father's name, the next obstacle for Kojo was to get it shipped from Europe to Ghana and to do so free of the heavy import duties that

Third World countries ordinarily apply to luxury cars. Kojo called a family friend, Abdoulie Janneh, who was then serving in Ghana as Resident Representative of the United Nations Development Programme (UNDP). He falsely told Janneh that the car was for the personal use of the Secretary-General in Ghana. Janneh never verified Kojo's story with the Secretary-General. Janneh cleared the way for the duty-free import of the car by filing a formal certification under seal of the UNDP claiming that the car was being imported "for personal use by Mr. Kofi Annan, UN Secretary-General."

Kojo saved himself $20,000 by buying and shipping the car in his father's name. His savings included both the diplomatic price discount as well as the waiver of Ghana's customs fees. After his fraudulent scheme was exposed by the IIC, Kojo agreed in January 2006 to pay restitution to Ghana for duties owing on the import of the car.[6]

LESSONS FOR PROCUREMENT

The UN's initial selection of contractors for the program in 1996 repeatedly placed politics over the integrity of the UN's procurement rules. Perhaps the political concerns were justified, yet their concealment was not. The events of 1996 demonstrated the importance of adhering to the merit requirements of the procurement rules and, if not, then disclosing the true reasons for action to all constituents of the procurement process. Fairness and transparency demand no less.

As for the selection of Cotecna, all concerned candidly acknowledged that it presented an apparent conflict of interest for the UN to award a contract to a company employing the son of the Secretary-General. Ironically, however, in the absence of a financial interest accruing to a UN official, or the official's spouse or dependent children, the UN's procurement rules did not prohibit the award of the inspection contract to Cotecna. Nor did the procurement rules generally require disclosure by company bidders and UN officials of any familial relationships that foster the appearance of conflict of interest, including whether a contractor employs a relative of any UN official with potential influence over the award of the contract. These gaps in the UN's procurement rules persist today. The lack of transparency and protection in the UN's procurement rules against the specter of favoritism is an obvious candidate for future reform.

Finally, there was the failure of responsible UN officials, from the Secretary-General through the chiefs of OLA and OIOS, to initiate promptly and conduct an appropriate investigation of the Cotecna contract award. This underscores the need to revitalize the UN's internal institutions that are charged with assuring the legality of the UN's activities and investigating well-founded allegations of improper conduct.

4

SADDAM'S SLUSH FUND:

OIL ALLOCATIONS AND SURCHARGES

It was a basic assumption of the Oil-for-Food Program that Saddam—not the UN Secretariat or the Security Council—would choose to whom Iraq would sell oil and from whom it would buy humanitarian goods. A report of then Secretary-General Javier Pérez de Cuellar in 1991 observed that "the most efficient way of selling Iraqi petroleum and petroleum products is for Iraq to carry out the marketing . . . in conformity with its normal trading practices" and that "it would be highly unusual if the United Nations were to engage in trading Iraqi oil directly or through a third party." This assumption was never seriously challenged by any of the parties involved in the negotiation or establishment of the program.*

The ill-fated decision to allow Saddam to choose his contracting partners unwittingly empowered him with political and economic leverage to advance his broader agenda. He used this leverage to

*Unless otherwise noted, the narrative in chapter 4 is drawn from the following reports of the Independent Inquiry Committee: *Manipulation of the Oil-for-Food Programme by the Iraqi Regime*, October 27, 2005, chapter 2 ("Oil Transactions and Illicit Payments"), and chapter 4 ("The Escrow Bank and Conflicting Interests").

build and maintain political support for his efforts both to overturn the sanctions regime and to circumvent sanctions by collecting illicit income from companies that did business under the program.

From the start of the program, he gave preferential access to contracts with companies from Russia, China, and France. As permanent members of the Security Council, these three countries seemed best positioned and possibly inclined to effectuate Iraq's goal to be free of the sanctions.

Russian companies garnered more than $19.3 billion of Iraqi oil under the program. This was nearly one-third of all the program's oil sales and about four times more than any other country. For Russia, in an era when its economy was still in recovery from the Cold War, the stakes were large. For each phase of the program, Russia's Ministry of Fuel and Energy sent to the Iraqi Ministry of Oil a proposed list of specific Russian companies, parties, and individuals and the amounts of oil to be sold to each. Russian officials described this as "a strictly internal agency procedure" about which it would not share information with the IIC's investigators. In any event, some Russian companies, including companies owned by the Russian government, benefited greatly. For example, Iraq gave almost $3 billion of oil contracts to Zarubezhneft, a Russian state-owned company that bought more oil from Iraq than any other company.

Chinese companies ranked second in oil deals, with $4.9 billion in purchases. This included more than $2.2 billion of sales to a British subsidiary of Sinochem, a state-owned company of the People's Republic of China. Sinochem was the second largest purchaser of oil under the program.

French companies ranked a close third among all recipients, with $4.4 billion in contracts. Accordingly, nearly half of Iraq's oil sales under the program ($28.3 billion of $64.2 billion) were to companies from the three countries that were the permanent members of the Security Council most sympathetic to Iraq's political point of view and as a result most favorably positioned to relieve Iraq from the crushing burden of sanctions.

Although the United States and Britain were also permanent members of the Security Council, their hard-line stance on sanctions meant that their companies did not fare so well with business from Iraq. Initially, Iraqi Vice President Taha Yassin Ramadan and Minister of Oil Amer Rashid convinced Saddam Hussein to seek to soften the U.S. position on Iraq by selling Iraqi oil to many of the major U.S. oil companies, such as Texaco, Mobil, and Chevron. By mid–1998, however, Iraq changed course to blacklist almost all U.S. companies. One of the few exceptions was Phoenix International, LLC—the company headed by Samir Vincent, a trusted friend of the Iraqi regime.

Still, despite Iraq's blacklisting of U.S. companies, more than one-third of Iraqi oil eventually found its way through intermediaries and resale to satisfy the voracious energy demands of the U.S. market. And some of the major financiers of Iraqi oil purchases by non-U.S. companies were from the United States. Bayoil, operated out of Texas by David Bay Chalmers Jr., financed the purchase of more than 400 million barrels of oil valued at more than $7.3 billion. Chevron Texaco financed the purchase of more than 83 million barrels of oil through more than $1.7 billion in letters of credit, and Coastal Petroleum of Texas purchased either directly or through intermediaries more than 70 million barrels of oil at a cost of more than $1.2 billion.

In Baghdad, the State Oil Marketing Organization—known as SOMO—was in charge of selling Iraqi oil. SOMO was a division of the Ministry of Oil, which also managed Iraq's facilities for producing and distributing crude oil. SOMO did business the old fashioned way. In the ordinary course, a buyer of Iraqi oil came in person to SOMO's office in Baghdad to negotiate and sign a contract, often for millions of barrels of oil at one time.

Once a contract was signed, it was faxed to the UN's "oil overseers" in New York for their review and approval. The overseers were oil industry experts selected by the Security Council's 661 Committee. They advised the 661 Committee whether prices proposed by SOMO corresponded to fair market value. It was important to require Iraq to sell its oil at a price as close to fair market value as possible so that the maximum amount of revenue was collected for humanitarian purposes. Prices too far below fair market value would allow a margin for Iraq to extract illicit payments from buyers in return for their rights to purchase oil.

Upon recommendation of the oil overseers, the 661 Committee approved a pricing formula each month for use in determining the price of the oil sold by SOMO during the following month. The formula linked the price of Iraqi oil to benchmark published prices for other types of world crude oil (Brent and West Texas Intermediate crude oils), with adjustments for transport and other costs and risks unique to the Iraqi market.

The oil overseers reviewed the signed contracts to make sure these included the proper pricing mechanism and other required contract terms. If there were no irregularities, the overseers issued an approval notice that cleared the way for Saybolt's on-site inspectors to allow lifting of the oil from either of the two approved points for Iraqi oil export: the Mina al Bakr terminal in the Persian Gulf or the Turkish port of Ceyhan on the Mediterranean Sea.

Beyond favoring companies from Russia, China, and France, Iraq also decided to furnish allocations of oil to friendly political figures, diplomats, and other individuals of perceived influence who supported political positions favorable to Iraq. At the beginning of each six-month phase of the program, SOMO drew up a list of proposed oil allocations. This list was passed up the chain to Iraq's Command Council, which included Oil Minister Amer Rashid, Finance Minister Hikmat Al-Azzawi, Deputy Prime Minister Tariq Aziz, and Vice President Taha Yassin Ramadan. The list was then subject to Saddam's final review. Iraq did not share its allocation lists with the UN or with the vast majority of its beneficiaries. Nevertheless, Iraq counted on its beneficiaries to support efforts to lift the sanctions regime, either by their acts and statements or by funding groups that advocated for the lifting of sanctions.

Not surprisingly, most political figures who received oil allocations from Iraq were not in the oil business. They certainly had no desire to have their name appear on a contract with SOMO to buy oil. For this reason, political beneficiaries often nominated companies to exercise their allocation rights, and these companies were the ones to sign formal contracts with SOMO to buy the oil. Accordingly, the company's name—rather than the intended political beneficiary's name—appeared on the contract paperwork sent to the UN for approval. The UN would not be advised at all of the political beneficiary's role or interest in the transaction. With a UN-approved contract, the contracting company might then lift the oil itself or transfer its rights to the oil to a major oil company or an oil trader, which would lift and then resell or refine the oil.

A political beneficiary of an Iraqi oil allocation did not have to assume any of the risks or make any of the logistical arrangements for the transaction. Nevertheless, the beneficiary typically received a commission of between 1 to 5 cents per barrel. An allocation for two million barrels could net a risk-free payoff to the political beneficiary of $100,000—all without the knowledge of the UN. In this manner and without having to draw down its own scarce reserves of hard currency, Iraq could use its control of oil sales to seek and maintain favor with foreign officials and public figures of influence.

Did the program or sanctions prohibit Iraq from using its oil riches to favor certain countries and individuals? No—and this was an obvious defect in the program's design. No rules capped the amount of contracts Iraq could give to companies of any single country. No rules required sales only to known or qualified oil companies. No rules prohibited buyers from paying off political officials or other figures of influence, though the laws of many of the countries outlawed such acts. Even where these laws existed, many authorities were unable to detect or unwilling to pursue reports of this activity. Saddam was free to use the Oil-for-Food program to cultivate and maintain political influence he hoped would topple or weaken the entire sanctions regime.

Among the most favored political beneficiaries were politicians and political parties in Russia. For example, Iraq allocated 125 million barrels of oil during the program to the Communist Party in Russia, which controlled a faction of the State Duma, the lower chamber of the Russian parliament. More than 106 million barrels of this oil were ultimately lifted at a value of more than $1.8 billion. The Communist Party reliably opposed the sanctions regime and any military action against Iraq. In February 1999, Gennady Zyuganov, the head of the Communist Party and a one-time runner-up in the vote for the Russian presidency, wrote to Tariq Aziz seeking an increase in a particular oil allocation while also expressing "our invariable solidarity with the just struggle of the Iraqi people against the barbarian aggressive actions of the USA and its allies." Neither Zyuganov nor the Communist Party responded to the IIC's request for an interview or information about their benefit from transactions under the Oil-for-Food Program.

According to records from Iraq's Oil Ministry, Iraq allocated about 73 million barrels of oil to Vladimir Zhirinovsky, the flamboyantly outspoken leader of the right-wing Liberal Democratic Party of the Russian Federation and also a member of the State Duma. More than 62 million barrels of this oil was lifted at a value in excess of $1.1 billion. Zhirinovsky openly opposed the sanctions regime and military action against Iraq. In March 2000, for example, he wrote to Secretary-General Kofi Annan urging him "to end the regime of economic sanctions against the Republic of Iraq." Zhirinovsky frequently visited the Iraqi embassy in Moscow and also traveled to Baghdad. According to one Russian news source, Zhirinovsky still displays a gold, sixty-kilogram statue of a dog that Saddam gave him as a gift.[1]

The money trail for Zhirinovsky's oil allocations leads back to his son, Igor Lebedev, also a member of the Liberal Democratic Party. Oil allocated for Zhirinovsky was bought in the name of various Russian companies. Many of these purchases were financed by Bayoil, a Houston-based oil trading company that is now under criminal indictment in the United States for illegal activities relating to the Oil-for-Food Program. Bank records show a string of payments in this same period of more than $1.6 million from Bayoil, transferred through an intermediary account to a bank account in Cyprus "in favor of Igor Lebedev." Zhirinovsky has publicly denied benefiting from oil allocations and declined to speak with the IIC about his involvement with the program.

Among the many French beneficiaries of Iraqi oil allocations was Jean Bernard Mérimée, France's former ambassador to the UN at the time that Resolution 986 was passed by the Security Council. Mérimée was one of the key officials involved in the negotiations that established the program. He also advocated the lifting of sanctions once Iraq had satisfied its weapons inspections obligations under UN resolutions. In August 2001, Iraq gave Mérimée an oil allocation of 2 million barrels, which when lifted was ultimately worth more than $30 million. This came two years after Mérimée left his UN ambassadorship but while he was serving as Special Advisor to the Secretary-General on European matters.[2] When voluntarily interviewed by IIC investigators, Mérimée admitted that Aziz had offered him an oil allocation during a visit to Baghdad and that it was tied to his previous work in establishing the program. According to Mérimée, he received an allocation because he was a "fair negotiator" in support of the program while serving as UN ambassador. Mérimée sold his oil rights through businessman Elias Firzli to Fenar Petroleum, Ltd., a Liechtenstein company operated by officials of the Taurus Group, a major European oil trader. Mérimée arranged to have $165,000 of the oil sale proceeds wired by Fenar Petroleum to his bank account in Morocco, in order to avoid the use of French financial institutions.

France's former Minister of Interior, Charles Pasqua, appears in Iraqi Ministry of Oil records as the designated beneficiary of 11 million barrels of oil. More than 10 million barrels of this oil was lifted at a value of more than $234 million. Pasqua had previously met with Aziz on two occasions in 1993 and 1995, the first occasion at a time when the two countries did not have diplomatic relations. According to U.S. intelligence sources quoted in the *Washington Post*, Pasqua was "coaching the Iraqis behind the scenes" in 1994 on ending sanctions.[3]

Pasqua's diplomatic adviser, Bernard Guillet, was a frequent visitor to Baghdad and, when interviewed, recalled reporting back to Pasqua on these visits. During one of his visits, Guillet met with Aziz, who stated that he wished to give oil allocations to Pasqua. Guillet reported the offer back to Pasqua, and Pasqua jokingly exclaimed, "I will be king of petrol!" but then immediately said he hoped Guillet had not accepted the offer. For his part, Pasqua denied to the IIC ever discussing oil allocations with Guillet.

The allocations were nevertheless made, though apparently only to Guillet's benefit. As with Mérimée, the oil allocated in Pasqua's name was sold to an oil trader through Elias Firzli. According to Firzli, Guillet asked for his assistance in selling the oil, and Firzli agreed to pay Guillet 2 to 3 cents per barrel. Eight times from October 1999 to October 2000, after each oil lifting, Guillet traveled from Paris to Geneva to withdraw a total of $234,000 in cash from Firzli's Swiss bank account. Pasqua has adamantly denied any involvement in the sale of the oil or receiving proceeds from the oil sales. Guillet has also denied receiving any commissions from these oil sales and strongly questioned the evidence collected by the IIC. He did acknowledge, however, that he withdrew cash from an account of Firzli and used it to pay Firzli, Iraqi nationals in Switzerland who sought medical treatment, and religious leaders who could help Iraq.

Other French figures received allocations. Businessman Claude Kaspereit, son of French Parliamentarian Gabriel Kaspereit, received more than 8 million barrels of oil. Since the company he used to buy the oil, E.O.T.C., was essentially a shell entity and had no means to purchase or sell the oil, he quietly arranged for an established oil trader, Marc Rich + Co., to finance and carry out the transactions. The company was headed by Marc Rich, a notoriously successful oil trader who was a fugitive from U.S. criminal charges until awarded a highly controversial pardon by President Bill Clinton in early 2001.

At times the purpose of oil allocations was unambiguous. Giles Munier, Secretary-General of the French-Iraqi Friendship Association (AFI), received more than 11 million barrels of oil in allocations. The AFI opposed military action against Iraq and advocated the lifting of sanctions. Munier arranged his allocations in a meeting with Tariq Aziz and later with SOMO officials. Although Munier denied receiving commissions for his allocations, he submitted AFI-related expense invoices for reimbursement to both a French company, Aredio Petroleum S.A.R.L., which he nominated to contract for the oil that was allocated in his name, and to Taurus Group, the oil trader that controlled Aredio. Taurus paid Munier more than $240,000.

Iraq also allocated 11 million barrels of oil in the name of George Galloway, a member of the British Parliament and an outspoken opponent of the sanctions in the British Parliament during the late 1990s. More than 6.5 million barrels of this oil was lifted at a value of more than $138 million. In 1998, Galloway became chairman of the Mariam Appeal, named after an Iraqi child whom Galloway had flown from Iraq to Britain for medical treatment. According to Galloway and the Mariam Appeal, the organization was devoted to furnishing medical aid to Iraq and to the care of this one little girl. It also spent considerable resources campaigning against the sanctions regime. From 1999 through 2002 it funded a ten-country bus tour by Galloway to campaign for the end of sanctions and it paid for other foreign travel by Galloway for the same purpose.

Galloway's interest in oil allocations was noticed by oil trader Augusto Giangrandi. According to Giangrandi, he saw Galloway in Baghdad, and Galloway asked him how the allocation process worked and how commissions were negotiated. When told by the IIC of this account, Galloway said the account was a "cock and bull story."

Some of the oil allocations that bear Galloway's name also bear the name of Fawaz Zureikat, a prominent Jordanian businessman. Iraqi officials explained to IIC investigators that many of the allocations in the name of Zureikat were intended to benefit Galloway's anti-sanctions work, and Zureikat himself mentioned to Iraqi officials that his allocation was for "George" or the Mariam Appeal. One early allocation that was jointly listed in the name of Galloway and Zureikat also bears the name of businessman Burhan Al-Chalabi. According to Iraqi Deputy Prime Minister Tariq Aziz, some of Galloway's allocations were allocated in the name of Al-Chalabi.[4]

Bank records show that some of the money from the sale of Iraqi oil was paid through Zureikat to support the Mariam Appeal in England. Zureikat received approximately $3 million from the Taurus Group and other companies that sold the allocations. These funds were deposited in accounts that Zureikat used at the Arab Bank, Jordan National Bank, and Citibank. Almost half a million dollars of these funds were transferred to the Mariam Appeal. In addition, from October 2001 to July 2003, nine cash withdrawals totaling more than $1 million were made from Zureikat's account at the Arab Bank.[5]

The IIC's investigation did not disclose proceeds from these sales of Iraqi oil going directly to George Galloway. However, financial records obtained by the IIC and U.S. Congressional investigators revealed that approximately $270,000 was transferred to the account of Galloway's wife, Dr. Amineh Naji Daoud Abu Zayyad, who was the medical and scientific officer for the Mariam Appeal.

These transfers were made from accounts that had just received deposits of the proceeds of oil sales. A Congressional report states that a portion of oil revenues was transferred to an account in the name of Ron McKay, a Galloway aide ($15,666). In addition, proceeds were transferred to accounts in the name of then Iraqi chargé d'affaires in London, Mudhafar Amin ($150,000).

Galloway, who was interviewed by IIC investigators and who voluntarily appeared before a U.S. Senate investigating committee, adamantly denied having any involvement in oil allocations or deals and questioned the legitimacy of any evidence to the contrary. He has repeatedly acknowledged that Zureikat was one of the benefactors of the Mariam Appeal and has stated that he never asked any of these benefactors how they made the money they donated to the Appeal. He has also informed the IIC that his wife has stated that she never received the money in question from Al-Chalabi or anyone else.[6]

Another vocal sanctions opponent and designated allocation beneficiary was a Vatican priest, Father Jean-Marie Benjamin. Father Benjamin produced a documentary on Iraq, traveled on an unauthorized flight to Baghdad in 2000 in protest of sanctions, and in 2003 helped organize a trip to the Vatican for Aziz during which Aziz met with Pope John Paul II. In 2001, Father Benjamin accompanied Alain Bionda, a Swiss oil trader and friend of Father Benjamin, to a meeting with Aziz for the purpose of soliciting an oil allocation. Father Benjamin called Bionda after the meeting to advise that the allocation had been granted. An allocation for 2 million barrels appears in Iraqi records in the name of Father Benjamin and was contracted for in the name of Bionda's company, Zyrya Management Services. Behind the scenes, Taurus Group lifted the oil and financed the entire transaction, valued at more than $25 million, while paying more than $800,000 to Bionda. According to Bionda, he then felt a moral obligation to donate some of his money to Father Benjamin.

Father Benjamin told the IIC that the money he received was a charitable donation to a religious foundation and not to him personally. Bank records told an interesting story. Father Benjamin had a Swiss bank account that received $140,000 in oil sale proceeds from Bionda. On the same day that this money arrived in Benjamin's account, more than $20,000 was taken out in cash and then more than $90,000 was retransferred to Benjamin's personal bank account at the Istituto per le Opere di Religione (also known as the IOR or the Vatican Bank). Of this amount that was transferred to the account at the Vatican Bank, only $25,000 was given to the religious foundation, and more than $50,000 was withdrawn in bank notes. When asked about these withdrawals, Father Benjamin claimed that cash was needed, among other things, for his travel in Iraq, for production of a documentary film about Iraq, and for the cost of Aziz's trip to the Vatican in 2003. He promised to give the IIC a formal accounting of his use of the money he received, but he never did.

Oil allocation beneficiaries also included officials in Italy. According to Iraqi records, more than 27 million barrels of oil were allocated in the name of Roberto Formigoni, the President of the Lombardy Region in Italy, the most prosperous industrial region of that country. More than 24 million barrels of these allocations were lifted at a value of more than $422 million. Formigoni had become friendly with Aziz in 1990, when he traveled to Baghdad to negotiate the release of Italian hostages. He traveled to Baghdad several times during the program and was openly against the sanctions.

In meetings and correspondence with Aziz and Iraqi officials, Formigoni recommended Marco Mazarino de Petro, his adviser and friend of thirty years, to do business with Iraq. De Petro was employed as a consultant in the Office of the President of the Lombardy Region and traveled regularly to Baghdad. He met with SOMO to obtain oil contracts for an Italian company that had little crude oil trading experience, Costieri Genovesi Petroliferi (CO.GE.P). Although de Petro denied using Formigoni's name in the meetings with SOMO officials, others who attended the meetings recall that Formigoni was mentioned as a beneficiary of oil allocations. De Petro acknowledged telling Formigoni about his relationship with CO.GE.P. He also stated that at his request Formigoni had asked Aziz to "keep CO.GE.P in mind."

Over the course of several years of the program, CO.GE.P contracted for more than 24 million barrels of oil allocated by Iraq in Formigoni's name, and it paid nearly $800,000 in commissions to de Petro. Available bank records do not show any of the oil revenues going to Formigoni, and de Petro denied making any payments to Formigoni, although de Petro's wife and Formigoni acquired ownership in a boat in 2002, during the period in which de Petro was paid by CO.GE.P. Formigoni refused to meet with IIC investigators and in a letter to the IIC, he disputed its findings and stated, "I never received oil allocations from Iraq."

Iraq's oil largesse extended to officials in South Asia as well. Among the listed beneficiaries of oil allocations was Natwar Singh, the Foreign Minister of India and the Congress Party, the ruling political party of India. Iraq allocated four million barrels of oil in Singh's name, and 1.9 million barrels were lifted at a value of more than $46 million. After the IIC disclosed Singh's name as an allocation beneficiary, he was stripped within two weeks of his duties as Foreign Minister and then resigned from the Indian cabinet in December 2005, pending India's ongoing investigation of him and at least seventeen others in connection with the program. Singh has denied any wrongdoing.[7]

Iraq forged close political ties with South Africa during the years of the program. Aziz visited South Africa, and South Africa's deputy foreign minister met with Saddam and other high-level Iraqi officials in Baghdad. When U.S.-led forces invaded Iraq in March 2003, Kgalema Motlanthe, Secretary-General of the African National Congress—South Africa's ruling political party—assured Iraq of his party's support for all "efforts to end the unilateral aggression" of the United States and other countries.

Sandy Majali, a self-proclaimed advisor to the African National Congress and South African President Thabo Mbeki, visited Baghdad as part of a trade delegation through which Majali sought oil allocations. He and his business partners eventually secured allocations in the name of "Sandi Majali—Advisor to the President of South Africa." His allocations resulted in contracts for two South African companies and ultimately the lifting of more than 5.8 million barrels of oil under the program.

Oil Surcharges

More than three years into the program, Iraq decided for its own financial advantage to skim from oil revenues destined for the UN escrow account and to do so by requiring its oil buyers to pay a "surcharge" directly to the control of the Iraqi government. When many of the regular buyers of Iraqi oil balked at the new surcharge demand, a black market emerged almost overnight among oil traders eager to enhance their market share of Iraqi oil. A handful of traders with the daring and sophistication to conceal their control of transactions and financing of surcharge payments soon came to dominate Iraqi oil transactions and to facilitate free from UN control Iraq's receipt of $228 million in illicit income.

In August 2000, SOMO started asking its oil buyers to pay voluntarily a surcharge of 10 cents per barrel directly to it rather than to the UN's escrow account. This kind of direct financial transaction with Iraq violated the UN's sanctions and the rules of the program that required all proceeds from oil sales to be channeled through the UN's escrow account.

Iraq's oil buyers generally declined to pay the voluntary surcharges. Iraq then sought but failed to gain official approval for surcharges from the UN. In early November 2000, Iraq's Minister of Oil Amer Rashid wrote to the Secretary-General to complain that Iraq did not receive money under the program for the costs it incurred to operate its oil production and distribution facilities. Rashid requested that the UN provide for a payment of €1.5 per barrel (about $1.25) and for these sums to "be remitted to a special account designated by SOMO." The Secretary-General referred the request to the 661 Committee, which acknowledged at a meeting that such direct payments to Iraq would contravene the sanctions regime. No action was taken on Iraq's request.

Not receiving a response from the UN, Iraq seized the initiative at the end of November 2000 to make mandatory each oil buyer's payment of a surcharge and also to raise the surcharge amount to 50 cents per barrel—all without notifying or seeking approval from the UN. At the same time, to make it more financially attractive for buyers to pay the surcharge, SOMO proposed to the UN's oil overseers a well-below-market-price formula for oil to be sold during the upcoming month of December 2000. The oil overseers and the 661 Committee refused to agree to the lower price, and with no approved pricing mechanism in place, Iraq shut down its oil trade for the first twelve days of December 2000. When exports resumed, far fewer companies elected to lift oil because of the market instability and their general reluctance to agree to Iraq's excessive surcharge demand. Total exports plummeted, and the imbroglio cost the program about $2 billion in lost revenues.

Iraq soon decided in January 2001 to lower its surcharge demand to between 25 and 30 cents per barrel. By June 2001, its oil exports steadily approached near pre-surcharge levels. While a smaller circle of companies remained willing to buy Iraqi oil, the void in demand was filled mostly by a handful of oil traders who were willing to go along with the surcharge scheme.

This market metamorphosis was not lost upon the UN's oil overseers or members of the Security Council. The overseers warned the Security Council in dire terms that "practically all Iraqi oil" was now sold to "contract holders" that "do not get involved in shipping, financing or other risk bearing activity," and that "this is rather unprecedented in the oil industry and only exists in this shape and form in the case of Iraq." The Security Council's general failure to redress the surcharge policy is discussed in the next chapter.

Iraq continued its surcharge policy for two years, until September 2002. The majority of surcharge payments were made to Iraqi-controlled "bridge" accounts at banks in Jordan and Lebanon. To disguise the Iraqi regime's control of these accounts, they were kept in the personal names of SOMO officials or other Iraqi individuals. The money deposited to the bridge accounts was regularly transferred within the banks to separate accounts in the name of the Central Bank of Iraq. Employees from the Central Bank of Iraq then withdrew cash from these accounts and transported it to the Central Bank in Baghdad.

Nearly one-third of the surcharge payments were made directly

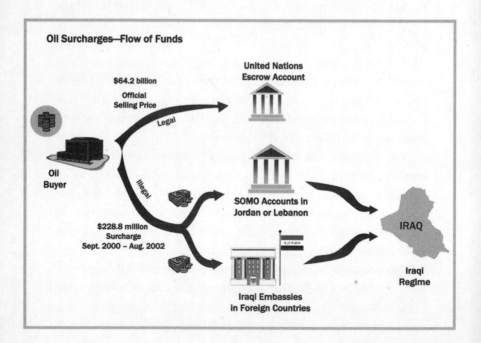

Oil Surcharges—Flow of Funds

$64.2 billion
Official Selling Price
Legal

United Nations Escrow Account

Oil Buyer

Illegal

$228.8 million Surcharge Sept. 2000 – Aug. 2002

SOMO Accounts in Jordan or Lebanon

Iraqi Embassies in Foreign Countries

IRAQ

Iraqi Regime

in cash to various Iraqi embassies abroad, including those in Egypt, Greece, Italy, Malaysia, Russia, Switzerland, Syria, Turkey, and Vietnam. By far the most payments—more than $52 million—were made in the name of Russian companies (including state-owned companies controlled by Russia's government) to Iraq's embassy in Moscow.

At Iraq's embassy in Moscow, Russian company representatives stopped by on a regular basis to drop off cash surcharge payments. For example, Iraqi payment records reflect nearly $8 million in surcharges paid in connection with oil sold to Zarubezhneft, the state-owned company that was the program's largest oil purchaser.

Iraqi Ministry of Oil records also show that surcharges of more than $5 million were imposed on contracts allocated to Vladimir Zhirinovsky. For two of these contracts, cash payments were made to the Moscow embassy, but Zhirinovsky fell behind in payments. In early 2002, Zhirinovsky wrote to Aziz offering to pay his outstanding surcharges by transferring the title to a building he owned in Moscow to the government of Iraq. The fact of this transfer appears in Moscow title registry records, with Zhirinovsky's son identified as the transferor of the building. The building was reportedly being used by the Iraqi embassy as a school.

The Moscow embassy payment scheme was confirmed by the firsthand accounts of numerous Iraqi witnesses and corroborated by scores of cash payment receipts and ledgers maintained by the Ministry of Oil. The authenticity of these records was not subject to legitimate question and in certain instances was self-evident. For example, some of the payment receipts obtained from Iraqi records had telltale fax-ribbon marks at the top reflecting their origin from a Russian company known as Zangas. These marks were the same as the fax-ribbon markings on Zangas's fax correspondence to the UN in New York.

Despite the extensive documentation and testimony regarding surcharge payments through the Moscow embassy and admissions of the scheme's existence by its own official during a 661 Committee meeting, Russia denied to the IIC that surcharges were ever paid by its companies. But when asked by the IIC for an opportunity to interview relevant officials of Russian state-owned companies that appeared in records as having made illegal payments, Russia refused the request. Russia did not disclose any transaction documentation to support its general denial of the fact of payments being made. Recently, Russia has announced that it will not investigate its own companies for illegal payments to Iraq in violation of the UN sanctions.[8]

After Russian companies paid their cash to the Moscow embassy, Iraqi diplomats ferried the cash in diplomatic pouches on jet charter flights from Moscow to Baghdad. When interviewed by IIC investigators, the jet company's owner denied knowledge of transporting the cash. But Iraqi Ministry of Oil records disclosed 5 million barrels of oil allocated personally to the jet owner and also a letter signed in his name on company letterhead requesting an allocation of oil.

Outside of Russia, a small group of well-financed oil traders emerged as dominant players in the Iraqi oil market, especially in the ninth phase of the program beginning in December 2000, when Iraq made surcharges mandatory and many prior buyers refused to go along. This "ninth phase crisis" nearly led to the collapse of the program for lack of oil exports. Only the intercession of certain oil traders, who saw an opportunity to acquire immense amounts of Iraqi oil, succeeded in propping up the program and eventually reshaping the market for Iraqi oil during the next two years of the program.

For an oil trader dealing in surcharge-tainted oil, anonymity was paramount. The oil traders rarely lent their own names to a contract with Iraq but still became the true parties-in-interest to the contracts by buying the rights from political beneficiaries or advancing front companies to act as nominal contract purchasers. As with earlier transactions with allocation beneficiaries, the traders arranged both the financing of the purchases and the logistical arrangements for transporting the oil to its destination. Various front companies and agents channeled payments of illegal surcharges, minimizing the risk for the oil traders that the illegal money trail could be traced back to them.

But the traders' control was not apparent from the documentation submitted to the UN. Large resources of the IIC were consumed in detecting and untangling the traders' global network of payments and corporate fronts devised to obfuscate their complicity in Iraq's surcharge scheme. The results of the investigation laid bare the traders' domination of the market for Iraqi crude oil and their bankrolling of Saddam's illicit surcharge revenue stream.

Bayoil was owned and managed by David Bay Chalmers Jr. of Houston, Texas. Its headquarters was in Houston, with a trading subsidiary in the Bahamas. Chalmers had traded in Iraqi oil since the 1980s, and at the start of the program Bayoil won two oil contracts with Iraq under the program. After Saddam stopped selling to U.S. companies, however, Chalmers switched to acquiring Iraqi oil rights from other companies—mostly Russian—that had received oil allocations. For those transactions Bayoil operated as the true purchaser of the oil, arranging the lifting, transport, and resale to other traders or refiners in the market. By program's end, Bayoil lifted more than 400 million barrels of oil at a value of more than $7.3 billion. This ranked Bayoil as the single largest true market participant for Iraqi oil—an ironic distinction in light of Saddam's general blacklisting of U.S. companies from the Iraqi oil market.

Chalmers worked closely with an Italian businessman, Augusto Giangrandi, who spent a good deal of time seeking business in Baghdad. Before Iraq initiated its surcharge policy, Chalmers and Giangrandi tried to use the name of an Italian entity, Italtech SRL, to obtain Iraqi oil allocations. But Iraq refused. Tariq Aziz told Giangrandi at the time that Iraq did not want to sell to Bayoil or Italtech directly because these companies were conduits for other direct beneficiaries to cash in their allocations. Iraqi officials thought it ironic to have a U.S. company indirectly financing its lobbying efforts to undermine support for the sanctions.

Chalmers apparently saw Iraq's imposition of mandatory surcharges and the market shutdown in late 2000 as an opportunity for Bayoil. The ensuing depressed market and Iraq's need to resume sales now rendered it amenable to giving allocations to Italtech. Italtech amassed contracts for 29 million barrels of oil that were lifted by Bayoil within the first three months of the new surcharge demands. As a result of these and prior oil purchases during the surcharge period, Italtech owed SOMO more than $11 million in surcharges.

When Bayoil and Italtech delayed in paying the surcharges, Oil Minister Amer Rashid summoned Giangrandi to a meeting in March 2001 to demand payment. The meeting was not pleasant. Rashid warned that Saddam himself had directed Italtech to make good on its debt and advised Giangrandi not to leave Baghdad before making the payment arrangements. To placate Rashid and to buy time to talk with Chalmers, Giangrandi wrote $8 million worth of checks on an empty account and left Baghdad to consult with Chalmers.

After Giangrandi spoke with attorneys and discussed the surcharges with Chalmers, the two men agreed there was no choice but to pay if they wanted to continue to do business with Iraq. In April 2001, Bayoil wired over $6 million—more than half of the surcharge debt—to an Italtech bank account. From this account, Giangrandi funneled payments to Al Wasel & Babel General Trading, LLC, a half-owned Iraqi front company in Dubai, and Al Wasel & Babel then passed the money through to SOMO. In case questions were raised about the reason for Italtech's payments to Al Wasel & Babel, phony invoices and contracts were fabricated to make it appear as if Italtech had bought oil from Al Wasel & Babel. For good measure, the phony contracts included a warranty sanctimoniously vowing that no surcharges had been paid in connection with the oil transactions.

The next month, Giangrandi transferred over $1 million through his company, United Management, to Al Wasel & Babel for the payment of surcharges on oil contracts financed by Bayoil. Also in 2001 and into 2002, Bayoil routed more than $3 million in surcharge payments to SOMO through a different front company, Al-Hoda International Trading Company of the United Arab Emirates, which was half-owned by Iraq's Ministry of Trade and Ministry of Oil.

In addition to Chalmers, another Texas oilman in the Iraqi oil market was Oscar Wyatt, the outsized owner of Houston-based Coastal Petroleum. Wyatt had been buying oil from Iraq since at least 1972. During the hostilities of the Gulf War in 1990, Wyatt used his connections to meet with Saddam, and he intervened successfully to secure the release of twenty-one American hostages in Iraq. Wyatt kept in good graces with Iraq's representatives in the United States by donating furniture to the Iraqi mission in New York and a car to the Iraqi embassy in Washington. When Iraq's long-serving UN ambassador Nizar Hamdoon fell ill with cancer and moved to New York for treatment at the Memorial Sloan Kettering Cancer Center, Wyatt guaranteed and paid a significant portion of Hamdoon's hospital bills.

Coastal Petroleum received the very first oil contract from Iraq under the program in December 1996. It was one of the few U.S. companies that continued to secure contracts from Iraq after Iraq took to blacklisting U.S. companies midway through the second year of the program in 1998. During the first four years of the program and before Iraq started demanding surcharges, Coastal Petroleum signed contracts with SOMO to buy almost 50 million barrels of Iraqi oil. Wyatt himself personally handled contract arrangements in Baghdad.

When Iraqi officials first asked Wyatt to pay surcharges, he was noncommittal. But then, according to an Iraqi official, Wyatt decided to go along. Yet he did not lend Coastal's name to a contract for surcharge-tainted oil. Instead, for Wyatt's post-surcharge oil allocations, two newly created companies from Cyprus—Nafta and Mednafta—became the contracting parties.

Despite Wyatt's effort to distance himself from the transactions, it was apparent that he was involved. In UN records, for example, Wyatt identified himself as director for one of these two companies, and banking records reveal that Wyatt or one of his Houston companies paid $15 million to one of the Cyprus-based company's bank accounts. Ultimately, more than $7 million of surcharges found its way to SOMO's coffers in connection with the oil bought by these two Cyprus companies, although the precise financial trail remains unclear. Through his attorney, Wyatt has denied he financed the oil transactions of these two companies or that he financed the surcharges that were paid.

Federal prosecutors in the United States have now indicted Chalmers, Wyatt, their companies, and others who worked with them relating to the payment of illegal surcharges to Iraq.[9] As of June 2006, they were awaiting trial on these charges.

Three more European oil trading firms—the Taurus Group, Glencore International, and the Vitol Group—figured prominently in Iraqi oil sales and surcharges. They helped prop up the beleaguered Iraqi oil market during the first few months of surcharges in late 2000 and early 2001.

Taurus was owned by Ben Pollner, a U.S. national and former protégé of David Chalmers at Bayoil. It financed the purchase of at least 256 million barrels of Iraqi oil sold under the program. Yet Taurus never received any oil allocations in its name or signed any contracts with Iraq. Instead, Taurus invariably acquired rights to Iraqi oil from allocation beneficiaries, then financed the letters of credit, and arranged for the oil to be lifted and resold to other companies.

Like Bayoil, Taurus mostly acquired Iraqi oil through various Russian company beneficiaries, such as Zarubezhneft and Zangas. For one of the first Zangas surcharge payments, Taurus's finance director Martin Schenker made payment by wire of $230,221 directly from a Taurus account in Switzerland to a SOMO account at the Fransabank in Lebanon. Schenker sought to conceal any involvement of Taurus in the surcharge payment. He included a note on the wire transfer form requesting the bank to "kindly effect this payment without any mention to Taurus Petroleum Ltd." and to identify the source of funds simply as from "one of our customers." Zangas paid the next installment of the surcharge directly in cash to the Iraqi embassy in Moscow.

To distance itself from the purchase of surcharge-tainted oil, Taurus eventually decided to do business through two shell companies it created in Liechtenstein—Alcon Petroleum, Ltd., and Fenar Petroleum, Ltd. For Alcon, Schencker installed Amr Bibi, a former Taurus oil trader, as director and beneficial owner. According to Iraqi officials, Pollner went with Bibi and another Taurus manager to SOMO in Baghdad to discuss oil allocations and paying surcharges. By July 2001, Taurus had opened Swiss bank accounts for Alcon and Fenar to use to buy Iraqi oil. Alcon and Fenar contracted with SOMO for nearly 120 million barrels of oil, and bank records show that Taurus financed at least 80 percent of the liftings of oil for Alcon and Fenar contracts.

For all this oil, Alcon and Fenar racked up more than $26 million in surcharges owed to SOMO. Taurus paid many of these surcharges to SOMO accounts in Jordan. Rather than making direct payments, it routed the funds from Taurus accounts in Switzerland through Alcon and Fenar accounts and then through two bank accounts in the names of "Petrocorp" and "Jabal" at a bank in Lebanon, all before the funds finally passed to SOMO's account in Jordan. Apart from the multiple layers of transactions, some of the bank records disguised the purpose of these surcharge payments with descriptions such as "loading fees."

As discussed above, former French ambassador Jean Bernard Mérimée sold his rights to an Iraqi oil allocation to Fenar. According to Ministry of Oil records, surcharges of approximately

$621,471 were paid for this oil contract. One of the bank advices for a surcharge relating to this contract reflects that payment was made "by order of Jean Bernard."

Pollner and Schenker refused to meet with the IIC's investigators, and lawyers for Taurus have denied that it paid or financed any surcharges. Alcon and Fenar representatives denied any wrongdoing and suggested that if there was any malfeasance on the part of Jabal and Petrocorp, "this is their fault," and each of those companies "has to be blamed for that." Of course, the whole point of using shell companies such as Jabal and Petrocorp is to obscure the transactional trail and allow blame to be heaped on the shell company rather than others who were truly in control.

Glencore International is a privately held commodity trading company in Switzerland. It was founded by the notorious Marc Rich, but by the time of Glencore's participation in the program, he had divested his interests in the company. Like other major oil traders, Glencore put few Iraqi oil contracts in its own name but still financed, lifted, and resold massive amounts of Iraqi oil.

Soon after Iraq began demanding surcharges in late 2000, Glencore financed the purchase by other companies of about 40 million barrels of oil for the next six-month phase. For these contracts, millions of dollars in surcharges were paid to SOMO from monies that Glencore paid to two of its agents, Talal Hussein Abu-Reyaleh and Murtaza Lakhani. In addition, for one of its deals involving oil that was bought in the name of Zangas of Russia, bank records show that Glencore wired a commission of 7 cents per barrel to Zangas and then a payment of 30 cents per barrel to a Swiss bank account in the name of Verplank Holding, Ltd., and from which in turn was soon wired the same amount to SOMO's bank account in Jordan.

When interviewed by IIC investigators, Glencore's agent Murtaza Lakhani admitted paying about $1 million of surcharges to Iraq with large cash payments he received from Glencore. He paid the surcharges in cash deposits to Iraq's UN mission in Geneva. To corroborate his claim, Lakhani disclosed a copy of a Glencore-issued "petty cash voucher" for $415,000 and bearing a date of May 15, 2002. Iraqi records independently show that $400,000 in cash was deposited to the Iraq mission in Geneva two days later.

Glencore also bought oil allocated in the name of Sandy Majali, advisor to the South African President Thabo Mbeki. After Majali had failed to pay surcharges for his first contract, Iraq was hesitant to give him another. According to a letter written from Majali to Oil Minister Rashid, there was a meeting on May 10, 2002, involving Aziz, Rashid, Majali, and ANC leader Kgalema Motlanthe at which Majali's interest in another oil contract was discussed. Majali promised in writing to pay the back-due surcharges, but only $60,000 was paid. For its part, Glencore denied to the IIC any knowledge or payment of any surcharges to the Iraqi regime. Majali denied ever agreeing to pay or paying surcharges on this contract and maintains that the $60,000 was incorrectly credited as a payment on this contract.

The Vitol Group is another major European oil trader headquartered in Rotterdam, the Netherlands, and Geneva. Beginning in the second year of the program, Vitol's Swiss subsidiary acquired eight oil contracts with Iraq that had been allocated to Serge Boidevaix, a retired French diplomat and an opponent of the sanctions against Iraq. As head of the Franco-Iraqi Economic Cooperation Association and the French-Arab Chamber of Commerce, Boidevaix was well positioned to make friends in Baghdad, where he frequently visited. Iraq allocated 35 million barrels of oil in his name. He signed contracts with SOMO representing himself as president of "Vitol-France," despite the fact that there was no such company as "Vitol-France." Boidevaix's credentials offered a helpful French angle for SOMO's approval of generous allocations that would ultimately benefit Vitol. Boidevaix himself earned more than $350,000 in commissions from Vitol for his efforts.

When Iraq started demanding surcharges in late 2000, Vitol was willing to go along but disguised its surcharge payments. It employed an entity called Peakville Limited, with a bank account at HSBC Bank in Hong Kong. More than $1 million in surcharges were routed through this Hong Kong account to a SOMO-controlled account in Lebanon. Banking records reveal "Peakville Limited" to be "c/o Mr. R. Favre—Vitol SA" and with a street address for one of Vitol's offices in Geneva, Switzerland. The reference to "R. Favre" is apparently to Roland Favre, one of Swiss Vitol's financial directors and a signatory on Vitol's behalf of its consultancy contract with Boidevaix.

When interviewed by IIC investigators, Boidevaix acknowledged learning from SOMO of the surcharge policy, but he stated that he advised Vitol not to pay the surcharges and that he never was aware of surcharge payments. Curiously, however, two handwritten notes were recovered from Boidevaix that refer to "Peakwilli Hong Kong" and the number "250217.25"—the amount, to the penny, of one of the surcharge installments paid through the Peakville Limited bank account on a load of oil in May 2001.

When asked about these notes, Boidevaix said that he had been given this information by an employee of Vitol and was told to write it down. He explained that immediately after he had been provided this information he tried to contact Vitol trader Robin D'Alessandro. Upon reaching her a few days later, he told her that Vitol should not pay surcharges. According to Boidevaix, D'Alessandro agreed and later informed him that, because Vitol and Boidevaix would not pay surcharges, Iraq would no longer sell oil to Vitol. But nine months after this transaction, Boidevaix nominated yet another company, Devon Petroleum of Panama, to contract for more oil that had been allocated in his name (although oil was never ultimately lifted under this contract).

Apart from oil it acquired with the help of Boidevaix, Vitol made deals with several other allocation beneficiaries. One of them was Faek Ahmad Shareef, an Iraqi-born businessman who lived in

Malaysia. Shareef had family ties to the deputy prime minister of Malaysia, and he arranged trade delegations to visit Iraq. Shareef and some business partners revived a previously dormant Malaysian company, Mastek Sdn Bhd, to act as formal signatory to contracts with SOMO for Iraqi oil.

According to Shareef, during the ninth phase crisis in December 2000, Oil Minister Rashid called him to set up a meeting and explained the difficulty Iraq was having with exporting its oil because of the reluctance of buyers to go along with surcharge demands. Rashid called upon Shareef to perform his "national duty for Iraq" and help keep Iraqi crude oil flowing. Shareef and his business partners agreed they would pay the surcharges, and SOMO gratefully reciprocated with an oil allocation of 39.5 million barrels. It was the single largest allocation of oil during the program. Vitol ended up financing and lifting at least 33 million barrels of this allocation. Mastek and its representatives did the dirty work in paying the surcharges to Iraq, apparently by using monies it received as commission from Vitol.

Vitol also did business with Hamida Na'ana, a Syrian journalist who ingratiated herself to Tariq Aziz because of her efforts to write a book and articles about Iraqi leaders. She received allocations in 2001, and contracts were put in the name of Devon Petroleum of Panama (the same company to which Boidevaix had assigned one of his allocations). Despite the presence of Devon Petroleum as nominal contractor, all Na'ana's dealings were with Vitol. A Vitol trader instructed Na'ana that payments had to be paid as "taxes" due to the Iraqi regime. For these contracts, Na'ana paid more than $700,000 of surcharges directly to a SOMO surcharge account in 2001 and 2002, using money she received from Vitol for this purpose.

Sometimes Vitol was not so careful about covering its surcharge payment tracks. For one contract it obtained in 2001 from a Russian company named Machinoimport, a Vitol subsidiary in Bahrain wired more than $300,000 from its bank account in London directly to a SOMO account in Jordan to pay the surcharge.

Despite all this evidence of its surcharge-related activities, Vitol denied to the IIC that it paid surcharges or knowingly financed their payment by others. Vitol pointed out that it included in most of its purchase contracts a provision requiring third-party purchasers to guarantee that no surcharges or other such payments had been or would be made. It specifically denied any knowledge that Na'ana had paid surcharges and stated that when she asked about surcharges, it had assured her that she had no obligation to pay them.

Among the most brazenly illegal activity during the program was the smuggling in 2001 of several hundred thousand barrels of oil from Iraq's loading terminal at Mina al-Bakr. The scheme might never have come to light but for a Greek sea captain—Theofanis Chiladakis—whose tanker was twice used to smuggle Iraqi oil and who decided after the fact to report the scheme to a UN oil overseer. According to Captain Chiladakis, his tanker, the *Essex*, loaded oil from Mina al-Bakr in May and August 2001, and each time it "topped off" its load with more than 200,000 barrels in excess of what it was authorized to lift under the program.

For Iraq, smuggled oil was far preferable to oil sold under the program. A buyer of smuggled oil paid hard currency directly to Iraq, free from UN interference and free from the requirement of the program that all oil sales proceeds be paid to the UN escrow account. Iraq made the "top off" of the *Essex*'s loads possible by paying more than $100,000 in bribes to Armando Carlos Oliviera, the supervising on-site inspector for Saybolt at Mina al-Bakr. Oil Minister Rashid personally cleared the bribe arrangement with Tariq Aziz.

Both the *Essex* shipments of oil were nominally purchased from Iraq in the name of a French company, Ibex Energy/Multi-Prestation S.A.R.L. Ibex was another preferred French political beneficiary of

Iraq, but it lacked the financial resources to fund this kind of multi-million-dollar oil deal. The financing and lifting of Ibex's oil was controlled by one of the world's major oil traders, Trafigura Beheer N.V., through its London-based subsidiary. Ibex and Trafigura teamed up because Ibex was owned and run by a Frenchman, Jean-Paul Cayre, who had been a business partner of Rui Cabecadas de Sousa, a facilitator of Trafigura's business in Iraq.

For both the *Essex* top-off loads, Ibex entered into two agreements with Trafigura—one for financing the oil lawfully purchased from Iraq under the program and one for financing the smuggled, top-off portion. Because the smuggling deal was illicit, the paperwork for that portion of the deal did not use the principal company names. Instead, the papers were put in the name of an Ibex subsidiary in the British Virgin Islands and Roundhead, Inc., an off-the-shelf company in the Bahamas that was operated by Trafigura. Both the British Virgin Islands and the Bahamas have been known as off-shore havens that furnish easy incorporation of off-the-shelf, post-office-box business entities for transactions in which anonymity and concealment are essential.

After Trafigura sold the oil from the first *Essex* shipment, it sent more than $4 million of the proceeds to a bank account for Ibex's subsidiary. This payment was for the smuggled portion of the *Essex* loading. The Ibex subsidiary in turn wired more than $3 million to a bank account in the name of Windmill Trade, Ltd., in Beirut, Lebanon. When interviewed by IIC investigators, Ibex's Cayre denied knowing of Windmill Trade. But this claim proved untrue, as later-acquired financial records showed that Windmill Trade was just another off-the-shelf company from the British Virgin Islands that was beneficially owned and operated by Cayre. Within a day of the money being sent to Windmill Trade, the same amount was forwarded from Windmill Trade to a SOMO-controlled account at another bank in Lebanon.

Ibex in turn sent about $380,000 back to Trafigura. This was apparently Trafigura's share of profits from the smuggled portion of the first *Essex* load. The two companies covered up the true nature of this transaction with a false invoice identifying the reason for the payment as a rebilling of demurrage (delay fees) incurred by a vessel known as the *Argo Hebe*. The invoice was manifestly fraudulent because Ibex had nothing to do with Trafigura's chartering of the *Argo Hebe* and could not have owed money to Trafigura for this reason.

A similar pattern of payments followed for the second *Essex* loading. SOMO derived more than $8 million from the smuggled loads. In addition, as to the UN-authorized portion of the *Essex* shipments, Cayre dutifully complied with Iraq's surcharge policy, making about $1 million in surcharge payments, routed again through his Windmill Trade account to a SOMO-controlled bank account in Lebanon. Even after the UN detected the top-off scheme in 2001, neither Ibex nor Trafigura was criminally prosecuted by any national law enforcement authorities.

DIVIDED LOYALTIES AND THE ESCROW BANK

Banque Nationale de Paris S.A., now BNP Paribas, acted as the UN's escrow bank throughout the program. The story of Iraq's oil surcharge scheme cannot be told without describing BNP's role in arranging the financing and transactions that helped oil trader clients conceal their true roles in surcharge-tainted transactions under the program.

To comprehend BNP's role in the program it is necessary to understand BNP's duties to provide letter-of-credit financing under the terms of its service contract with the UN. A letter of credit is a written promise of a bank to pay a seller for goods, usually upon the delivery of the goods, if the seller does not receive payment from the buyer. Letters of credit have long been indispensable to transnational business transactions because sellers cannot always trust buyers to make good on their payment obligations. When a bank *issues* a letter of credit, it is guaranteeing in the first instance that the buyer will pay. By contrast, when a bank *confirms* another bank's letter of credit, it is guaranteeing payment only if the issuing bank defaults on its duty to make payment on behalf of a buyer.

BNP's primary role as set forth in its service contract with the UN was to confirm letters of credit issued from other banks on behalf of prospective buyers of oil. It was double protection for Iraq—if the first bank did not pay, then BNP as escrow bank would ensure that the funds were credited to the account. But BNP also retained an option under the terms of the service contract to issue letters of credit on behalf of oil buyers. And in most cases under the program it ended up doing so. Either BNP in France or one of its various global subsidiaries and affiliates, including BNP's office in Geneva, Switzerland, issued 72 percent of all letters of credit for oil transactions during the program.

BNP was surely within its contract rights to issue letters of credit for oil buyers. But this role planted the seeds of a conflict of interest. On the one hand, BNP's primary customer was the UN, and it had an allegiance to the terms of Resolution 986 "to ensure the transparency of each transaction" under the program. Indeed, the requirements of Resolution 986 were incorporated as "essential and fundamental terms and conditions" of BNP's service contract with the UN. On the other hand, by issuing rather than merely confirming a letter of credit, BNP acquired a second customer—the oil buyer or financier. If the oil buyer or financier could gain because a transaction was *not* transparent and its particulars *not* fully disclosed to the UN, then BNP's loyalties would stand irreconcilably divided. This is precisely what happened beginning in late 2000, when Iraq initiated its surcharge scheme and the true purchasers of Iraqi oil sought to conceal their role in the program's oil transactions.

Although many purchases of Iraqi oil under the program were

direct transactions between SOMO and the contracting party, numerous other transactions involved third-party oil traders that financed the purchase in the name of the nominal contracting party and physically took possession and control of the oil from lifting to resale. Many of these third-party oil traders were customers of BNP, mostly BNP's affiliate in Geneva, which despite its obligation under the UN contract did not disclose its involvement during the program even to other branches of BNP, much less to the UN.

BNP officials explained to IIC investigators that such financing arrangements and the nondisclosure of third parties involved in these transactions were routine in the oil industry. They pointed out that the third-party purchaser client requested nondisclosure, that the disclosure would cause complications in the UN review process and risk rejection by the UN of the letter of credit if a name other than the purchaser was identified, and that disclosure might violate Swiss bank secrecy laws.

These explanations did not withstand serious scrutiny. BNP's concealment of the involvement of third parties was contrary to its agreement with the UN, and both BNP and the third party were aware that the standard contracting terms and program procedures prohibited assigning or transferring letters of credit, which was the essential effect of these third-party financing transactions. The transparency that the program procedures were meant to provide compelled disclosure of the third-party's involvement. As for the stated concern of BNP officials for Swiss bank secrecy, this apparently did not prohibit large-scale disclosure of information to the bank's parent or prevent the bank from seeking a waiver from its third-party client, as it had done during the IIC's investigation.

Two examples—involving Glencore and Texaco—reveal how BNP was faced with competing interests of the UN and its oil-purchasing clients and how the needs of those clients won out. In late 2000, Iraq allocated 9 million barrels of oil for the benefit of the Russian Communist Party. The oil was contracted in the name of a

Russian entity known as ACTEC (Council for Trade and Economic Cooperation with Middle East and North Africa Countries). ACTEC ranked as the eighth largest purchaser in the program, signing contracts for nearly 72 million barrels of oil. Yet ACTEC was not an established oil company. It was merely a nameplate company that temporarily leased office space during the program at a Russian foreign service training school in Moscow. The company has now abandoned the space and appears no longer even to exist. During the IIC's investigation, investigators made a number of efforts to locate and interview Vladimir Zair-Bek, the company's president and signatory on contracts, but he was nowhere to be found.

The UN's records reflect that ACTEC secured letters of credit from BNP in Geneva for its purchase of 9 million barrels of oil in the ninth phase of the program, just as Iraq's surcharge policy went into effect. In reality, Glencore financed two of the three letters of credit supporting this purchase. The UN did not know Glencore's role because Glencore specifically instructed BNP Geneva not to reveal its name. Glencore's correspondence with BNP Geneva makes clear that Glencore, and not ACTEC, was the true party in interest and principal behind the transaction: it stated that Glencore had full responsibility for the transaction and that the costs of the transaction were to be drawn from Glencore's credit line with the bank.

Glencore's request for concealment of its identity was repeated three times in its request to the bank for a letter of credit. In addition to its first request, Glencore wrote: "We repeat that Glencore International AG's name must not appear on any correspondence you send to third parties. . . . We remind you that there must be absolutely no mention of the name of Glencore International AG." BNP honored Glencore's request, and so far as the UN's documents reflected, ACTEC was the true party to this transaction.

ACTEC gave the bank a power of attorney assigning its rights to Glencore for the oil. This violated a provision of the UN-approved contract between SOMO and ACTEC that prohibited the assignment of the oil buyer's rights without approval of the 661 Committee. The bank did not disclose this violation to the UN. Instead, it furnished the financing to effectuate Glencore's secret substitution as the true party in interest to the contract with SOMO. Nearly $1.2 million in cash surcharges was later paid in ACTEC's name to the Iraqi embassy in Moscow for the oil sold from ACTEC's allocation.

In the same way, BNP concealed Texaco's role in another oil deal with Iraq, and this time it was BNP's New York office that did so, despite the fact that the New York office had primary responsibility for the UN's escrow account. A Romanian company known as Bulf Drilling and Oil obtained a contract with SOMO in February 2001. Bulf promptly gave power-of-attorney rights to a U.S. company, Midway Oil of Reston, Virginia, who in turn exercised the power of attorney to allow Texaco to open a letter of credit for the purchase of 1 million barrels of oil from this contract. Midway agreed that Texaco would have full authority regarding any future transactions related to the financing of the letter of credit, as well as to the possession of the oil. This was effectively an assignment of rights in violation of the UN-approved contract and known to BNP New York but not disclosed to the UN. Continuing the appearance that Bulf was the true party in interest, BNP in New York issued multiple letters of credit in Bulf's name without disclosing Texaco's involvement (except apparently by accident on one transmittal document). Midway paid more than $400,000 in surcharges relating to Bulf's contract. Midway eventually pleaded guilty in New York court because of this illegal activity.[10]

Given BNP's involvement in issuing letters of credit at the direction of its third-party clients, its failure to scrutinize related transactions for obvious signs of illegal or money-laundering activity was even more puzzling. Of all the banking institutions that should have had safeguards to prevent its facilities from serving as instrumentalities for illegal payments to the Iraqi regime, BNP as the UN's escrow account manager should have done so. Yet BNP's own branches, subsidiaries, and affiliates served as instrumentalities for approximately $10 million of surcharge payments—with most of the payments flowing through BNP accounts in Geneva. These included numerous transactions with textbook characteristics common to illegal and money-laundering activity. A number of different BNP clients involved in the purchase of Iraqi oil during the surcharge period made sizeable transfers of funds into the same obscure banks and accounts (some located in countries known to be money-laundering havens). BNP processed several large payments to many of the same key Middle Eastern banks and accounts from shell companies such as Italtech, Alcon, and Fenar in the same period of time that it was financing oil purchases for these clients.

BNP had good reason to examine these fund transfers. Its officials in Geneva and New York acknowledged awareness at the time of the Iraqi oil surcharge policy. The anti–money-laundering training program at the bank directed bank officials to scrutinize large, unusual proposed transactions or a series of large incoming deposits followed shortly thereafter by large disbursements, a pattern employed by a number of BNP's oil purchasing clients. BNP compliance officials had even been aware in 2000 that Augusto Giangrandi of client Italtech had been involved in legal proceedings in connection with the illegal sale of controlled technology and money laundering; one compliance officer proposed that Giangrandi's accounts be closely monitored. BNP did not do so. Despite all of these signs, BNP implemented no policy to identify and prevent suspected surcharge payments.

In short, although Iraq and the companies that paid surcharges were primarily at fault, BNP's conflicted loyalties inhibited it from taking steps to impede the success of the surcharge scheme. BNP failed to disclose the involvement of third-party oil traders in program transactions and failed to take reasonable precautions to monitor its client accounts for signs that illegal payments were flowing to the Iraqi regime.

Kickbacks-for-Contracts:

Iraq's Collection of Kickbacks

on Humanitarian Contracts

Just as with its oil deals, Iraq also manipulated transactions for the purchase of humanitarian goods under the Oil-for-Food Program. It steered business to companies from its ostensible allies on the Security Council, while mostly shutting out companies from Britain and the United States. It diverted large amounts of humanitarian imports for prohibited use by the Iraqi military. And then beginning in the summer of 1999, it squeezed about $1.5 billion in illegal kickback payments from more than 2,200 companies that sold goods to Iraq under the program.*

Iraq favored companies from Russia, France, and China when it came time to buy humanitarian supplies under the program. Russian companies ranked first among humanitarian suppliers, with $3.8 billion of sales, and French companies ranked third, with $3 billion of sales. Chinese companies ranked eighth, with $1.7 billion. Together, companies from these three countries accounted for about 25 percent of Iraq's humanitarian purchases.

---

*Unless otherwise noted, the narrative in chapter 5 is based on the following report of the Independent Inquiry Committee: *Manipulation of the Oil-for-Food Programme by the Iraqi Regime*, chapter 3 ("Humanitarian Goods Transactions and Illicit Payments").

By contrast, in keeping with the generally hard-line position of their governments against Iraq, companies from the United States and Britain were usually shut out from receiving contracts. U.S. companies ranked twenty-sixth, and British companies ranked thirtieth among supplier countries, with combined sales to Iraq of barely more than $400 million. This was less than 2 percent of Iraq's total humanitarian purchases under the program and far disproportionate to the worldwide market presence of U.S. and British companies.

Iraq bought at least some of its goods from very well-known companies with established reputations for producing quality goods (such as DaimlerChrysler, Volvo, Siemens, and General Electric). But the general preference given to goods from politically favored countries translated to a lower quality for the goods it received. For example, Iraq's former Minister of Transport advised the IIC that his ministry sometimes had to purchase lower-quality goods—such as Russian instead of German cars—to comply with the requirement that it buy from political priority countries. Numerous former Iraqi officials recalled instances when Iraq received substandard goods, including animal feed, cars and other vehicles, wheat, medicine, generators, batteries, and chemicals. There were instances in which spoilage occurred, and Iraq received out-of-date goods. Officials recalled purchasing substandard goods from particular suppliers—notwithstanding previous shipments of low quality goods—in order to satisfy the political considerations of buying from particular countries, as directed by senior members of the Iraqi regime.

Iraq had little legal recourse against a supplier who furnished substandard goods. Because the program did not allow the Iraqi government access to money, Iraq could not require suppliers to post performance bonds. About the most Iraq could do was decline to give future contracts to suppliers who furnished substandard goods.

The typical Iraqi citizen was not free to enter into contracts to buy goods under the program. Instead, almost all goods purchased by Iraq during the program were bought in the name of an Iraqi ministry or state-owned entity. Some Iraqi ministries regularly diverted the goods they bought to be used for prohibited, non-humanitarian purposes. These ministries were allocated funds beyond their specified budgets in order to purchase goods for other military-related entities—such as the Ministry of Defense, the Ministry of Military Industrialization, the General Security Directorate (*Mukhabarat*, or intelligence division), and the Presidential Diwan—that could not participate as contractors in the program. For example, the Ministry of Agriculture routinely fronted as a purchaser for the Ministry of Defense.

All in all, nearly $2 billion of the more than $34 billion of goods bought by Iraq under the program was diverted to other Iraqi entities that were not themselves eligible to buy goods under the program. This included $1.4 billion to the Ministry of Defense. Commonly diverted items included trucks (in particular, a model used for pulling artillery), tires, batteries, forklifts, and even date palm excavators, which were used to uproot palm trees and transport them to Saddam's presidential palaces.

According to officials of Iraq's Ministry of Agriculture, staff members initially feared being caught diverting goods but soon realized that the UN was generally ignorant of the practice and would not act to prevent it. One Ministry of Transportation official stated that if UN inspectors ever asked about particular diverted goods, they were told that the items had been lent to another ministry for a few days and would soon be returned. If UN inspectors wanted to inspect a vehicle transferred to another ministry such as the Ministry of Defense, the purchasing ministry would make a delaying excuse and then "borrow" the vehicle back long enough for the inspectors to check, only to later return the vehicle permanently to the prohibited ministry.

Iraq appears to have used some of the goods it purchased under the program in illicit trade with other countries. According to UN trade data, Iraq exported $286 million of goods (excluding oil) between 1996 and 2002. This is a surprisingly high number for a country subject to comprehensive economic sanctions and that, in theory, was not permitted to export anything but oil as allowed under the Oil-for-Food Program. At least some of the items that Iraq exported, such as cotton yarn, are not known to be produced within Iraq. These goods were apparently imported to Iraq under the program and, rather than being put to the use of the Iraqi people, sold to customers in some other country.

As the program endured, Iraq paid higher and higher prices for the goods it bought with the UN escrow money. According to the IIC's comparisons of prices for 1,600 contracts comprising about one-third of products bought under the program, the rise in prices could not be explained solely by the risky operating environment of Iraq or the extent (as discussed below) to which contractors inflated their prices to finance corrupt kickbacks for the Iraqi regime. This evidence of price inflation was consistent with an earlier study of the U.S. Department of Defense estimating more than $600 million of overpricing in connection with a sample of $3 billion of contracts financed under the program.

Iraq's suppliers doubtless had an incentive to engage in price gouging. Iraq may have been willing to accept this behavior because of the collateral political benefits it sought from the award of contracts to companies from favored nations and because the increasing costs could be painlessly passed on to the escrow account without financial repercussion to the Iraqi government's own budget or available resources.

KICKBACK PAYMENTS ON HUMANITARIAN CONTRACTS

More than two years into the program, Iraq decided to start demanding kickbacks from companies that supplied humanitarian goods. The first step occurred in June 1999, when Iraq's Economic Affairs Committee, headed by Finance Minister Hikmat Al-Azzawi, issued a directive ordering all government ministries making purchases under the program to impose on vendors the payment of nonnegotiable "transportation fees" for any goods requiring inland delivery by Iraqi trucks.

Most of the goods entering Iraq under the program landed at the sea port of Umm Qasr, several hundred miles south of Iraq's main population center in Baghdad. Because Iraq was run by an authoritarian regime, foreign company suppliers could not easily hire or deploy their own trucks and transport facilities to make inland deliveries to Baghdad. Instead, inland trucking was done by Iraq's Ministry of Transportation. The new inland transport payment policy was ostensibly part of an effort to recoup the Iraqi government's costs for transporting program goods within Iraq.

Was the new policy legal? No—the program rules strictly controlled the use of escrow money, allowing it for the purchase of essential goods but not for paying the government's general administrative costs, such as to truck goods within the country. Rather than securing consent from the UN to use escrow money for inland transport costs, Iraq resorted to extracting secret payments directly from its suppliers. The payments were direct financial transactions with Iraq, in violation of the UN sanctions. And they posed precisely the risk of Iraq's unrestricted access to funds that the sanctions were meant to stop. The UN had no way to monitor the payments from suppliers to ensure that they were comparable to the actual costs of inland transport. Nor did the UN have any way to verify that the fees collected by Iraq were actually used for the trucking of goods rather than to enrich Saddam or to rebuild his army.

Despite the illegality of the payments, Iraq had little trouble collecting the fees from suppliers eager to maintain their business in Iraq. Neither the Security Council nor the UN Secretariat scrutinized or cracked down on the new policy (as discussed in the next two chapters). The success of the "inland transport" kickback policy ultimately emboldened Iraq to expand its kickback demands about one year later. In the late summer and fall of 2000, just as the Ministry of Oil was separately initiating its oil surcharge policy, Iraq's Command Council expanded the kickback policy to impose across-the-board kickback fees for all humanitarian contracts. This new fee was *in addition* to the inland transport fees.

Vice President Taha Yassin Ramadan announced the new policy in an official memorandum to all ministries, referring to the new kickbacks as "after-sales service" fees levied for purposes of "making additional revenues for commercial contracts" under the program. At first, the required kickback amounts varied between 2 percent to 10 percent, depending on the type of goods involved. But in October 2000, the Command Council decreed that the after-sales service fee should be at least 10 percent. Any amount more than 10 percent that individual ministries could extract from contractors would be viewed as "commendable." For the rest of the program, the standard levy was 10 percent, but in some instances fees ranged as high as 30 percent.

Along with the initiation of the 10 percent after-sales service fee, Iraq increased its inland transport fees. For example, Iraq's largest supplier of rice saw its inland transport fee increase within the space of eight months, from $25 per ton up to $59 per ton. The extent to which these transport fees increased without apparent basis betrayed any claim by Iraq that the inland transport fees corresponded to true costs incurred for trucking.

For many companies that had previously been shipping bulk goods to Umm Qasr and paying inland transport fees, both of the new kickback components—the 10 percent after-sales service fee and the higher inland transport fee—were combined into a single, very high, so-called transportation fee. By contrast, some companies were saddled with paying only the 10 percent after-sales service fee if they shipped their goods for entry into Iraq by land rather than sea. In any event, by late 2000, almost no prospective suppliers of goods to Iraq would see their bids approved by Iraqi ministries without agreeing to pay a kickback.

Some ministries required companies to sign formal side agreements stipulating their agreement to pay the required kickback. A company agent or manager signed the side agreement at the time he or she signed the main contract to furnish goods, and both agreements were ordinarily affixed with the company's seal to substantiate the agent's power to sign on the company's behalf. Of course, only the main contract itself was forwarded for review and approval by the UN, while the Iraqi ministry retained for itself the secret side kickback agreement. The IIC recovered more than 1,600 examples of these side agreements from Iraqi ministry files.

For goods arriving by sea, the Iraqi Ministry of Transportation oversaw the collection and enforcement of kickback fees. Vessels berthing at Umm Qasr required the approval of the Iraqi State Company for Water Transport (ISCWT), an administrative unit of the Ministry of Transport. Absent proof that a supplier had paid the kickback fee, the supplier's goods could not be unloaded at Umm Qasr. A supplier who neglected to make an advance payment faced costly or ruinous delays while its goods sat stranded at sea. Iraq unhesitatingly threatened to block the unloading of cargo to collect kickbacks from its suppliers.

Iraq could scarcely count on its suppliers to pay kickbacks if the payments would cut into the suppliers' bottom line. To sidestep this problem, Iraq ensured that the costs of the kickbacks were passed on to the official price proposed in contracts submitted to the UN for approval. Once a company bid on a contract and Iraq decided to accept the offer, Iraq inflated the real price terms to incorporate the costs of the kickback fees. If a company offered tires at $50 each and there was a 10 percent kickback, Iraq submitted a contract with a $55 price to the UN for approval. Kickbacks became essentially costless for suppliers, and this was a powerful incentive for suppliers to acquiesce in making illegal payments to the Iraqi regime.

Suppliers paid their kickback fees in many ways. Most simply, they could pay them directly in cash to the ISCWT at Umm Qasr or by cash deposit to banks in Baghdad. Alternatively, suppliers could wire funds to various Iraqi-controlled bank accounts in Jordan and Lebanon. As it had for the oil surcharge scheme, the Central Bank of Iraq opened dozens of clearing bridge accounts to receive kickback payments. At banks in Amman, Jordan, the accounts were registered in the personal names of Iraqi government employees (sometimes with first and last names transposed). In Beirut, Lebanon, the funds went to numbered but unnamed accounts. Every twenty-four hours, balances within the bridge accounts were transferred automatically to other accounts within the same banks that were controlled by the Central Bank of Iraq.

This layering of accounts made it more difficult for any sanctions enforcement authorities to identify and "freeze" Iraqi accounts. A review of the wire transfers to the bridge accounts would not reveal any Iraqi government involvement, and the internal transfers from these accounts to the Central Bank accounts could not easily be seen outside of the bank. This system also allayed any suppliers' concerns about the appearance of making payments directly to Iraq or to the name of an Iraqi entity. Once the funds were safely lodged in the Central Bank's accounts in Jordan or Lebanon, they were routinely withdrawn in cash and transported—often by diplomatic pouch—to Baghdad.

On a daily basis, the banks holding bridge accounts transmitted advices to the Central Bank reflecting the amounts paid by suppliers and the corresponding contract numbers provided with the incoming transfers. The Central Bank advised the relevant Iraqi ministries which suppliers had paid their fees, and this cleared the way for goods to be allowed entry to Iraq. The Central Bank circulated monthly fee reports to all ministries and to Saddam's Presidential Diwan.

Yet another method of kickback payment was by wire to various front companies, usually owned in part by the Iraqi government and located in Jordan or the United Arab Emirates (UAE). For a supplier, payment to a front company outside Iraq was least suspect for bookkeeping purposes and, if questioned, could most easily be justified as a legitimate business expense.

In classic money laundering style, the front companies promptly retransferred funds they received to Iraqi-controlled bank accounts in Jordan and Lebanon, among other countries. The major front companies used by Iraq included Al Wasel & Babel and Al Hoda in the UAE, as well as Alia for Transportation and General Trade in Jordan. When Al Wasel & Babel's owner was asked about the commissions his company earned for laundering kickback payments, he replied: "Why not get easy money?"

And it was big money for Iraq. By the end of the program in 2003, Iraq collected more than $1.5 billion from its humanitarian kickback fees. This included about $1 billion generated from the 10 percent after-sales service fee and about $527 million from inland transport fees. Because contractors passed on the costs of the kickbacks to their contract prices, the kickback scheme was in effect funded from the UN's escrow account.

What did Iraq do with the kickback money? Iraqi officials offered differing accounts, and precious few records were obtained that reflect the disposition of these funds. Some suggested that the fees were for genuine internal administrative costs, but none claimed that the money in fact was spent in this manner. Isam Rashid Al-Huwaysh, the former Governor of the Central Bank, stated that all but $10 to $15 million of the after-sales service revenues were maintained as a cash reserve. Oil Minister Rashid conceded that the after-sales service fees had nothing to do with services or internal costs.

Other Iraqi officials, including Finance Minister Al-Azzawi, asserted that money held by the Central Bank was routinely allocated to other entities and ministries at the request of the Presidential Diwan or the ministries themselves. These officials also noted that some of the largest recipients were Iraqi ministries that could not participate in the program, such as the Ministries of Defense and Military Industrialization, the *Mukhabarat* (Iraqi intelligence), and the Presidential Diwan itself.

Although the source of the cash reserves is unclear, a large portion of the cash reserves maintained by the Central Bank was taken by a member of Saddam's family. Shortly after U.S.-led forces attacked Iraq in March 2003, Qusay Hussein—one of Saddam's sons—arrived at the Central Bank with a note signed by Saddam ordering the withdrawal of nearly $1 billion in cash. The Central Bank's officers complied with the request and loaded the cash into more than two hundred boxes that Qusay Hussein took away.

All in all, more than 2,200 companies paid kickbacks on hu-

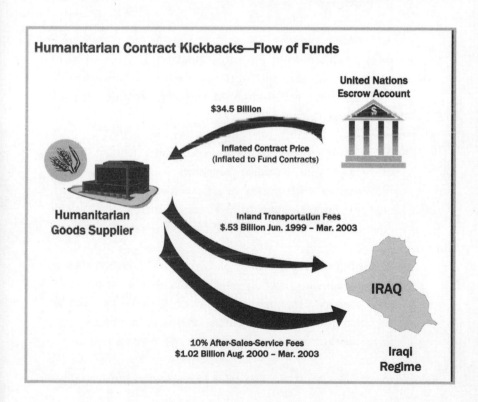

Humanitarian Contract Kickbacks—Flow of Funds

United Nations
Escrow Account

$34.5 Billion

Inflated Contract Price
(Inflated to Fund Contracts)

Humanitarian
Goods Supplier

Inland Transportation Fees
$.53 Billion Jun. 1999 – Mar. 2003

IRAQ

10% After-Sales-Service Fees
$1.02 Billion Aug. 2000 – Mar. 2003

Iraqi
Regime

manitarian contracts from 1999 to 2003. The IIC's investigation focused on about two dozen of the most significant companies that collectively accounted for more than $500 million in the kickbacks that were paid. The companies examined by the IIC fell into four general groups:

- *Major Iraqi front companies*: These companies, such as Alia, Al Wasel & Babel, and Al Hoda, were registered outside Iraq but partly owned by the government of Iraq, and they facilitated the kickback scheme by serving as collection agents for payments to the Iraqi regime from other contractors and, in some instances, by participating as favored contractors under the program.

- *Major food suppliers*: These companies included grain and dairy producers from Australia, Thailand, Egypt, and Vietnam, and they generally obtained the largest humanitarian contracts under the program, paying huge amounts of purported "inland transport" fees.

- *Major trading companies*: These companies included several of the major general trading companies that played large roles in furnishing a wide array of general merchandise and that also paid large amounts of kickbacks in return for program contracts.

- *Major industrial companies of Europe and North America*: These companies generally paid kickbacks on a smaller scale than larger program participants, but nonetheless they did so despite reputations and organizational resources that should have safeguarded against making illegal payments.

Many of the companies that paid kickbacks on humanitarian

contracts also won rights to Iraqi oil allocations—not surprisingly, they paid illegal surcharges as well.

The five largest suppliers to Iraq during the program were all foodstuffs companies: AWB, Ltd., of Australia (AWB); Chaiyaporn Rice Company, Ltd., of Thailand; the Holding Company for Food Industries of Egypt; the Vietnam Northern Food Corporation; and the Vietnam Dairy Joint Stock Company. These five companies collectively accounted for about $5 billion in contracts—nearly one-sixth of all humanitarian payments from the UN escrow account.

Commonly known as the Australian Wheat Board, AWB is the exclusive manager and marketer of all Australian bulk wheat exports through a supply pooling system arrangement with Australia's wheat growers. For the first years of the program, it functioned as a statutory authority of the Australian government to control the domestic and export marketing of Australia's wheat. In July 1999, legislation transferred control to a grower-owned group of companies, and in August 2001, AWB was placed on the Australian stock exchange as a publicly traded company.

AWB was far and away the program's single largest humanitarian contractor. It sold 6.8 million tons of wheat to Iraq, for which it received more than $2.3 billion from the UN escrow account. This was nearly 7 percent of Iraq's total purchases under the program, more than twice as much as any other humanitarian contractor.

During each phase of the program, AWB negotiated several contracts with the Iraqi Grain Board for up to several hundred thousand metric tons of wheat per contract. Each contract ordinarily required up to ten or more individual shipments in ocean freighters from Australia to Iraq's port of Umm Qasr.

As Iraq first imposed inland transport fees in mid–1999, AWB started paying these fees to Alia for Transportation and General Trade of Jordan. According to AWB, it believed Alia was a legitimate trucking company and that it was permissible to make payments to a company in Jordan. In fact, however, Alia was half-owned by the Iraqi government and did not actually furnish trucking services. Iraq's Ministry of Transportation furnished all trucking services.

From 1999 to 2003, AWB paid more than $221 million to Alia, and Alia in turn remitted these funds to Iraqi government bank accounts. Alia served simply as a pass-through account. The total of AWB's payments was more than 14 percent of all kickbacks paid by all contractors on humanitarian contracts to Iraq, and Iraq derived nearly as much illicit income from AWB as it gained from its entire oil surcharge scheme ($228 million).

Did AWB know that its payments to Alia were actually passed through to Iraq? Although AWB denied knowledge when questioned by IIC investigators, the circumstances and other evidence suggested a strong likelihood that AWB knew. First, the relationship between AWB and Alia bore little resemblance to an ordinary arms-length commercial relationship. AWB did not select Alia in the first place to provide transportation services. Instead, Iraq told AWB that Alia would do the trucking. AWB did not negotiate with Alia about its prices or even enter into a contract at all with Alia. AWB knew that Iraq's Ministry of Transportation dictated the prices that Alia would charge. This alone should have alerted AWB to the probability that the Ministry of Transportation derived some benefit from AWB's payments to Alia.

AWB was also suspiciously indifferent to unexplained increases in alleged trucking fees. For the first three contracts that AWB agreed to pay trucking fees, transport costs ranged between $10 to $12 per metric ton. But then from 2001 to 2003 the costs sharply increased without any apparent explanation to between $45 and $56 per metric ton. AWB did nothing to question Iraq's raising of the trucking fees.

Although AWB's contracts required the transport of wheat to Baghdad, AWB did not tell the UN that it was paying any third party, let alone Alia, to truck its wheat. AWB's contracts with Iraq

Flow and Distribution to Iraqi Ministries of AWB "Inland Transportation" Fees in June 2002

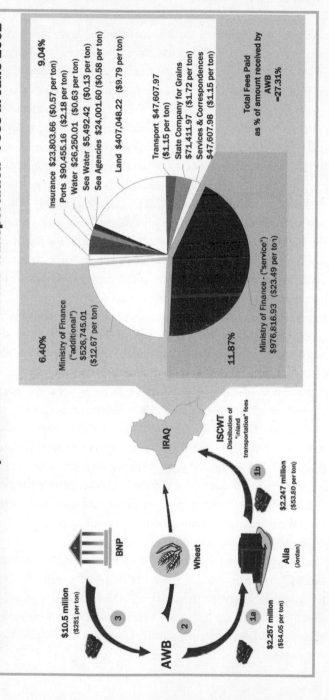

9.04%

Insurance $23,803.66 ($0.57 per ton)
Ports $90,455.16 ($2.18 per ton)
Water $26,250.01 ($0.63 per ton)
Sea Water $5,492.42 ($0.13 per ton)
Sea Agencies $24,001.60 ($0.58 per ton)

Land $407,048.22 ($9.79 per ton)

Transport $47,607.97 ($1.15 per ton)
State Company for Grains $71,411.97 ($1.72 per ton)
Services & Correspondences $47,607.98 ($1.15 per ton)

Total Fees Paid as % of amount received by AWB =27.31%

6.40%

Ministry of Finance ("additional") $526,745.01 ($12.67 per ton)

11.87%

Ministry of Finance - ("service") $976,816.93 ($23.49 per ton)

IRAQ

ISCWT
Distribution of "inland transportation" fees

1b

$2.247 million ($53.80 per ton)

BNP

$10.5 million ($251 per ton)

Wheat

Alia (Jordan)

1a

$2.257 million ($54.05 per ton)

AWB

3

2

conspicuously failed to disclose to the UN how much AWB was paying for alleged trucking fees. When trucking fees were first imposed, AWB's contracts advised that payments of "discharge costs" up to $12 per ton would be made to unnamed "Maritime Agents." As the trucking fees increased, AWB did not reveal the growing proportion of the contract costs devoted to alleged trucking fees. Indeed, by the later years of the program, more than 25 percent of AWB's total contract price was consumed for the alleged cost of trucking its wheat from Umm Qasr to Baghdad.

AWB's files also contained many documents from Alia and the government of Iraq suggesting a likelihood that payments made by AWB were made to or for the benefit of the Iraqi regime. For example, a fax in November 1999 from Alia to AWB reported a complaint from Iraq's ISCWT that AWB had not yet paid its inland transportation charge, and Alia asked AWB to "remit the subject funds to them." The mere discussion of the fact that ISCWT was complaining about AWB's nonpayment of fees to Alia suggested AWB's awareness that the government of Iraq was privy to its specific payments and arrangements with Alia and that the government of Iraq was possibly the true beneficiary of those payments.

And some discussions were quite explicit. Another example was a fax sent in October 2001 from Alia to AWB in which Alia warned AWB that "you are totally aware of the instructions issued by the ISCWT to pay the inland transportation charges (5) days before vessel[s] arrive to the port" and stating that Alia customarily "notif[ied] the ISCWT that we have received the inland transportation charges for AWB's vessels . . . before actually receiving the funds in our account."

Similarly, in September 2002, Alia sent a fax marked "URGENT" to AWB about a payment that had not yet been received for a wheat shipment that had arrived in port and warning AWB that "ISCWT informed us that *you should credit their account* [emphasis added] with the amount of Euro 203303 immediately today otherwise they will stop the discharging of vessel and would not permit it to leave the harbour until money is received." This explicit statement that the funds were going to the Iraqi government again suggests that AWB was at the least on notice of Iraq's direct financial interest in payments made by AWB.

AWB's dealings with the Iraqi Grain Board also suggested its awareness of Iraq's direct financial interest in AWB's payments. AWB routinely advised the Board of the status and amount of its payments to Alia, and the Board occasionally reminded AWB of its obligation to pay transportation fees. In May 2001, for example, the Board sent a telex to AWB instructing it to "contact Alia" in order to "transfer [the] total amount of inland transport charges" for cargoes specified in an e-mail that AWB had sent to ISCWT. The Board noted that only after these payments were made would AWB's ships be permitted to discharge.

Alia gave IIC investigators a telex that it received from a former AWB employee in Baghdad that bespoke of very unusual and secretive terms of their relationship. In this telex, the AWB employee complained that AWB did not wish "to be threatened to stop vessel[s] from sailing unless trucking fees [were] received" and warned that "any discussion/message concerning trucking/ and trucking fees should be sent only repeat only from your office in Jordan to myself or [another AWB employee] home fax—not by telex to AWB office and not from Basrah." The AWB employee also noted in the telex that he would send Alia "wording of 7 letters to cover trucking fees," and that he would send this "wording" from his home fax, and Alia should reply to the same coordinates.

AWB denied knowing the true destination of its payments to Alia. But after the IIC reported the results of its investigation of AWB, an Australian Royal Commission began an investigation of the payments. The Royal Commission subpoenaed many additional documents from AWB that AWB did not give to the IIC and obtained testimony from AWB employees who were not available to the IIC.

According to media reports, this additional evidence has made abundantly clear AWB's knowledge that its payments to Alia were channeled to the Iraqi regime, in violation of sanctions and the rules of the program. AWB's president and chief executive officer has resigned in the midst of the Royal Commission's investigation, and the Royal Commission's ongoing investigation has included testimony from Australia's Prime Minister and Foreign Minister about whether the Australian government may have known of AWB's illicit payments.[1]

In addition to AWB, Iraq's other major food suppliers also paid tens of millions of dollars in kickbacks. Chaiyaporn of Thailand sold rice to Iraq and paid $42.8 million in kickbacks (mostly through payments to Alia), as well as about $1.5 million in surcharges for Iraqi oil allocations. The Holding Company for Food Industries of Egypt paid more than $30 million in kickbacks. The company admitted to the IIC knowing that its payments were for the Iraqi regime. Two Vietnamese food companies—Vietnam Northern Food Corporation and Vietnam Dairy Products Company—collectively paid more than $60 million in kickbacks through Alia. While the first company denied knowing Alia was passing the money through to Iraq, the second company admitted knowing its payments to Alia were for the Iraqi regime.

Another major source of kickbacks for Iraq was from various trading companies that acquired large contracts to sell nonfood supplies to Iraq. The Belhasa Group of the UAE was Iraq's largest *non*food contractor with nearly $750 million of contracts. It knowingly paid more than $45 million in kickbacks, usually by means of payments to Iraqi bridge accounts in Jordan. The Ginza Company of Egypt was the top seller of construction supplies to Iraq, and it dispensed more than $10 million in kickbacks.

The Russian Engineering Company was among the top twenty suppliers of humanitarian goods, with contracts of $210 million to furnish foodstuffs, cars, trucks, construction materials, and equipment that it obtained from other companies. The company kept an office in Baghdad during the program, and its chairman, Sergei Isakov, frequently traveled there to meet with high-level Iraqi officials, including Saddam and Aziz.

Iraqi ministry files include at least thirty-two kickback side agreements signed by Russian Engineering. The company paid more than $5.8 million in kickbacks. Isakov's close relations with Iraqi officials also led to allocations for more than 24 million barrels of oil. The company paid more than $6.5 million in oil surcharges through cash payments to the Iraqi embassy in Moscow. According to some of the payment receipts, Isakov personally delivered large amounts of cash to the Iraqi embassy in Moscow.

Like almost all Russian companies, Russian Engineering refused to meet with the IIC's investigators, even after the IIC furnished the company with copies of its side letter agreements and receipts for cash payments it delivered to the Iraqi embassy. In response to the IIC's investigation, Isakov wrote a letter asserting that his company "undeviatingly followed all recommendations of the Ministry of Foreign Affairs and strictly observed all rules, norms, and restrictions of the sanctions regime."

Sinochem is a Chinese state-owned company that is one of the world's largest trading companies, specializing in the areas of petroleum, fertilizers, and chemicals. It ranks on the Fortune 500 list of the world's largest companies. Through one or more of its numerous subsidiaries, Sinochem sold more than $20 million of piping supplies to Iraq's North Oil Company, a division of the Ministry of Oil. For some of these contracts, Sinochem signed side agreements to pay "handling charges," and it paid a total of nearly $670,000 in kickbacks.

Sinochem was also the second-largest purchaser of Iraqi oil— 114 million barrels worth more than $2.2 billion. According to SOMO records, Sinochem paid more than $5 million in illegal oil surcharges. Sinochem declined to meet with the IIC's investigators to discuss the evidence of its illegal payments. Sinochem is a state-owned company, but the Chinese government did not ensure that Sinochem cooperate with the IIC's investigation. When the IIC's investigators met with Chinese diplomats in Beijing, China declined the IIC's request to arrange meetings with any of the major Chinese companies that secured contracts under the program.

Many major European companies did business with Iraq under the program, and some of them also decided to pay kickbacks. DaimlerChrysler AG of Germany is one of the world's largest car and truck companies, including top-of-the-line brand names such as Mercedes Benz. One of Daimler's sales managers in the Middle East was Wolfgang Denk, a longtime company employee who had worked for the company in Iraq in the 1980s. By 1998, Denk was Area Sales Manager for Daimler's overseas department at the company's headquarters in Stuttgart, Germany.

In 1998, Denk traveled to Baghdad—where DaimlerChrysler still maintained a service office—seeking to revive the company's sales business that had vanished during the sanctions regime. He soon learned, however, that Iraq had blacklisted Daimler from receiving program contracts because Daimler had a pending claim against Iraq with the UN Compensation Commission arising from damage caused by Iraq during the first Gulf War. To clear the way for Daimler to do new business with Iraq, Daimler's management decided to withdraw the company's compensation claim. In the summer of 2001, Denk returned to Iraq, where he went to the Ministry of Oil to sign on the company's behalf a contract to sell a mobile box truck. This truck was in essence an armored van to be used by the Oil Ministry to transport cash from its banks to its offices.

Nine days before Denk signed the contract for the truck, he also signed a side agreement to pay a 10 percent kickback. The one-sentence letter agreement stated: "DaimlerChrysler AG undertakes to pay to the Oil Products Distribution Company a sum of DM 13.589,50 equivalent to 10 percent of the total amount [of the contract] upon the establishment of the Letter of Credit." The cost of this kickback was added to the real price offered by Daimler for the truck, and then a contract incorporating the kickback-adjusted price was submitted to the UN for approval.

Denk's kickback side agreement was recovered by the IIC from the Ministry of Oil's files. But when the IIC asked Daimler for copies of any side agreements to pay kickbacks, Daimler claimed it did not have any.

When interviewed, Denk remembered negotiating and signing the contract for the mobile box truck. He said that he had heard rumors at the time that Iraq was requiring vendors to make side payments in the form of after-sales service fees. When he was then shown the side agreement signed in his name, he claimed not to remember the agreement—though conceding that the signature appeared to be his (and it is the same signature that appears on the UN's official contract paperwork). Denk suggested that he may have signed the one-sentence agreement but did not understand what he had signed.

Denk did not act alone to pay the kickback. Daimler routed the kickback by wire transfer to an Iraqi-controlled account at the Housing Bank of Jordan. It was sent through a Swiss bank account controlled by Hussam Rassam, a former sales agent for Mercedes-Benz in Iraq. During the program, Rassam operated service centers for Mercedes-Benz vehicles in Iraq, and Denk acknowledged when interviewed by IIC investigators that he knew Rassam.

Rassam's Swiss bank account was not in his own name. Instead, it was put in three names—his son, his accountant, and his Swiss lawyer. A fourth person—Azar Bawwab, another former Middle East sales agent for Mercedes-Benz—opened the account for Rassam. When interviewed, Bawwab said he believed that a purpose for the account was to make illegal payments to Iraq.

Rassam himself refused to meet with the IIC about the kickback payment. But when his lawyer was asked about the transaction, he falsely claimed that it was a commission payment that had nothing to do with the program. When the lawyer was asked if he had personally authorized the payment, he tellingly responded that he could not say who authorized the transaction without violating attorney-client privilege.

Although the Daimler kickback was only about $7,100, Denk signed at least two more side agreements to pay approximately $73,000 more in kickbacks. These contracts do not appear to have been executed or the kickbacks paid. When shown these signed agreements, Denk professed perplexity again about the appearance of his signature. Yet Daimler never challenged the authenticity of Denk's signature on any of the kickback agreements. Daimler did more than $5 million of contracts with Iraq during the program.

Siemens AG of Germany is one of the world's largest electrical engineering and electronics companies. Through various subsidiaries or affiliates in France, Turkey, and the UAE, Siemens did nearly $125 million of business with Iraq during the program. Records from Iraq's Ministry of Electricity and Ministry of Oil, in conjunction with bank records of an Iraqi-controlled account in Jordan, confirmed several kickback payments related to Siemens contracts. The available evidence suggests that Siemens paid more than $1.6 million in kickbacks.

For example, in November 2000, Siemens-France entered into a contract with the Ministry of Electricity to sell turbine system equipment and spare parts for €538,175. The Ministry's internal records reveal that this price was inflated to account for a 10 percent kickback of €48,925 and that this kickback was paid in full. Bank records from the Housing Bank of Jordan independently confirmed all but €5,000 of the kickback payment for this contract. An Iraqi witness whose name appeared on the kickback deposit account advised the IIC that a Siemens employee in Jordan made the cash deposit. What is more, Siemens-Turkey also made payments to this same Jordanian bank account used on behalf of Siemens-France, and the deposit records for both the Siemens-France and the

Siemens-Turkey transactions reflect the same unknown depositor name.

Siemens officials offered limited cooperation and refused to produce records of the contracts for which the kickbacks had been paid. IIC investigators met with officials at a Siemens-France office near Paris and asked to speak to Pascal Lullier, one of the Siemens officials who signed contracts for which kickback payments were made. Siemens-France officials stated that the personnel who had worked in that division, including Lullier, had left and were no longer employed there. But within days IIC investigators located Lullier, who was in fact employed at another Seimens-France office a few miles away. Siemens-France refused to make Lullier available for interview.

As for Siemens's affiliate in the UAE, files from the Ministry of Oil revealed three side agreements to pay kickbacks. The agreements were each signed on behalf of the affiliate by "Wilfried Grunewald, Sales Manager," whom the IIC could not locate. When contacted and given copies of the evidence of its kickback payments, Siemens claimed that it could not confirm the IIC's kickback information.

The Volvo Group of Sweden describes itself as "one of the world's leading manufacturers of heavy commercial vehicles and diesel engines." Among its business subsidiaries is Volvo CE, a large manufacturer and worldwide seller of heavy construction equipment vehicles, including excavators, haulers, wheel loaders, and motor graders. Volvo CE sold nearly $12 million of equipment to Iraq during the program. In December 2000, its Swedish marketing director, Hakan Nirstedt, signed a contract to provide thirty-five wheel loaders (bulldozers) to the Ministry of Housing and Construction for approximately $6 million.

Two weeks later, Volvo CE announced its intention to do business with Iraq through a Jordanian sales agent rather than directly with Iraq. Volvo CE's president signed a formal "Authorization Announcement" appointing the International Engineering Group of

Jordan to act as "our sole distributor and consultant for the Iraqi market" and authorizing it "to bid and submit offers on our behalf, enter into contracts with Iraqi purchasers, supply spare parts to Iraq as well as handle all aftersales [*sic*] services."

The decision of Volvo CE to switch to the use of a Jordanian agent occurred within just a few months after Iraq had initiated its 10 percent kickback policy. Volvo CE did not tell the IIC why it needed a Jordanian agent to do its bidding in view of the fact that Volvo CE had already successfully signed five prior contracts with Iraq under the program. Companies that pay kickbacks commonly do so by paying commissions to local agents, who, in turn, pay the kickbacks for them. This type of arrangement conveniently distances the main company from any later claim of complicity in illegal payments.

In May 2001, Volvo CE's new agent signed another contract with the Ministry of Housing and Construction to sell ten Volvo CE wheel loaders and spare parts. Banking records from an Iraqi-controlled account at the Housing Bank in Jordan show that kickbacks of nearly $320,000 were paid for both wheel loader contracts—the one signed by Volvo and the one signed by its agent. The records reflect that the deposit for the first contract was on behalf of "the Swedish company Volvo" and related to the same official ministry contract number that appears in the UN's contract file.

According to Mohammad Al-Farraj, the general manager of Volvo's agent in Jordan, he was aware of Iraq's 10 percent kickback policy and personally paid kickbacks on behalf of Volvo CE. Al-Farraj stated that Volvo CE was aware of everything and that no transactions were conducted without Volvo CE's full knowledge.

Although Al-Farraj was willing to admit his culpability, Volvo CE stonewalled the IIC's investigation. The IIC furnished Volvo CE with relevant transaction records, but Volvo CE refused to meet with the IIC's investigators or to furnish any information. It is estimated that Volvo CE caused to be paid about $535,000 in kickbacks stemming from three equipment contracts it had under the program.

The Weir Group of Scotland in the United Kingdom is a large engineering services company that employs nearly eight thousand people and conducts business operations in numerous countries across the world. Along with its French and UAE subsidiaries, Weir obtained nearly $80 million in contracts under the program to provide mostly industrial pumping equipment to the Ministry of Oil and the City of Baghdad.

In July 2004, when the IIC was just starting its investigation, Weir issued a press release announcing that its internal review of program contracts had disclosed that its contract prices had been inflated and that several million dollars of unexplained payments were made to "an agent" for Weir. According to Weir, it was not known if these payments had gone to Iraq. In response to a followup inquiry from the IIC, Weir advised that it had been assured by its agent that the money did not go to the Iraqi regime. Weir further stated that its own investigation had not revealed evidence of any agreement between one of its own employees and the Iraqi regime to pay kickbacks and that none of its own employees had been terminated as a result of its investigation.

Despite Weir's claim that its own employees did not approve kickbacks, Weir refused to let the IIC interview Andrew Macleod, a general sales manager whose name appeared as the signatory for Weir on all the contracts at issue with Iraq and who worked at Weir's headquarters in Scotland. Unbeknownst to Weir, the IIC had recovered several side agreements from the Ministry of Oil's files that were signed by Macleod and agreed on Weir's behalf to pay more than £700,000 to Iraq. The agreements stipulated that Weir would make the payments "in cash or through a mechanism, which is to be agreed upon between the two sides." The agreements made no mention of any agent acting on Weir's behalf. In addition, records from an Iraqi-controlled account at the Rafidain Bank in Jordan showed several kickback deposits related to Weir contracts.

Although Weir refused to make any of its employees available for IIC investigators to interview, the IIC managed to track down

Weir's agent in Baghdad. According to the agent, he dealt with Macleod, who came to Baghdad to negotiate Weir's contracts. After Iraq initiated its policy of requiring 10 percent after-sales service kickbacks, the agent said that Macleod talked with him about a mechanism to pay the fee, and Macleod suggested that the agent act as an intermediary. The agent arranged for payments to be made through a Swiss entity to his account in Jordan and then to the Rafidain Bank.

To corroborate his account, the agent provided the IIC with copies of two e-mails from Macleod in January 2002 that requested the agent's assistance with kickback payment arrangements. In one of these e-mails, a Weir financial manager in France advised Macleod of "this '10% AFTER SALES TAX'" imposed by Iraq and the need to make sure that the shipping company had proof of payments before "Iraqi Authorities" will "let the vessel discharge the goods." Macleod forwarded the e-mail to the agent with a list of four contract numbers and asked the agent to "supply" the payment information for these contracts. He added: "Trust you will [take] action accordingly." The available evidence suggests that Weir knowingly paid about $4.5 million in kickbacks to the Iraqi regime.

After Weir refused to arrange a meeting with Macleod, an IIC investigator tracked down Macleod by telephone to advise him that the IIC had the side letter agreements that were signed by him. Macleod still declined to be interviewed but not before telling the investigator that "I work for the company, and I did as I was told." He added that he knew it sounded like a "soldier's excuse, but I'm sure you understand I did what was required in Baghdad."

Indeed, what was required in Baghdad were illegal payments for the Iraqi regime. Thousands of companies paid so they could buy Iraq's oil and sell Iraq a wide range of goods. Both the Security Council and the UN Secretariat knew to varying extents of these illegal payment schemes, and the next chapters turn to assess what they knew and what they did—or did *not*—do about it.

6

Stumbling in the Security Council:

The Failure to Redress Program Abuses

What did the UN know about Iraq's massive exploitation of the Oil-for-Food Program, and what did it do about it? The question depends on what is meant by the term "the UN." For many, "the UN" conjures an image of a stately Secretary-General or perhaps the sleek silhouette of the UN headquarters' skyscraper perched on the edge of the East River in New York City. But in truth "the UN" is its 192 member states—the nations when joined in deliberation and decision that inspire its purpose and its name. Yet, so far as the Oil-for-Food Program was concerned, "the UN" was far less than the full member state roster. Only fifteen countries served on the Security Council at any one time, and the Security Council alone dictated the terms of the sanctions against Iraq.*

The Oil-for-Food Program existed only at the pleasure of the Security Council and could survive only if reauthorized every six months by a new resolution from the Council. Beyond broadly au-

---

*Unless otherwise noted, the narrative in chapter 6 is based on the Independent Inquiry Committee, *The Management of the Oil-for-Food Programme*, vol. 2, September 7, 2005, chapter 3 ("The Security Council: Response to Surcharges and Kickbacks") and chapter 4 ("Smuggling").

thorizing the program, the Security Council also assigned itself a role through its 661 Committee to review most contracts for oil and goods under the program. Indeed, to the extent that Iraq's efforts to extract illegal surcharges and kickbacks were known (and became known), any single member of the Security Council could have responded by freezing the program in its tracks. The consensus rule within the Security Council's 661 Committee meant that a single member could simply withhold approval of an oil pricing mechanism or place an indefinite "hold" on the approval of goods contracts, most of which were required to be approved unanimously by the 661 Committee.

This is not to suggest that sweeping action, with its potential humanitarian cost, was warranted as a response to what was known about Iraq's abuse of the program. But the breadth of each Security Council member's authority underscores the degree to which the fundamental power and responsibility to control the program, as well as to set the tone for its enforcement in the teeth of its abuse by Iraq, resided first and foremost with the member states of the Security Council.

There is much to say about what the Secretary-General and UN staff members knew and failed to do in response to Iraq's exploitation of the program. These topics await the next chapter. The focus of this chapter remains the unique role of the Security Council, and the actions of its five permanent and most powerful members—Britain, China, France, Russia, and the United States.

The Security Council's basic design of the program contained inadequate safeguards to prevent Iraq's manipulation efforts. When Iraq almost immediately began steering its award of contracts for political purposes to undermine the sanctions regime, the Security Council appears not to have anticipated this practice or to have cared to redress it when it became apparent. For example, there is no record that the Security Council considered any measures to limit the number or volume of contracts that Iraq could give to companies from any one member state. Of course, companies from several key members of the Security Council richly benefited from Iraq's contractual preferences.

Nor did the Security Council restrict Iraq from offering allocations of oil to individual, political beneficiaries. An individual's acceptance of an allocation from Iraq was, in effect, an unauthorized financial transaction with Iraq in violation of the sanctions regime. Yet the rules of the program did nothing to enforce the rule of sanctions—to prohibit Iraq from dispensing these kinds of individual gifts or to inhibit political figures from agreeing to accept oil allocations from Iraq.

More problematic still was the Security Council's response to Iraq's $228 million oil surcharge scheme. Indeed, well before Iraq initiated its surcharge policy in late 2000, inaction by the Security Council rendered the program vulnerable to Iraq's exploitation.

OIL OVERSEERS AND OIL SURCHARGES

For starters, the 661 Committee failed to ensure an adequate number of oil overseers to monitor Iraq's oil transactions. From the outset of the program, when the number of oil contracts was at its smallest, the committee's rules required it to select "at least four independent experts in international oil trade" to assist with ensuring that Iraq sold oil only at fair market value and to examine contracts in order to ensure that the transactions did "not contain any attempts at fraud or deception." As oil trade experts, the overseers were far better positioned than the career diplomats who served on the 661 Committee to deal with Iraq's State Oil Marketing Organization (SOMO) and to assess the fairness of pricing mechanisms proposed by SOMO.

In the summer of 1996, when the program began, the 661 Committee filled the oil overseer positions with individuals from four different countries: France, Russia, the United States, and Norway. Perhaps not by coincidence, three of these countries were permanent members of the Security Council. But within several months, the Norwegian overseer resigned, and then, in mid-1998, the U.S. overseer had to resign for health reasons. The program was down to just two overseers—one from Russia and one from France.

The 661 Committee members squabbled about who would be chosen as replacement overseers. China, who had lost out initially on having one of its nationals appointed an overseer, and who believed that it had been promised rights to fill the next overseer vacancy, insisted that one of the replacement positions go to a Chinese oil expert. The United States, however, would not agree, because it did not trust a combination of Russian, Chinese, and French overseers. It would not agree even when offered the option of having a U.S. overseer appointed along with a Chinese overseer.

The two positions stayed vacant month after month as billions of dollars in oil deals coursed through the program. Because of the 661 Committee's consensus rule, this dispute between China and the United States meant that the committee could not take any action to appoint replacement overseers. In the meantime, the need for overseers dramatically increased when the Security Council decided in February 1998 to allow Iraq to sell more than double the amount of oil—from $2 billion to more than $5 billion per six-month phase of the program. The situation grew worse in June 1999, when the French overseer resigned. The entire overseer workload shifted to just one overseer—Alexandre Kramar of Russia. Of all the overseers, Kramar was by far the least experienced in international crude oil marketing.

Yet another year and billions more in oil deals passed without the appointment of any new overseers. Finally, in the summer of 2000, the United States and China decided to let the Secretary-General decide on new overseers. In August 2000, Secretary-General Annan appointed two more overseers with extensive industry experience—

Michel Tellings of the Netherlands and Morten Buur-Jensen of Denmark. These two and Kramar of Russia would end up serving through nearly the end of the program.

The overseer fiasco was just one example of the 661 Committee's ineffectual oversight of the program in the face of political differences and rivalries. Another example was the committee's handling of the issue of "port fees" that Iraq wanted to charge for oil tankers and other seagoing vessels that used Iraqi terminals at Mina al-Bakr and Umm Qasr. It is standard maritime practice for sea vessels to pay reasonable port fees for the costs incurred by port facilities to accommodate vessels as they load and unload their goods. But payment of port fees to the Iraqi government would be a direct financial transaction with Iraq in violation of the sanctions. The program rules did not contain an allowance for the payment of port fees to the Iraqi regime.

When this conundrum was raised with the UN's Office of Legal Affairs (OLA), its legal counsel, Hans Corell, issued an opinion suggesting that the payment of port fees would not contravene the sanctions regime so long as these fees did not "exceed what is customary in such circumstances." Corell's opinion did little to explain why such direct payments to the Iraqi regime were authorized and not a violation of sanctions.

Although Corell no longer works at the UN, when the IIC asked OLA if there was any basis for his conclusion that direct payments of port fees did not violate the sanctions regime, OLA was unable to identify any legal basis for this conclusion. This was not an isolated instance. As discussed in earlier chapters, Corell had served as one of the members of the Iraq Steering Committee that supported the award of the program's inspection contracts on the basis of political preference, and he had also thought it unnecessary for the UN to investigate the tainted award of the goods inspection contract to Cotecna.

Although Corell and OLA did not seem to be worried about direct cash payments made to the Iraqi regime, a trade group of oil tanker owners wrote to the UN in June 2000 to note that the port fees charged by Iraq had "increased dramatically" and that direct payments of this kind to Iraq could be illegal. OLA responded with yet another legal opinion, now modifying its position to conclude that payment for port fees remained permissible but only if paid in the form of Iraqi dinars, rather than U.S. dollars.

This new position bordered on the absurd. A requirement to pay port fees in Iraqi dinars—a nonconvertible currency—would essentially require tanker owners to break sanctions by engaging first in a prohibited transaction with the Iraqi regime to purchase Iraqi dinars prior to using the dinars to pay the port fees. The tanker owners pointed out that its members were therefore presented with an "unacceptable" choice: refuse to pay port fees (and not lift oil) or pay port fees and break the sanctions.

The UN's legal office washed its hands of the matter, and the issue came to the 661 Committee. Britain proposed a simple solution: incorporate the cost of port fees into each oil buyer's contract and then allow payment of the port fees through the UN escrow account. This would ensure that the amount of port fees was subject to UN review and approval and that Iraq did not receive direct and unregulated payments of money.

The 661 Committee, however, took no action on the British proposal. The issue was simply ignored, and thus the 661 Committee effectively acquiesced to illegal transactions with Iraq in violation of the sanctions regime. For Iraq, the UN's tolerance of port fees doubtlessly signaled the UN's lack of resolve to prevent the payment of other so-called fees, such as purported "inland transport fees" and "after-sales service fees," from which Iraq would eventually reap about $1.5 billion dollars in illegal income.

Of equal concern as the 661 Committee's failure to regulate port fees was its failure to do anything about Iraq's sale of oil predominantly to "middleman" buyers. Well before the onset of sanctions,

it had been Iraq's practice to sell oil only to "end-user" buyers—
that is, to companies that owned or had access to refinery facilities
to process the oil. This practice was memorialized in SOMO's standard oil sales contract, which had long prohibited any buyer from
reselling Iraqi oil. The contract stated in relevant part:

> It is expressly understood that BUYER will process crude oil sold
> under this contract in its own processing facilities or under process-
> ing arrangements with other refiners for BUYER's own account for
> which SELLER's prior approval must be obtained. BUYER also un-
> dertakes that *under no circumstances shall BUYER resell or ex-
> change the said crude oil in its original form or blend it with any
> other crude oil* or crude oil derivatives for purposes of resale or ex-
> change. [emphasis added]

The end-user requirement that SOMO had long insisted on offered some obvious benefits for the program. First, it could help ensure that the full value of any oil sold was captured for the benefit of
the escrow account. The involvement of an oil trader or other middleman implicitly meant that a portion of Iraq's potential gain from
an oil sale would be diverted to the trader or middleman. Second, an
end-user sale requirement would have promoted the transparency
and integrity of transactions under the program. If questions arose
about a particular transaction, an end-user requirement would mean
a shorter transactional trail following the oil from pipeline to refinery for an auditor or investigator to review. Moreover, end-users are
ordinarily well-established businesses with assets such as refineries.
An end-user can be more readily located and held to account than a
middleman company, which may—and in this case did—exist
merely as a nameplate glued to a door, a telephone or fax machine,
or a post office box somewhere.

During MOU negotiations, SOMO's standard sales contract was
circulated within the UN's negotiating team as a basis for discus-

sion of the terms of Iraq's oil sales. But despite the concern at the time over the transparency of the program and its transactions, neither the UN negotiators (led by Corell) nor the 661 Committee saw fit to require Iraq to adhere to its past practice of selling its oil only to end-users. As the committee's official secretary would matter-of-factly concede, the end-user requirement simply "was overlooked by the Committee."

Not only did the 661 Committee decline to limit sales only to end-users, but also it declined to impose any kind of meaningful qualification requirements for companies to take part in the purchase of oil under the program. The program's rules allowed member states to nominate and forward to the 661 Committee the names of oil buyers "authorized to communicate with the oil overseers." This registration procedure was a mere formality. It did not require companies to show that they had assets, credit, or other bona fide experience in the oil industry, or even to vouch that they were not owned and operated by criminals or con artists, let alone owned by the Iraqi government. Few, if any, member states scrutinized the background of companies before nominating them to the UN as qualified participants in the program.

Even when directly confronted with the issue, the 661 Committee passed up its chance to limit oil buyers only to end-users. In August 1996, Italy inquired of the 661 Committee's chairman if Iraqi oil bought under the program could be resold. After circulating the letter to the full committee, the chairman wrote back to the Italian ambassador to advise simply that "Resolution 986 (1995) does not prohibit the resale of the Iraqi oil." This one-sentence response was literally correct: Resolution 986 did not expressly prohibit the resale of Iraqi oil. But the response was also woefully incomplete. It failed to account for the end-user requirement of the SOMO standard sales contract and to account for the authority of the 661 Committee to require in its own contract review rules that each sale comply with the end-user requirement of the SOMO contract.

When the committee's chairman was interviewed by IIC investigators, he acknowledged that his answer should have included more specific details.

For its part, SOMO continued throughout the program to include the end-user requirement among many other standard, boilerplate provisions of its oil contracts. This practice continued long after SOMO had shifted to selling its oil to a vast range of front companies and oil traders that were paying surcharges and reselling the oil to other middlemen or true end-users. But because the end-user requirement was not incorporated into the program's own rules, it was meaningless. It was neither enforced by SOMO nor required as a precondition for contract approval by the oil overseers. With some embarrassment, one overseer admitted to the IIC that he had not been aware of the SOMO contract's end-user requirement.

The likelihood that Iraq would exploit the program to derive kickbacks from its oil deals was clear and publicized well before Iraq decided to do so. James Norman was an experienced investigative reporter for *Platts Oilgram News*, one of the world's leading oil industry publications. Norman had previously investigated and authored a *Forbes* magazine article—"Oilman, Trader, Banker, Spy"—about David Chalmers's allegedly illegal dealings with Iraq before the Oil-for-Food Program.

Now, in late 1998, Norman noticed from price data published by *Platts* that Iraqi oil prices as approved by the 661 Committee seemed suspiciously low in comparison to other world benchmark crudes. To confirm his suspicions, Norman spoke with Maurice Lorenz, a U.S. citizen who had recently resigned for health reasons from his post as oil overseer, and Lorenz agreed that the prices were too low.

On November 19, 1998, Norman published an article headlined "Petrodollars" that prophetically described Saddam's likely exploitation of lowball pricing to derive illegal payments for his pernicious purposes:

How does Saddam keep funding his huge army and adding new weapons?

In part, it could be through lucrative kickbacks and money laundering wittingly or unwittingly built in to the UN's little-watched Iraq oil pricing regime.

Ever since the UN let Iraq resume selling crude in 1995 under its "oil-for-food" program, Iraq has consistently proposed prices far BELOW the market. UN overseers have had to repeatedly prod Iraq to bring its prices UP. Why?

.   .   .

By underpricing his oil, Saddam can create up to $1-mil a day at times in phantom funds to either pay past debts, buy new arms, or simply line his own pockets.

How does the scam work? By controlling which obscure trading companies win the right to buy that oil, Iraq can direct the flow of these discounts. That would explain why major western refiners have been bumped off the Iraqi buyer list and replaced by more and more unknown names. Increasingly, Iraq's customers are trading companies with no use for the crude except to quickly resell it.

Gone are Shell, BP, Exxon, and Chevron. Instead, Iraq is selling to a dozen Russian trading houses and has recently added half a dozen Chinese firms. Whether or not these firms actually are conduits for arms payments or kickbacks, sources say the system clearly is rigged to launder money.[1]

Norman's warning was picked up in two major mass media sources. On November 30, 1998, *Time* magazine reported that "according to a recent report in *Platts Oilgram* the Iraqi leader may be involved in another ingenious scheme to fill the regime's coffers: selling oil under the U.N. program to Russian and Chinese middlemen at artificially low prices and then siphoning off kickbacks from the dealers when the crude is resold on the world market."[2] A month later, the *Financial Times* also mentioned the possibility of Iraqi authorities "offering bigger than usual discounts to some Russian and Chinese oil buyers as part of a kickback scheme."[3]

Norman's article quoted Lorenz as "a frequent critic of Iraq's lowball formulas." When interviewed by IIC investigators, Lorenz confirmed that after he left his overseer post in June 1998, he had several times raised his concern about low pricing with the two remaining French and Russian overseers and also with the U.S. mission to the UN.

Then, after Norman's article came out, Lorenz sent a copy to the U.S. mission, and the article was eventually forwarded through Benon Sevan's office to the overseers with an urgent request for a response. The French overseer did not respond. By contrast, the Russian overseer (Alexandre Kramar) replied in a one-page memo denouncing the article as based on "groundless allegations, provocative suggestions and factual 'mistakes.'" He added: "Apparently the author, who as I was told is known for his articles of such kind, does not [possess] neither understanding of the process nor real information about it."

When Kramar was interviewed by IIC investigators about his response, he was asked what basis he had for his assertion that he "was told" that Norman previously had published "articles of such kind" and that Norman did not have "real information" about the process. Kramar replied that that he had learned this information from none other than David Chalmers, who was frequently in contact with the overseers throughout the program to urge them to agree to lower prices for Iraqi oil.

According to Kramar, Chalmers told him that Norman had previously written an article falsely alleging Bayoil's involvement in arms trade and that, if Norman's allegations were true, he already would have been in jail. Ironically, several months after Kramar recounted this to the IIC, Chalmers was indeed arrested upon his indictment by U.S. law enforcement authorities for participating in a scheme through Bayoil to pay massive amounts of illegal oil surcharges to Iraq.

The extent of Kramar's dealings with Chalmers is unclear. However, after Kramar left employment with the UN as an overseer, he went back to Russia, where he began work as an adviser to the general director of government-owned Zarubezhneft—the program's single largest buyer of Iraqi oil and the source of more than $8 million in illegal cash surcharges paid through the Iraqi embassy in Moscow. Zarubezhneft was a frequent business partner of Bayoil in transactions under the program.

In any event, after Kramar's refutation of the *Platts* article, the issue died out at the UN. Curiously, no one at the UN contacted Lorenz to discuss the concerns he had voiced in the article. Nor did the U.S. mission forward the article to other members of the 661 Committee or raise it for discussion by the 661 Committee.

About two years later, Iraq launched its surcharge policy in late 2000. The onset of the policy was widely reported in oil industry media, and the Secretary-General received and forwarded to the committee a letter from Iraq's Oil Minister, Amer Rashid, advising of Iraq's intent to start charging buyers €1.5 per barrel in order to fund maintenance of Iraq's oil infrastructure. The United States, joined by France and Britain, took the position that payments by buyers to an account for Iraq outside UN control would be unacceptable.

Faced with the UN's unwillingness to pay surcharges from the escrow account, Iraq realized that its ability to induce oil buyers to pay a significant surcharge depended on lowering the UN's official selling price below fair market value. Unless the price was lowered, oil buyers might not earn a large enough margin on the resale of Iraqi oil to afford payment of a surcharge back to Iraq. The oil overseers soon learned of Iraq's strategy. In mid-November 2000, one of the UN's three overseers, Michel Tellings, was with a UN mission visiting oil facilities in Iraq, and Oil Minister Rashid proposed that Tellings have dinner with a senior official of SOMO to discuss how Tellings could be of assistance on pricing. Rashid added, "We don't forget our friends." Tellings believed that a bribe was being proposed, and he declined the dinner invitation.

Upon his return to New York, Tellings advised the other overseers of the incident, and a chill thereafter pervaded the relationship between the overseers and SOMO. The overseers examined the premiums and pricing mechanisms more closely, while SOMO pressured the overseers to agree to lower prices. The overseers advised the 661 Committee in late November 2000 that SOMO's proposed pricing mechanism for the upcoming month of December was too low, and the committee therefore rejected SOMO's pricing proposal. As a result, through early December 2000, there was no agreement on pricing and no exports of Iraqi oil. The committee finally accepted the lower price because of damage to the market's confidence in the stability of the Iraqi oil supply and the risk to the funding of humanitarian efforts due to lack of oil exports.

By mid-December 2000, all three oil overseers advised the 661 Committee of information they had received from their market sources substantiating the existence of Iraq's surcharge policy. The committee, however, immediately divided on what to do. The United States proposed issuing a letter to all buyers warning that payments to Iraq outside the escrow account were not allowed. But Russia questioned this proposal because "there was no official confirmation of the surcharges, and further interruption in sales could cause losses to the oil-for-food-program, the Iraqi people and the companies in the oil market." Britain countered that it would be "naive" to expect Iraq to acknowledge that it was demanding surcharges and "negligent" for the 661 Committee not to make clear the illegality of payment of surcharges. Russia apparently relented, and the oil overseers faxed out official warning notices to all oil buyers on December 15, 2000.

But the warning notice did not stop surcharges. Media reports in late December 2000 suggested that Iraq was still requesting surcharges, but because of buyer resistance had reduced its demands from a level of 50 cents per barrel to about 30 cents per barrel. One of the oil overseers advised the 661 Committee in early January 2001 that Iraq had exported lower than normal levels of oil for the month of December because of cancellation of loadings and delays as a result of the surcharge demands. Media reports observed that Iraq was now awarding oil contracts to "little known" and "obscure" oil firms "based in countries such as Belarus and Liechtenstein."

In early February 2001, the United States formally requested a report from the oil overseers about how to address the surcharge policy. The overseers responded with a report describing how among Iraq's oil purchasers "there are very few companies that can be classified as end-users of crude oil." The report added that "contract holders seem to be intermediaries who are not known in the petroleum industry" and "are very small in size and seem to have limited credit facilities." According to the overseers, Iraqi oil sales under the program had "gradually evolved" from SOMO "directly selling to end-users," then "selling via traders to end-users," and "now . . . selling via intermediaries to traders who on-sell to end-users." The overseers also noted "end-users can consistently only buy Iraqi crude oil at a premium of 20–50 cents per barrel" over the UN's official selling price. According to the overseers, their "direct contacts with traders and end-users in the oil industry confirm[ed] in broad terms" what was appearing in media reports: that buyers were paying surcharges to Iraq.

At a meeting of the 661 Committee on February 26, 2001, one of the oil overseers vividly described the character of the current market for Iraqi oil. Iraqi oil buyers often "were small companies with no financial standing, many of which had no equipment beyond a fax machine and a telephone." He added that "it might well be asked how intermediaries with such limited resources could purchase oil," and he explained that "their procedure was the following: after a brief visit to Baghdad, they contacted a number of trading companies to which they proposed to sell oil if the companies in question agreed to their price (the official sales price plus the premium), issued them a letter of credit, chartered a ship and paid them." Accordingly, "it was the trading companies and, in some cases, the end-users who financed the operation."

To deter surcharge payments, one of the overseers suggested that the committee "should advise Governments to set stricter standards for inclusion in the register of companies." Another overseer added that buyers should be required to show assets of about $100 million and proof of trading experience in oil or other goods. He also proposed that potential oil purchasers be asked to pay a registration fee into the escrow account to deter intermediaries lacking the necessary financial guarantees and know-how.

On March 16, 2001, the 661 Committee met informally and discussed a formal U.S. proposal to redress surcharges, including: (1) renewed warnings to buyers; (2) reregistration of buyers with qualification criteria including proven creditworthiness and experience; (3) payment by buyers of a nonrefundable fee to the escrow account; (4) new warnings to end-users and refiners not to buy surcharge-tainted oil; and (5) increased publicity of the prohibition against surcharge payments.

Britain supported the U.S. proposal, but France, China, and Russia all objected. France and China suggested that the measures were too focused on buyers rather than end-users. France further suggested that "all of the proposed measures were in blatant contradiction to the agreed procedures of the Committee in that the latter did not envisage the Committee's interference in the process by which Iraqi oil was traded."

Toward the conclusion of the meeting, Russia voiced doubt that Iraq actually was imposing surcharges. It indicated "strong concerns over the procedures as a whole" and that the committee "was attempting to address a violation of sanctions for which it had no evidence." Of course, the largest purchases of oil under the program were by Russian companies—including government-owned companies that were subject to Russia's control. Yet Russia's inexplicable objection to the lack of evidence did not suggest that it had initiated any inquiries of its own companies to determine if Iraq was demanding illegal surcharges.

One month later, the 661 Committee met again to discuss the surcharge issue, and the United States circulated a copy of a letter it had sent to U.S. oil companies urging them to "take all necessary steps to ensure that any Iraqi-origin crude you acquire has not been tainted by the payment to Iraq of an illegal surcharge." The United States asked for more "feedback" from other members on its reform proposal from the last meeting. France replied that it could support the "spirit of the proposal," but only if it were "part of a comprehensive approach to Iraq and the Oil-for-Food Program, in which such issues as the impact of sanctions on third states and applications on hold were also reviewed." Despite the passage of one month's time, Russia replied that it had not yet received a response from Moscow on the U.S. reform proposal. The U.S. proposal does not appear to have been discussed again.

Later in the spring of 2001, Britain and France offered proposals directly to the Security Council to have the Secretary-General develop screening criteria for the qualification of oil buyers under the program. But the Security Council never voted on these proposals. Neither the Security Council nor the 661 Committee ever took any steps to require increased screening of buyers of Iraqi oil.

A similar fate befell an initiative by Britain in August 2001 to shorten the committee's oil pricing period from a monthly schedule to just ten or fifteen days. A shorter pricing period would mean that the prices would be reset more frequently to correspond to true market conditions, and this would decrease the likelihood of windfall profits—and of a margin from which contract holders could pay surcharges—if market prices increased during the month after they had been set. As the overseers noted, SOMO conspicuously sought far more downward revisions of the official selling price than upward revisions. Along with SOMO, Russia, China, and France all objected to shortening the pricing period to ten days. When the United States and Britain countered with a proposal to reset prices every fifteen days, the committee languished in disagreement and did nothing to modify its usual monthly pricing schedule.

Nor could the committee reach consensus on a proposal to ensure that it had full information about the accuracy of "fair market value" pricing. This proposal in September 2001 would have required a weekly report from the overseers on the difference between the committee's official selling price of Iraqi oil and the price Iraqi oil was being resold to end-users on the world market. According to the overseers, the amount of this premium could be derived from publicly available data, and the premium currently was between 30 to 40 cents per barrel. Russia objected that the overseers "had no authority to monitor the profits of the oil companies" and that the "sanctions were not against companies, but against Iraq."

With the committee deadlocked on both proposals for shortening the pricing period and weekly reporting on the price premiums, these issues were elevated to the full Security Council, where the overseers gave a briefing in late September 2001. The overseers explained that "practically all" Iraqi oil was sold to contractors that "do not get involved in shipping, financing or any other risk bearing activity," and that this market structure was "rather unprecedented in the oil industry and only exists in this shape and form in the case of Iraq." The overseers also stressed the extent of risk free profit that accrued to Iraq's contractors, with a consequent loss of potential revenue for the escrow account. The per-barrel premiums gained by contractors on resale of Iraqi oil rarely had gone below 30 cents per barrel since December 2000—far more than a normal industry profit level of no more than 5 cents per barrel.

Britain and the United States voiced continued support in the Security Council for reducing the pricing period to fifteen days, and now France also agreed, but Russia remained opposed. Accordingly, the Security Council took no decision on the shortened pricing period but did ultimately agree to allow the overseers to report weekly on the size of the market premium for the resale of Iraqi oil.

With the Security Council unable to agree on any meaningful reform to combat surcharges, the United States and Britain acted unilaterally to bring about pricing reform beginning in October 2001. They decided to use the 661 Committee's consensus rule as a tool in their favor by simply withholding approval of SOMO's proposed monthly pricing mechanism until the end of each month for which the approval had been sought. Then at that point it could be determined if SOMO's pricing mechanism corresponded to actual historic market value, and the pricing mechanism would either be approved or rejected and revised to correspond with historic market conditions.

This after-the-fact review of the pricing mechanism became known as "retroactive pricing." Russia and China protested the new stratagem, but there was nothing they could do about it. Retroactive pricing made it less profitable for Iraq's contractors to pay surcharges, yet it came at a cost to the program of far fewer Iraqi oil exports, because fewer buyers would agree to buy Iraqi oil without knowing at the time what the price would be. As for Russia, it continued to claim that there was no evidence that Iraq was requiring companies to pay oil surcharges. And China also resisted further pricing reforms, citing an old Chinese proverb, "If the river is too clean, there are no fish."

Retroactive pricing persisted though 2001 and 2002. As oil sales steadily declined, Iraq finally decided in August 2002 to abandon its surcharge policy, while holding out hope that the United States and Britain would relent on their retroactive pricing policy. Russia took on the role of Iraq's advocate in the 661 Committee, now conceding for the first time that Iraq had imposed the surcharges. During a meeting of the 661 Committee in August 2002, Russia defended the surcharges as necessary "because [of] Iraq's need to offset the cost of maintaining its oil industry [that] had been ignored for many years."

Not only did the Russian representative confirm the existence of surcharges, but he offered a deal on behalf of Iraq to end them:

> The current situation, which had been confirmed to the Russian Federation in contacts with Iraqi representatives in Baghdad, was that Iraq would be prepared to abolish surcharges immediately if the Committee was finally able to solve two key problems affecting the humanitarian programme: ending retroactive pricing, and approving the cash component for the oil industry.

Thus Iraq would be prepared to abolish surcharges immediately if the committee would end retroactive pricing and approve disbursements from the escrow account for the costs of maintaining Iraq's oil infrastructure. Russia proposed that the committee accept the Iraqi conditions so that "the surcharges so often discussed would disappear, and Iraqi oil could be extracted and exported under normal conditions."

Despite conceding in the 661 Committee the existence of Iraqi surcharges, Russia retreated to its original denials of surcharges when it came time to respond to the investigation of the IIC. When questioned about surcharges by investigators of the IIC, Russian diplomats insisted again that there was little evidence that Iraq ever imposed surcharges, much less that Russian companies paid them.

In any event, the 661 Committee did not agree to Iraq's conditions for ending surcharges, but Iraq ended them anyway. Iraqi oil exports soon doubled to about two million barrels per week.

The Iraqi regime and the companies that agreed to pay surcharges doubtlessly bear primary responsibility for the abuse of oil sales under the program. But it is clear that the Security Council and 661 Committee acquiesced to lax oversight and the evolution of "middleman" market conditions that lay fertile ground for the success of the surcharge scheme. Then, once the surcharge scheme took root, the Security Council and the 661 Committee were unable—for lack of consensus—to mount a timely or unified response.

OIL SMUGGLING

Although Iraq garnered more than $200 million of illicit income from its oil surcharge scheme, this paled next to Iraq's illicit income—about $11 billion—from outright smuggling of oil outside the Oil-for-Food Program. Iraq smuggled most of its oil to Jordan, Turkey, and Syria. In the words of then-U.S. Ambassador James Cunningham, "smuggling steals money from the Oil-for-Food Programme and puts it to illicit purposes." But as with the oil surcharge scheme, the Security Council and its members—despite being aware of the smuggling—did little to stop it.

Of Iraq's neighbor states, perhaps none felt the consequences of the sanctions regime more strongly than Jordan. Before the sudden onset of sanctions in August 1990, Jordan depended on Iraq for about 85 percent of its crude oil supply.

Under Article 50 of the UN Charter, a country burdened by "special economic problems" arising from the Security Council's sanctions on another country "shall have the right to consult the Security Council with regard to a solution of those problems." Jordan advised the Security Council that its adherence to the sanctions would lead to "extreme economic hardships," including a "direct financial loss" of no less than $1.5 billion per year and even a "total collapse" of the Jordanian economy.

The Security Council acknowledged Jordan's plight but did little to help other than asking the Secretary-General to do a study of the problem and issuing a general appeal to all member states for any help they might offer. Even Saudi Arabia—the world's largest oil producer and neighbor to Jordan—did not come to Jordan's aid to provide a compensating source of oil supply.

And so within two months of the start of sanctions Jordan turned back to Iraq for its oil, while seeking tacit approval from the Security Council and member states, including the United States. To make its resumption of oil imports more palatable to those concerned about enriching the Iraqi regime, Jordan assured the Security

Council that Iraq's oil imports would be strictly for internal use and accepted merely as repayment of a preexisting debt between the two countries and that "no transfer of funds is being made to Iraq."

For its part, the United States did not at first accept Iraq's export of oil to Jordan. In late January 1991, U.S. war planes bombed five tanker trucks carrying oil from Iraq to Jordan. The United States declared that Jordan's trade was "a clear violation" of the sanctions and that the 661 Committee had "never approved an exception for Jordan" to import oil. Similarly, the chairman of the 661 Committee denied authorizing Jordan to import Iraqi oil.

Later, in the spring of 1991, Jordan wrote to the 661 Committee, stressing again its "great difficulties" in "finding a continuous and secure source" of oil from sources other than Iraq. Jordan reiterated its intention to fund the oil imports only by "drawing down on Iraqi debts to Jordan" rather than paying hard cash to Saddam. Moreover, Jordan committed to making a "report to the Committee each month on the quantities, value, and dates of imports of all Iraqi oil and oil derivatives."

By this time, the United States and others on the Security Council had evidently softened their position on Jordan. On May 21, 1991, the chairman of the 661 Committee suggested that, "given the unique position of Jordan with respect to Iraq," the committee should "*take note*" of Jordan's resumption of oil imports, "pending any arrangements" by Jordan "to obtain supplies from other sources." What did it mean to "take note"? This was never discussed and remains unclear to this day. What is clear is that neither the 661 Committee nor the Security Council ever voted to authorize an exception for Jordan from the sanctions to import Iraqi oil. Despite this lingering ambiguity, the "taking note" proposal passed without objection or comment, and the chairman of the 661 Committee sent a letter to the Jordanian ambassador advising him of the committee's decision not to take action.

Jordan soon entered into formal protocols with Iraq to provide for discount sales of oil. Now, however, it was no longer just oil-for-debt-reduction; the two countries agreed that Jordan would provide commodities in return for Iraq's oil. This of course departed from the terms on which Jordan had initially sought the 661 Committee's approval. In addition, Jordan only sporadically complied with its promise to make reports to the 661 Committee of its oil imports from Iraq. But that did not trouble the committee, even when presented with compelling evidence from UN official Paul Conlon that the limited trade data provided by Jordan to the committee was substantially understated and inconsistent with the data Jordan was providing to another UN department under a separate program. According to Conlon, in light of the debt figures provided by Jordan, the oil import figures Jordan provided to the 661 Committee indicated that "trade with Jordan now earns currency for Iraq."

Although smuggling oil to Jordan was well established by the time the Oil-for-Food Program started, the start of the program presented a prime opportunity for the ongoing Iraq-Jordan trade to be put under UN control. It did not happen. The Security Council made no effort to require the oil-for-goods trade between Iraq and Jordan to occur under the control of the program.

In return for oil shipments ranging between 60,000 to 100,000 barrels per day, Jordan shipped vast amounts of goods back to Iraq outside the program. None of it was subject to UN inspection. And this was so despite the fact that the program required the UN to send teams of inspectors from Lloyd's or Cotecna to be stationed at the Iraq-Jordan border.

Indeed, the fact that the UN hired border inspectors for the program may well lead one to think the inspectors would have taken part in the UN's overall mission to enforce the sanctions and to prevent the illegal flow of resources to Saddam. For if the UN had gone to the trouble of sending inspectors to stand at Iraq's border, why shouldn't the inspectors serve this vital sanctions enforcement purpose? But it was not to be so. In fact, the Security Council did not authorize the program's inspectors to examine smuggled goods or even to make reports to the UN about any obviously illegal cross-border trade. As thousands of trucks cascaded past the border station with smuggled oil and goods in violation of the sanctions regime, the inspectors concerned themselves only with goods entering Iraq under the Oil-for-Food Program.

In the meantime, Jordan financed inspections by the Lloyd's inspectors at its port of Aqaba to screen incoming items for goods potentially destined for Iraq in violation of sanctions. But as the Lloyd's inspectors noted in reports they sent to the 661 Committee, Jordanian authorities took an exceptionally broad view of what essential "humanitarian" foodstuffs were permitted to be imported to Iraq. Hence, between 1995 and 2000, Lloyd's released to Iraq more than 4 million cigarettes, nearly 2,500 metric tons of tobacco, more than 1.5 million liters of beer, more than 185,000 bottles of wine, more than 300,000 liters of vodka, and more than 700,000 bottles of whiskey. So far as the committee's meeting notes reflect, this report from Lloyd's to the committee caused no concern or response by the 661 Committee. Nor did the committee respond when Jordan simply terminated Lloyd's inspection services at the end of 2000 and failed to live up to a promise it had made to hire a replacement inspection company at Aqaba.

Oil is far easier to transport in bulk by sea than over land, and so by June 1997, Jordan decided to request approval from the 661 Committee to import Iraqi oil by sea. France favored granting Jordan's request, reasoning that the 661 Committee had "approved the export of Iraqi oil to Jordan, or at least had taken note of it," and that the manner of how the oil was transported to Jordan was "secondary." By contrast, the United States maintained that "the fact that the Committee had taken note of something did not mean or imply that it approved it." The U.S. representative added that the 661 Committee "had never formally approved Jordan's oil imports from Iraq" and "it was not clear" that the committee itself rather than the plenary Security Council could approve such trade. Britain added that "it was clear that the Committee had never approved imports of Iraqi oil to Jordan."

Despite the stated view of the United States that Jordan's trade with Iraq was in violation of sanctions, it tacitly encouraged Jordan's trade with Iraq by continuing to dispense large amount of foreign aid to Jordan. Under U.S. law, no foreign aid could be furnished to a country that was not in compliance with UN sanctions against Iraq. But a provision of this law allowed an exception if the President decided that such foreign assistance was "in the national interest." Successive U.S. administrations acknowledged Jordan's sanctions-busting trade but cited its cooperation in other foreign policy objectives and annually invoked the "national interest" exception in Jordan's favor. This cleared the way for the United States to donate $2.4 billion of aid to Jordan from 1991 to 2003.

By the beginning of 2003, Jordan was freely transacting in Iraqi oil without reporting to the 661 Committee what it was doing and certainly without fear of consequence from the United States or other Security Council members. This set the stage for Jordan to accomplish the single largest episode of oil smuggling to take place during the program and, surprisingly, to do so with help from the government of the United States.

The smuggling plan involved a Jordanian company loading massive amounts of Iraqi oil from a dilapidated Iraqi oil terminal known as Khor al-Amaya. This terminal lay about six nautical miles north of Mina al-Bakr, which was the only Iraqi terminal in the Persian Gulf authorized for the export of oil under the program. Both the Khor al-Amaya and Mina al-Bakr terminals are fed by a common sea pipeline network stemming from an onshore distribution center. Initially commissioned in the 1960s, the Khor al-Amaya terminal was severely damaged and made inoperable in the 1980s during the Iran-Iraq war.

Iraq had long sought to use some of the program's escrow funds

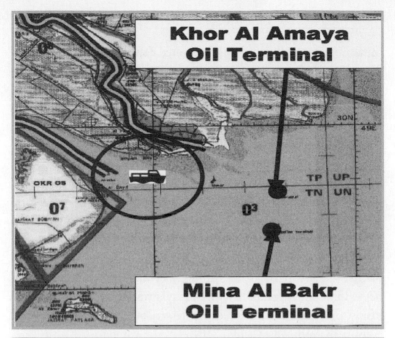

Khor Al Amaya
Oil Terminal

Mina Al Bakr
Oil Terminal

DIAGRAM OF MINA-AL-BAKR AND KHOR AL-AMAYA OFFSHORE OIL TERMI-
NALS AND PHOTO OF KHOR AL-AMAYA OFFSHORE OIL TERMINAL.

to restore Khor al-Amaya. But the United States had resisted these efforts. "When there are so many urgent needs in Iraq," explained U.S. Ambassador James Cunningham to the Security Council, "it is unconscionable for the Government of Iraq to divert precious resources to a facility which the Council has not decided that Iraq may use."

Nevertheless, Khor al-Amaya was evidently functional by early 2003, when Iraq received an offer to smuggle oil from this terminal. The Iraqi ambassador to Jordan telephoned Samir Al-Nejm, Iraq's new Oil Minister (who had replaced Amer Rashid), to inform him that a "Mr. Shaheen," a businessman and friend of the ambassador, was interested in purchasing oil from Iraq. "Mr. Shaheen" was apparently Akram Shaheen, who, according to an IIC confidential source, acted at the direction of his brother, Khaled Shaheen. In 2003, Khaled Shaheen was chairman and chief executive officer of Shaheen Business and Investment Group in Jordan, and Akram Shaheen was a senior official in the company.

In early 2003, Akram Shaheen met with Oil Minister Al-Nejm in Baghdad to express his interest in lifting oil from Khor al-Amaya. This was in the weeks leading up to the much-anticipated U.S.-led invasion of Iraq. In contrast to Mina al-Bakr, there were no UN oil inspectors from Saybolt stationed at Khor al-Amaya, and so there was nothing to stop a ship from loading Iraqi oil there. But Al-Nejm and another Iraqi official voiced concern to Shaheen that any lifting of oil from Khor al-Amaya could be noticed and was at risk of seizure by ships of the Multi-National Interception Force (MIF).

The MIF was a U.S.-led naval brigade that patrolled the waters of the Persian Gulf to interdict suspected sanctions smuggling activity. Throughout the sanctions years, the MIF had intercepted and boarded thousands of suspect ships. These rigorous maritime sanctions enforcement efforts stood in contrast to the absence of comparable safeguards to prevent Iraq's export and import of illegal goods over any of its land borders.

A large oil tanker without any UN authorization to carry oil would be easy prey for the MIF. But Shaheen assured the Oil Minister not to worry—he claimed to have strong friendships at the U.S. Department of Defense and the CIA, and he said he had taken some measures to ensure a smooth process. According to one Iraqi official, Shaheen spoke of having the Pentagon in one pocket and the CIA in the other.

Al-Nejm got approval from Vice President Taha Yassin Ramadan to deal oil to Shaheen. It was agreed that Iraq would sell the oil for a cut-rate price of $7 per barrel. This price was far below what the oil would fetch under the program, but Iraq would gain unrestricted use of the sale proceeds, rather than losing control of the proceeds to the UN's escrow account.

Not everyone in the Oil Ministry was prepared to divert oil to Khor al-Amaya. An official of Iraq's South Oil Company—which was in charge of distributing oil in southern Iraq—had originally refused to load the oil. But he was personally ordered to do so by Vice President Ramadan.

To carry out the oil liftings, the Shaheens used a company known as Millennium for the Trade of Raw Materials & Mineral Oils. The government of Jordan backed Millennium, and Jordan's Minister of Energy and Mineral Resources issued a power of attorney authorizing Millennium to act on Jordan's behalf. Millennium arranged with a U.S. company—Odin Marine of Connecticut—for the charter of several tankers to lift oil from Khor al-Amaya.

Communications among Millennium, the charter company, the ships lifting the oil, and their owners reveal that the U.S. government was aware of, if not actively assisting, the Khor al-Amaya lifts. The first tanker to lift the oil would be the *Argosea*, captained by Vladimir Egoshin. On February 9, 2003, Millennium sent instructions to Captain Egoshin advising him at first to proceed to Mina al-Bakr and advising that the "US Navy" was "already aware about your passage." In its written instructions to Captain Egoshin, Millennium stressed that he must maintain absolute secrecy about his mission—specifically, that "no information of any kind be given to any person // repeat any person // at the loading port with regard to arrangements made or mentioned here above."

Two days later, on February 11, the *Argosea* arrived in the vicinity of Mina al-Bakr. But there was no response from the terminal, which was not surprising because Millennium had not acquired any permission from the UN to load Iraqi oil from Mina al-Bakr. Millennium then sent directions to Captain Egoshin to change his port of call to Khor al-Amaya, including the following instructions: "If you are asked (I repeat[:] if you are asked) for authorization: inform them that a special authorization to load at [Khor al-Amaya] terminal is granted to Millennium Shaheen Business Investment Group." The owner of the *Argosea* later reported that the ship had received approval from the MIF to proceed to Khor al-Amaya:

> The vessel shifted from MINA AL BAKR anchorage to KHAWR AL AMAYA terminal. During this passage the vessel was contacted by [a] UN naval vessel to whom the Master reported that he is proceeding to load from KHAWR AL AMAYA terminal. The UN naval vessel acknowledged this advice and told the Master it was OK to proceed.[4]

Another two days later, on February 13, Captain Egoshin sent a message that he was at Khor al-Amaya. He marveled that the *Argosea* would be the first ship to load from Khor al-Amaya since 1980. The *Argosea* started loading on February 15 and took on 1 million barrels of oil.

It was also apparent that the U.S. government was aware of the *Argosea*'s unusual course. After the loading, Millennium instructed Captain Egoshin to proceed through the Persian Gulf not to Jordan but to Fujairah in the United Arab Emirates. Although this would require a journey across the heart of MIF-patrolled international waters, Millennium assured Captain Egoshin that he would have no problems: "The U.S. Navy will call you on the way for vessel inspection, they are already aware about your passage and itinerary."

The U.S.-led forces of the MIF let the *Argosea* go but, just as Al-Nejm had feared, the loading at Khor al-Amaya did not go altogether unnoticed. Because Khor al-Amaya shared the same pipeline source with Mina al-Bakr, the loading of the *Argosea* caused a noticeable drop in the oil flow rate at Mina al-Bakr, where UN-approved vessels under the program were also loading. Through binoculars, personnel at Mina al-Bakr could see activity at Khor al-Amaya, and a chorus of complaints sounded to the UN from Saybolt inspectors and other companies with tankers at Mina al-Bakr for which loading was delayed by the diversion of oil to Khor al-Amaya.

Saybolt's managing director, Peter Boks, contacted David Russell, an operations officer at the U.S. Navy's Maritime Liaison Office in Bahrain to make sure the MIF would do something about the apparent smuggling activity. Russell e-mailed back to Boks that "we're still checking on this curious event," and "I still don't understand it, or how these people think they can get away with this."[5]

But they did get away with it. When Russell contacted MIF Commander Harold French of the United States, he never got a response. Russell would later remark, "Those people that did know about it weren't very interested." Similarly, one of the UN's oil overseers alerted the U.S. representative to the 661 Committee about the apparent illegal activity. He never got a response. The overseers also contacted the captain of the *Argosea* on several occasions and informed him that the vessel was carrying oil in violation of UN sanctions.[6]

The *Argosea* was just the first of seven ships that Millennium sent to Khor al-Amaya. On February 21, 2003, *The Wall Street Journal* ran a detailed article describing the now well-known loadings from Khor al-Amaya. A spokesman for the U.S. ambassador to the UN denounced the Khor al-Amaya shipments as "immoral."[7]

The U.S. State Department would later assert that it had promptly forwarded the information it received about the loadings to the MIF for investigation.[8] But all available evidence suggests that the United States ultimately decided to go along with the smuggling scheme.

When Shaheen met for a second time with Al-Nejm in Baghdad to discuss more lifts from Khor al-Amaya, Al-Nejm complained about the publicity. Again, Shaheen assured Al-Nejm not to worry, because the U.S. government was already informed and he didn't think there would be more media coverage of the lifts in the future. Shaheen also advanced a political proposal to Al-Nejm: he said that he carried a message on behalf of the U.S. Department of Defense and the CIA to determine if the Iraqis were willing to negotiate to avoid the impending war.

Al-Nejm informed Saddam and Vice President Ramadan of Shaheen's proposal. With Saddam's approval, a meeting was soon set up with Shaheen, Vice President Ramadan, and the head of Iraq's secret services, Taher Al-Takriti. It is not known what transpired at this meeting. When interviewed by IIC investigators, Ramadan himself denied that he met with Shaheen or knew of a proposal to avoid the war.

In any event, Millennium continued to lift oil at Khor al-Amaya without interference from the MIF. It issued instructions to Odin Marine as to how ships were to communicate with the MIF and in particular with MIF Commander Harry French, as U.S. Naval officer:

> At anchorage, Master will contact Commander Harry French and get the NO OBJECTION message from him. Mr. Young of Odin Marine to contact Commander French as well in order to verify and confirm the communication between the Master and Commander French. Mr. Young will seek the NO OBJECTION message in the text and format agreed between us. . . .
>
> The message that should be sent by either the ship master or

Mr. Young is the following: "We are loading crude oil from the terminal at Khawr Amaya for Millennium: do you have any objection?"[9]

This procedure appears to have been followed with each of the remaining ships that loaded at Khor al-Amaya.[10]

On March 3, 2003, a leading oil trade news journal rhetorically asked "how, despite all the publicity, [the vessels] have been able to sail down the Gulf without being apprehended by the large fleet of ships belonging to the navies of the US and its allies which are gathering for a possible attack on Iraq."

In the midst of ongoing publicity, Odin Marine contacted Commander French on March 15, 2003, to make sure there was permission for another one of its ships, the *M/T Sea Victory*, to load oil from Khor al-Amaya. As reflected in contemporaneous notes obtained from Odin Marine's records, Commander French promptly called back "confirming 'no objection' to the loading of the M/T Sea Victory." Odin Marine's representative then added in a note to his file that "I have been over the past few weeks very comfortable that the liftings were authorized by the U.S. government. After this conversation [with Commander French] I am equally comfortable that they are UN authorized as well."

In fact, the UN never approved the lifting of oil from Khor al-Amaya. But this didn't stop high officials of Jordan from misrepresenting that Millennium's oil liftings were cleared by the UN. Both Jordan's Minister of Finance and Minister of Energy and Mineral Resources signed a letter of indemnity to one of the ship owners vowing that Millennium was "duly authorized to load up to full cargo of Iraqi Crude Oil at the Khor al-Amaya Terminal" and that "we confirm that this cargo is legitimate, lawful and authorized merchandise according to relevant U.N. Regulations and International law."

Equally telling were the repeated assurances Millennium provided to the concerned owner of the *Argosea*, who had been informed by the UN oil overseers of the illegal nature of its cargo and who demanded documentation demonstrating the legitimacy of the shipment. Millennium stressed that the transaction was permissible because UN naval forces had tight control of Arabian Gulf shipping and were responsible for verifying, scrutinizing, and taking action on any information received from UN headquarters in New York.

> Once again, we assure you based on our agreement that the owners will not be subject to any legal procedure initiated against them of whatsoever nature due to this operation. The fact that further documents and information could not be provided does not and should not lead to the impression that this is an illegitimate transaction.
>
> .   .   .
>
> More importantly, as you are fully aware, any vessel carrying illegal cargo is subject to confiscation and that the sole authority and party to carry out such confiscation is the UN Naval Forces. Considering that as stated above the ships are granted safe passage in and out by the UN Naval Forces only confirms the legitimacy of our operation.[11]

But these assurances did not stem Odin Marine's quest for further proof of the legality of the shipment. In response, Millennium provided a written explanation that the Khor al-Amaya shipments had been conducted under the 1990 Iraq-Jordan trade protocol, which, Millennium explained, had been entered into pursuant to Article 50 of the UN Charter and which "has been approved by the UN in general and the UN sanctions committee in particular."[12]

This justification was false. The Iraq-Jordan trade protocol applied only to land-shipped oil, and the 661 Committee had already rejected Jordan's request for shipment of oil by sea. Nor was the oil for Jordan's internal use, as contemplated by Jordan's Article 50 request. To the contrary, Millennium sought third-party purchasers for the oil, including U.S. companies, with the prospect of spectacular profits on resale because Iraq had sold the oil to Millennium at a steeply discounted price.[13] Finally, neither the Security Council nor the 661 Committee had ever approved the Iraq-Jordan trade protocol, and Jordan never reported its purchase of the Khor al-Amaya oil to the UN.

Odin Marine also contacted the U.S. Treasury Department's Office of Foreign Assets Control, which was the U.S. government office responsible for administering sanctions against Iraq. In response to this call, Odin Marine's counsel received a call from a U.S. State Department official. Odin Marine's counsel offered to turn the oil over to the United States, but the State Department official told him that the State Department "was aware of the shipments and has determined not to take action." When Odin Marine's counsel added that another shipment was being sought by Millennium, the State Department official merely repeated her statements and would say no more. Odin Marine felt reassured that the United States was fully informed and had no objection to the Khor al-Amaya shipments or to the involvement of a U.S. company in the shipments.[14]

Not surprisingly, the U.S. Department of Justice never filed charges against U.S.-based Odin Marine for taking part in the oil smuggling operation. Nor did the U.S. government take action against the Shaheen brothers of Jordan. Only several months after the smuggling operation, in October 2003, the Shaheen brothers' company sponsored the "American Jordanian Expo," at which Khaled Shaheen appeared as a discussion panelist and at which the U.S. ambassador to Jordan, Edward Gnehm, delivered a keynote address. In March 2004, the U.S. Department of Defense awarded the Shaheen brothers' company a contract for $71.8 million to furnish gasoline and diesel fuel for Iraq.

According to SOMO records, Millennium paid SOMO more than $53 million for about 7.7 million barrels of oil lifted from

Khor al-Amaya. The payments went to a SOMO bank account in Jordan and were then transferred to an account of the Central Bank of Iraq. Although these payments were a hefty sum, they were but a fraction of the oil's true market value. Had the Khor al-Amaya oil been properly sold under the program at fair market value, it could have earned approximately $200 million for the program's escrow account.

Neither the United States nor Jordan chose to respond to the IIC's queries about the Khor al-Amaya smuggling. Commander French told an IIC investigator that he could not recall the incidents. It remains unclear why the United States went along with the scheme and to what extent the Jordanian government shared in the proceeds of Millennium's resale of the Iraqi oil. The smuggling operation has left still unanswered questions about the selective commitment of the United States to enforcement of the UN sanctions.

All in all, Iraq smuggled about $3.4 billion of oil to Jordan from 1997 to 2003—all revenue that was foregone by the Oil-for-Food Program. Another major smuggling partner was Turkey, to the north of Iraq. Iraq smuggled about $800 million of oil to Turkey by overland truck shipments during the program, mostly through Kurdish territory and with assistance from Kurdish officials. The governments of Iraq and Turkey entered into a formal trade protocol that provided for Turkey to repay Iraq for its oil in part through the provision of goods and in part through cash.

As with Jordan and Turkey, the Security Council did little to stop Saddam from deriving billions more in illicit income from oil smuggled to Syria. Indeed, next to Jordan, Syria was Iraq's second largest market for smuggled oil—accounting for about $3.1 billion in oil sales.

The Syrian Arab Republic lies on the western border of Iraq. Since the 1930s, a transnational oil pipeline has run east to west across the country to transport oil from Iraq's northern Kirkuk fields to the coast of Syria. By the 1980s, the six-hundred-mile pipeline system ran to a refining facility in the Syrian city of Homs, with outlet extensions to refining facilities on the Mediterranean coast—at Baniyas to the north and Tripoli (Lebanon) to the south. Before the closure of the pipeline in 1982, it carried about 4 million tons of oil a year—about one-third of Iraq's annual production. But the pipeline was closed when Iraqi-Syrian relations broke down because of Syria's support of Iran in the Iran-Iraq war. Syria thereafter imported oil from Iran, rather than Iraq, at concessional prices.

As the sanctions started against Iraq in 1990, Syria and Iraq had begun talks to reopen the pipeline. Like Jordan, Syria petitioned the Security Council for relief from the sanctions under Article 50 of the UN Charter. But little relief came. When the Security Council passed Resolution 986 to authorize the Oil-for-Food Program, the Council allowed Iraq to export its oil only from Mina al-Bakr and by pipeline through Turkey. Iraq's ambassador wrote to the UN declaring that "the Iraqi delegation wishes to state that a third outlet

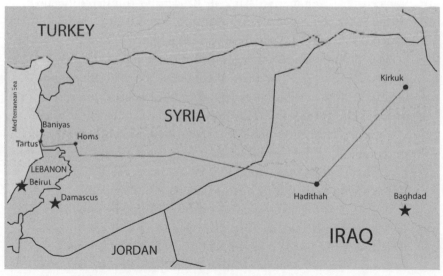

MAP OF SYRIA (JAN. 2004) (SHOWING EAST-WEST PIPELINE)

for Iraqi petroleum export could be via the Syrian Arab Republic."
However, the Security Council never authorized the export of Iraqi
oil through Syria.

Without UN approval, Iraq and Syria eventually took matters
into their own hands as bilateral relations improved. In March
2000, they negotiated a formal border trade protocol under the
terms of which Iraq would export oil to Syria, in return for which
Syria would pay Iraq partly in traded goods (60 percent) and partly
in cash (40 percent). The 60 percent "trade" account was maintained at the Commercial Bank of Syria in Damascus and used by
SOMO to pay Syrian suppliers of goods upon proof of delivery of
the goods to Iraq. Because these Syrian goods were not provided
under the program, they were not subject to any UN inspection
prior to entry into Iraq. The remaining 40 percent of oil sales proceeds were deposited by Syria into a "cash" account—another
SOMO bank account at the Commercial Bank of Syria. The cash
account funds were then transferred to a bridge account at the Syrian Lebanese Commercial Bank in Beirut and transferred again
within twenty-four hours to a separate account controlled by the
Central Bank of Iraq at the same bank in Beirut.

This entire arrangement was made without approval of or formal notice to the UN. Because of concerns that the trade monies
could be frozen or subject to attachment, the bridge accounts were
set up under individual Iraqi names rather than in the name of an
entity of the Iraqi government. Most of the money was transferred
to the control of the Central Bank of Iraq at a bank in Beirut, but
about $90 million was withdrawn in cash from the Commercial
Bank of Syria to be sent by diplomatic pouch to Baghdad.

At first, Iraq shipped its oil to Syria by truck and by rail. But the
greatest prospect for oil smuggling was to reopen the pipeline
through which enormous volumes of oil could most easily flow. As
early as 1998, Oil Minister Rashid publicly announced Iraq's intention to reopen the pipeline. In the meantime, in April and May

1999, other media reports suggested large-scale oil smuggling by trucks to Syria and Iraq's use of its sale proceeds to buy goods from Syria outside the program. Various Iraqi officials confirmed to IIC investigators that the pipeline was used to smuggle oil to Syria throughout the later years of the program.

At the time, Iraq disclaimed to the UN any intention to open the Syrian pipeline. In January 2000, a team of UN experts visited Iraq to discuss how Iraq could boost its oil production for more sales under the program. Their terms of reference for the trip included the review of potential alternative loading sites, with a visit to the Syrian pipeline. But the experts never visited the pipeline and instead relied on assurances from Iraqi officials that the pipeline was not a priority and would not be ready until 2002 at the earliest.

Iraq's assurances were soon cast in doubt. On October 31, 2000, the *Middle East Economic Survey* issued a "News Flash" stating that it had learned "from authoritative sources that Iraq and Syria have agreed to reopen the crude oil pipeline between the two countries—which has been closed since 1982—in November, probably around the middle of the month" and that "Baghdad will export around 200,000 [barrels per day] of Basrah Light crude to Syria." The article suggested that this development was a "clear signal to the US that it cannot turn a blind eye to the violation of the sanctions regime by its friends in the region (i.e. Jordan and Turkey) while expecting others to adhere to it" and that there was "widespread anger in the Arab world at the Americans' lack of even-handedness as far as the peace process and sanctions on Iraq are concerned." This article in turn formed the basis for several more news articles during the first week of November 2000. Later articles confirmed the opening of the pipeline and a flow of up to 150,000 barrels of crude oil per day.[15]

On November 21, 2000, Britain's representative to the 661 Committee circulated to other members of the committee some of the media reports about the reopening of the pipeline. Britain requested an "urgent meeting" of the committee and agreement that the committee should seek "clarification" of the pipeline matter from the government of Syria. Despite the urgency of Britain's request, the 661 Committee convened four more times over the next month without even discussing the Syrian pipeline question.

The pipeline question arose at the same time that Iraq had announced its surcharge policy. The full Security Council also had before it a new resolution to reauthorize the program for another six-month phase. Britain proposed that the new resolution require a report from the Secretary-General on recommendations to stop Iraq from smuggling, but the Security Council declined to agree to this language. Instead, on December 5, 2000, it passed a reauthorization resolution requesting the Secretary-General to study the feasibility of Iraq's opening a third major pipeline export route— presumably to bring Iraq's exports through the Syrian pipeline within the Oil-for-Food Program.

Iraq nipped this effort in the bud. When Iraq's assistance was requested for a team of UN experts to visit Iraq to discuss the opening of a pipeline, the Iraqi ambassador replied in January 2001 that this issue was "not among Iraq's current priorities" and that there was "no need for a special delegation to be sent by the United Nations to address this topic."

In the meantime, the 661 Committee's consensus procedures failed to yield even a letter of inquiry to Syria. On December 21, 2000, the committee met in formal session to address the pipeline issue and specifically to discuss Britain's request that a letter of inquiry be sent to the government of Syria. Joined by the United States, Britain urged sending a letter of inquiry. Russia, however, demurred for fear of giving offense. "While the question was neutral," explained the Russian representative, "merely raising it would seem political, since a question was halfway to an accusation." France joined Russia, stating that sending a letter "would be political" and adding that "any questions should be raised by a neutral party, such as the

Secretary-General." Canada rejoined that it "was alarmed to learn that France believed the Committee could not be neutral, even in simply requesting information."

France and Russia also raised concerns that Syria alone was being singled out for examination. This was apparently motivated by the favoritism of the United States toward Jordan. According to France, "the Secretary-General should be asked to prepare a report on all violations of the sanctions regime." Russia remarked that "the whole picture of sanctions busting and smuggling must be assessed, in order to avoid the use of a double standard." After China seemed to side with the concerns of Russia and France, the 661 Committee's chairman from the Netherlands openly voiced his frustration that the committee could not agree on something as simple as making a request for more information:

> Three of the five permanent members of the Security Council were objecting to the Committee requesting information on an occurrence that had been described by the media as a breach of the sanctions regime . . . [and] the five permanent members of the Security Council were supposed to be supreme guardians of legality in the United Nations.

The protest had no effect. Russia and France later rebuffed another effort in February 2001 to request more information from Syria about the pipeline.

Nor could the committee reach consensus on requesting that the Office of Iraq Programme (OIP) conduct its own investigation in Iraq to determine if the Syrian pipeline was actually in use. The Russian representative said he would have to get further instructions from his capital in order to agree that OIP should embark on this kind of inquiry. Instructions never came. Despite the presence of hundreds of OIP staff in Iraq, the Security Council never sought a report from OIP on whether Iraq was operating the Syrian pipeline.

For the next two years, the members of the 661 Committee sporadically quarreled about what, if anything, to do about the Syrian pipeline. The pipeline kept running. The committee ended up doing nothing, while Iraq pumped more than $2 billion of smuggled oil through the pipeline from 2000 to 2003.

By 2002, the flickering prospects for addressing the pipeline issue were doused when Syria itself was elected to join the Security Council for a two-year term. This development meant that Syria could simply veto any initiative in the 661 Committee to bring the pipeline within the program. Syria did so, while falsely assuring the committee that it "had not paid a single cent to Iraq" and insisting that the pipeline issue not be raised again.

But from February to July 2002, the Secretariat circulated more and more media reports about the continued use of the Syrian pipeline. In August 2002, the United States contended in a meeting of the 661 Committee that "Syria represented the largest single destination for Iraq's illicit oil exports," including about 180,000 to 200,000 barrels of oil that were shipped daily through the pipeline, resulting in an annual loss of $1.3 billion for the program. Syria responded by falsely denying again that the pipeline was in use and contending that "Iraq had received absolutely no payment for the experimental operationalization of the pipeline, which had been without result."

To the same effect, in late September 2002, Syria told members of the Security Council that discussions in the 661 Committee about the pipeline were like a "dialogue of the deaf," and it urged the Security Council not to focus "on unfounded allegations about a pipeline that was not operational." Both Russia and China sided with Syria, and France remained of the view that Syria should not be singled out among Iraq's neighbors for further inquiry.

Yet the difficulty with France's view against singling out Syria was not simply that Syria was by far the largest leak of oil revenue at that time from the Oil-for-Food Program. It was also that France had previously blocked a proposal from Britain in the Security Council in May and June 2001 that would have rendered *all* of Iraq's border trade with *all* of its neighbors subject to UN supervision. In essence, the British proposal—joined by the United States, Norway, and Singapore—would have carved an exception to the sanctions to allow Iraq to trade with its neighbors but made all the trade subject to UN inspection and channeled the revenues through monitored escrow accounts for each border country. But Iraq and its neighbors bridled at submitting to UN control their long-established smuggling trade. And so Russia, China, and France followed suit to oppose the British proposal, citing the objections raised by Iraq's neighbors. The British proposal died in early July 2001 without a vote in the Security Council.

HUMANITARIAN KICKBACKS

Unlike the open acknowledgment of oil surcharges and smuggling, the Security Council and the 661 Committee rarely discussed Iraq's extraction of kickback payments from its humanitarian contractors. Far more often, the members of the Security Council hotly debated the reasons for delays spanning many months or years in the review and approval of humanitarian contract applications.

This debate generally split along the same lines as debates about surcharges and smuggling, with Britain and the United States pitted against France, China, and Russia. Apart from delays caused by administrative backlogs at OIP, the United States—and to a lesser extent Britain—commonly blocked or placed temporary "holds" on approvals of humanitarian contracts because of "dual-use" concerns—that the civilian items involved could potentially be put to military use. France, Russia, and China, as well as Iraq and nonpermanent members of the Security Council, frequently criticized these holds and the toll they took on the welfare of the Iraqi people.

Despite the relative inattention to the issue of kickbacks, the Security Council was certainly aware of the possibility that Iraq would seek kickbacks from its contractors. But for reasons that are not clear the 661 Committee declined to institute comprehensive safeguards against kickbacks when crafting its internal procedures for the review and approval of humanitarian contracts. An early draft of the 661 Committee Procedures included a U.S. proposal for the Secretariat to employ "humanitarian contract examiners" who would be charged with assessing whether the contracts were "consistent with world prices and market trends," as well as "whether they appear[ed] to contain any attempt at fraud or deception." A note to the chairman of the Iraq Steering Committee from one of his assistants stated that the United States was "insist[ing] . . . on a mechanism that would allow the [661 Committee] to verify the 'fairness' of the price agreed for the purchases" because it was "afraid that Iraq might engage in fraudulent contracts involving illicit payments."

It is unclear why the U.S. proposal was not adopted. Instead, the 661 Committee Procedures tasked the Secretariat with a more generic responsibility simply to examine "the details of price and value," as well as to make sure that the items were within the scope of goods approved for distribution in Iraq and that there were funds in the escrow account to make payment. Customs experts within the Secretariat included their evaluation of this information in customs reports that they forwarded to the 661 Committee with each contract application.

For the first three years of the program, from 1997 to 1999, after initial processing by OIP, all humanitarian contract applications were submitted for the review and approval of the 661 Committee. Because of the sheer volume of contracts, the committee followed a "no objection" procedure—a contract was deemed approved unless any member of the committee affirmatively objected within a particular time period.

In December 1999, under pressure to expedite the processing of humanitarian applications and to reduce the number of contract holds, the Security Council adopted Resolution 1284 to create a fast-track procedure for approval of many kinds of humanitarian contracts. This authorized OIP—without the 661 Committee's involvement—to approve certain contracts, including items such as food and medicines that appeared on a preapproved "green list" of goods for which no dual-use possibility was foreseen.

Then, in May 2002, amid continued concerns about contract delays, the Security Council adopted Resolution 1409 to narrow again the category of goods that would be subject to review and approval by the 661 Committee. Under Resolution 1409, unless a contract contained items appearing on a "goods review list" that were known to have potential military significance, OIP retained authority to review and approve the contract without involvement of the 661 Committee.

Iraq initiated its inland transport fee in August 1999 and its general 10 percent after-sales service fee in August 2000. At least one of the Security Council members—France—was aware of the formal kickback policy. It learned from French companies in November 2000 about an announcement of the policy by Iraq's Trade Minister in Baghdad. According to France, it warned the Trade Minister and companies at the trade fair that kickback payments would be illegal. It does not appear, however, from the records of the 661 Committee that France raised what it knew about the kickbacks for discussion by the 661 Committee.

Apart from sporadic media reports and passing references at meetings of the 661 Committee or the Security Council to the possibilities of such kickbacks, there was no specific attention to the kickback issue until February 2001, when the United States queried OIP during an informal meeting of the 661 Committee what information OIP had about allegations that Iraq had been demanding a 10 percent kickback for awarding contracts to particular humanitarian goods suppliers. Farid Zarif, who was Chief of OIP's Contracts Processing Section, answered that OIP had not received "formal complaints from any permanent mission." As described in the next chapter, Zarif neglected to disclose that OIP had in fact received numerous complaints from companies about Iraq's kickback demands.

In mid-February 2001, Britain invited OIP to draft and circulate a paper addressing whether Iraq in fact was seeking kickbacks from firms supplying humanitarian goods through the program. Stephani Scheer, OIP's chief of office and second in command to Benon Sevan, replied "that OIP would look into providing what very little information existed" on this issue.

Two weeks later, Britain asked about OIP's report, only to be told again that there had been no *formal* complaints from missions (omitting any mention of the many complaints received from company suppliers). Britain and the United States noted their disappointment that OIP had not looked into or reported further on the matter. But Russia countered that OIP "did not have the capacity to investigate the allegations, nor did it have any other sources of information which would allow it to prepare an in-depth report." France added that OIP already had indicated "that any report would be 'thin'" and that informal sources of information had to be protected. By this time, of course, Iraq's humanitarian kickback policy was in full swing, and OIP never prepared a report for the 661 Committee.

Several days later, on March 7, 2001, the *New York Times* ran a major feature article concerning allegations of Iraqi kickbacks for humanitarian contracts. The article accurately described how Iraq incorporated "supplemental charges . . . often in side letters that are not part of a transaction's formal records" and included "bogus additional charges like 'inland transportation.'" The article cautioned, however that there was no written proof of the kickback policy and that Iraqi officials denied it.[16] Numerous diplomats, including the

661 Committee's chairman and the UN ambassadors from both Russia and the United States, agreed in published press reports that there was no hard evidence at the time of the kickback policy.[17]

On March 14, 2001, the United States proposed to the 661 Committee several modest measures to deter payment of kickbacks by means of ensuring that suppliers would know they were illegal. These measures included:

1. asking UN missions to instruct their home country suppliers not to pay kickbacks,
2. referencing in UN contract approval letters that kickback payments were illegal,
3. warning of the illegality of kickbacks on OIP's website, and
4. issuing a press release about the committee's anti-kickback initiative.

The U.S. proposal was greeted with a desultory and inconclusive discussion. Nearly a month later, when the proposal came up again, Russia and France advised that they still had not received instructions about the U.S. proposal from their capitals. So far as can be gleaned from the records of the 661 Committee, the U.S. proposal was never discussed again, and the committee did nothing to make sure that suppliers knew kickbacks were illegal.

When interviewed by IIC investigators, one U.S. official noted the challenge of trying to motivate the Security Council to take action against kickbacks: "We were trying to maintain a regime and improve it, while another very strong block was trying to walk it back. The result was the status quo; we cancelled each other out." Another U.S. official remarked that, even though goods suppliers were making "under the table payments," whenever this subject was broached at 661 Committee meetings, Russia typically would dismiss the information and stymie further investigation.

The Russian response was similar to its approach when confronted with evidence of oil surcharges and massive oil smuggling. On the one hand, Russia would disclaim the reliability of media reports, even reports appearing in highly specialized trade journals, and insist that findings of violations could not be founded on this kind of information. But then Russia would never initiate its own investigation of illegal payments, even though uniquely positioned to do so because its own companies—many of them owned by the government—were the largest contractors under the program. Finally, Russia would resist any proposal for the UN to conduct any kind of an official investigation more worthy of reliance than media reports. For Russia, mere media reports of corrupt activity were worthless and official inquiries to be otherwise discouraged.

The United States and Britain did more than other countries to stop the kickback scheme, but even their commitment quickly flagged. Neither country initiated their own inquiries of companies about whether Iraq was requiring the payment of kickbacks. The telltale sign of a kickback-tainted contract was an inflated contract price submitted to the UN for approval. Yet, except in one instance, neither the United States nor Britain ever placed a hold on a humanitarian contract because of concerns about high pricing. For example, OIP submitted a contract to the 661 Committee for computers with a warning that the price was "approximately 100% higher than normal market value." Similarly, for a school desk contract, OIP warned of 50 percent overpricing, and for a contract to buy tin, OIP warned of 30 percent overpricing. The warnings of high prices did not matter, as all these contracts sailed through to approval without objection.

In April 2001, a British diplomat wrote to OIP to complain of "unusual payment/service clauses that could mask payment of commissions to Iraq" in fifteen specific humanitarian contracts submitted for approval. The British diplomat "expressed surprise that OIP had chosen to circulate these contracts when they clearly offer Iraq the opportunity to obtain uncontrolled revenue" and that Britain was not "keen to let Iraq get away with blatant and profitable manipulation of the [program] to obtain hard currency outside UN control." Despite these concerns, the letter added that Britain would not itself block these contracts because of potentially adverse humanitarian consequences. According to a British diplomat, the letter was not circulated to the 661 Committee because it would have been "yet another agenda item in limbo."

In contrast to their failure to block contracts believed to contain inflated prices, the United States and Britain routinely placed holds on hundreds of contracts that were thought to involve items of potential military use. John Ruggie, a former high-level UN adviser and professor at Harvard, has suggested in retrospect that "it seems reasonable to infer that the U.S. and Britain held their noses and overlooked pricing irregularities in order to keep the sanctions regime in place and to put all their efforts into preventing dangerous technologies from getting into Saddam's hands."

But the difficulty with this explanation is that money alone empowered Saddam. By allowing Saddam to derive unrestricted revenue from kickbacks, the United States—and others—potentially enabled him to make black market purchases of weapons far more dangerous even than the ambiguously dual-use items that were the focus of the many contract holds placed by the United States. Indeed, because the United States and other members of the Security Council had long acquiesced to Iraq's smuggling of goods from Jordan, Turkey, and Syria, Saddam's ability to procure weapons was clear, so long as he could acquire the money from kickbacks to do so.

Iraq amassed hundreds of millions of dollars in kickbacks through 2001 and 2002 and into 2003 without further objection or action by the Security Council to investigate or put an end to the practice. Finally, after U.S.-led forces invaded in 2003, Iraq's massive kickback policy was quickly confirmed from Iraqi ministry records. For about three thousand program contracts that were approved but still unfulfilled, the UN unilaterally reduced the contract

price by 10 percent to remove all or most of the kickback compo-
nent. Some companies objected, but no longer did any members of
the Security Council deny the existence of the kickback scheme.

In short, the Security Council struggled in clearly defining the
broad purposes, policies, and administrative control of the program.
The members of the Security Council oscillated between treating
Iraq with enough flexibility to get its agreement to a program and
retaining sufficient control that any program would not become a
doorway to the clandestine reinvigoration of Iraq's ambitions for
weapons of mass destruction. In the end, far too much initiative and
decision-making was left to the Iraqi regime, while at the same time
the Security Council took the extraordinary step of retaining,
through its 661 Committee, substantial elements of operational control, at times in place of, and in tension with, the UN Secretariat.
That turned out to be a recipe for the dilution of individual and institutional responsibility. When things went awry—and they did—
when troublesome questions of conflict between political objectives
and administrative effectiveness arose, decisions were delayed, bungled, or simply avoided—no one was in charge.

7

"The Story Will Quickly Turn Negative":

Maladministration and Corruption

at the U.N.

From the start of the Oil-for-Food Program in 1996, the hazards assumed in doing business with Saddam were apparent. Just one day after the UN and Iraq finally came to terms on the program's MOU, one of Secretary-General Boutros-Ghali's aides wrote to him with a prophetic warning of the danger that lay ahead:

> Yesterday's Iraqi oil agreement was a great plus for the UN and you personally. Congratulations. But a word of caution! The story the press will be looking for next is how Saddam Hussein circumvents the agreement and diverts the oil for his own, or military, use. It will be critical for the UN's monitoring of the agreement, and delivery of medical aid to the needy, to be watertight. If there are flaws, the story will quickly turn negative.

There were indeed flaws, and the story turned negative as predicted—all at stunning cost to the perception and prestige of the United Nations. Was the warning ignored? This final chapter shifts to what went wrong with the administration of the program by the UN Secretariat and related UN agencies.*

Unfortunately, just as the Security Council did little to stop Iraq from smuggling and extracting surcharges and kickbacks from program contractors, the UN Secretariat played a key role in the overall mismanagement of the program. The Oil-for-Food Program was the UN's single largest financial enterprise, but Secretary-General Kofi Annan and Deputy Secretary-General Louise Fréchette took little interest in supervising the program or ensuring that its problems were redressed. They left the program to be run by Benon Sevan, who was secretly profiting from his receipt of Iraqi oil allocations. And perhaps because of Sevan's conflicted loyalties, his and OIP's response to reports of surcharges and kickbacks were anemic, with numerous instances in which significant information was not passed onto the 661 Committee and opportunities to confront the Iraqi regime were missed.

Apart from surcharges and kickbacks, OIP's administration of the program bogged down in confusion about its role to enforce sanctions and not just to dispense humanitarian relief. Auditing, when done, was almost wholly ineffectual, and little follow-up was done to ensure that the most significant problems identified were fixed. The auditors never examined the adequacy of the UN's contract review process. Had they done so, they may well have identified flaws that made the program most vulnerable to Iraq's surcharge and kickback schemes.

The UN-related agencies achieved considerable success in alleviating the suffering of Iraq's people, but they strayed at times beyond

---

*Unless otherwise noted, the narrative in chapter 7 is based on the following reports of the Independent Inquiry Committee: *Interim Report*, February 3, 2005, part 2, chapter 4 ("Benon Sevan and Oil Allocations"); *Third Interim Report*, chapter 1 ("The Conduct of Benon Sevan"); *The Management of the Oil-for-Food Programme*, volume 3, chapter 1 ("The Secretariat and the Office of the Iraq Programme: Functions and Responsibilities"), chapter 2 ("The Secretariat's Administration of the Programme from New York"); chapter 3 ("The Secretariat's Administration of the Programme in Iraq"); chapter 4 ("The Secretariat's Response to Sanctions Violations"), and chapter 5 ("The 38th Floor").

their core competencies in performing projects in northern Iraq. Moreover, the success of the agencies' work was marred by the UN's overpayment to them of more than $50 million, drawn from the escrow account, for services they performed under the program.

CORRUPTION AND BENON SEVAN

A native of Cyprus, Benon Sevan began his career with the UN in 1965. By 1989, he rose to the level of Assistant Secretary-General and served as the Secretary-General's Personal Representative in Afghanistan and Pakistan. Later assignments included high-level posts at the Department of Political Affairs and at the Department of Administration and Management. In October 1997, Secretary-General Annan chose Sevan as Executive Director of the newly created Office of Iraq Programme (OIP). He served at the level of Under-Secretary-General and remained at this post for the rest of the program through 2003.

With his appointment to lead OIP, Sevan assumed a position of significant power and far-flung responsibility. In New York, OIP had a Programme Management Division that set general policy for administering the program, compiled program statistical information, and prepared regularly required reports for the Secretary-General and Security Council. Separately, the Contracts Processing and Monitoring Division employed customs experts and other personnel to review the tens of thousands of contracts for goods purchased under the program. Out in the field, OIP operated through the United Nations Office of the Humanitarian Coordinator in Iraq to monitor the distribution of goods within southern and central Iraq, and worked in conjunction with the various UN-related agencies that distributed goods in the Kurdish areas of northern Iraq. All in all, Sevan oversaw the activities of hundreds of international staff both in New York and Iraq.

Beyond these administrative duties, Sevan was the unofficial ambassador and voice for the Oil-for-Food Program. His job included constant communications with the Iraqi government and numerous UN member states, including most prominently each of the members of the Security Council. If there was one human face of the UN's Oil-for-Food Program, it was that of Benon Sevan.

From Iraq's viewpoint, Sevan held great authority over a program that had become a lifeline for the Iraqi economy and people. He was well positioned to promote Iraq's hopes to expand the program, while softening the program's nettlesome contract review and monitoring requirements. Through the early years of the program, Iraq could sell only limited amounts of oil and import a relatively narrow range of goods. Iraq constantly pressed to sell more oil and to use escrow funds not just to buy food and medical supplies but also to buy general civilian and industrial sector goods.

During his first months in office, Sevan became intensely involved in efforts to obtain Security Council authority for an "oil spare parts" program—a program to permit Iraq to use funds from the escrow account to import parts and equipment for the repair and maintenance of its oil production infrastructure. This had always been a very important issue for Iraq. During MOU negotiations, the UN had declined Iraq's request to use some of the program's escrow funds for improving Iraqi oil facilities, and Iraq had formally reserved the issue for future discussion.

As the oil spare parts proposal came under consideration in 1998, the Security Council requested an expert study on how to increase Iraq's oil exports, and Saybolt was commissioned to do the study of Iraq's funding needs. When its group of experts traveled to Iraq in the spring of 1998, their mandate covered only the assessment of "upstream" crude oil pumping, storage, and distribution facilities (for which Iraq requested $210 million), not "downstream" refining equipment that was not related to enhancing Iraq's capacity to export its crude oil under the program. When the experts arrived, however, Iraqi officials pressed for an additional $90 million for "downstream" refinery facilities. The experts balked at considering this request or making any recommendations on it in their report, because it was outside of their mandate.

But Sevan did not let the matter end there; instead, he took the lead on behalf of Iraq's request for an additional $90 million in funding. Although the oil overseers were not charged with providing an opinion, they favored providing the $90 million in additional funding. Sevan forwarded the overseers' view to the experts and told them that he needed their position on Iraq's request for additional funding so that he could make a recommendation for a full $300 million. In response, the experts acknowledged in their final report that "while not strictly relevant . . . the request [for "downstream" funding] is considered to be reasonable."

The experts' report was then forwarded along with a cover letter from the Secretary-General to the Security Council urging approval of Iraq's request for $300 million in funding for an oil spare parts program. When OIP drafted the Secretary-General's cover letter, it misleadingly recast the experts' acknowledgement of the oil overseers' opinion as the oil overseers' endorsement of the experts' opinion, making it appear far stronger than it actually was:

[The oil overseers] share the view of the group of experts that the request by the ministry of oil for $300 million for spare parts— $210 million for upstream and $90 million for downstream operations—is reasonable and that it reflects only the most essential and urgent needs of the Iraqi oil industry.

Days later, Sevan personally advised the Security Council that he would have to reconsider his upcoming planned trip to Iraq if the Security Council failed to approve the oil spare parts request. Upon consideration of Sevan's statements and the Saybolt expert report with the Secretary-General's letter, the Security Council approved the entire $300 million request.

On June 21, 1998, just two days after the Security Council approved the request, Sevan left New York for Iraq. One of the official purposes of this trip was to meet with Iraqi officials and specialists from Saybolt about implementing the new program now that it was approved. Sevan met twice with Oil Minister Amer Rashid and once with Vice President Taha Yassin Ramadan.

During one of his meetings with Rashid, Sevan asked Rashid for an oil allocation to be given to a Panamanian oil trading company named African Middle East Petroleum Company, Ltd., Inc. (AMEP). Rashid, in turn, conveyed Sevan's request for an oil allocation to Vice President Ramadan. At some point just before or after his Iraq trip, Sevan also requested an oil allocation at the Iraqi mission in New York. Sevan told the Iraqi mission official that he wanted the allocation to "help a friend" from Egypt named "Abdelnour."

"Abdelnour" was Fakhry Abdelnour, a veteran oil trader who was president of AMEP. AMEP served as an agent for the Egyptian state-owned petroleum corporation for several years and claimed to be its biggest lifter of crude oil. Abdelnour ran AMEP from his home in Geneva, and he also kept a small operations office in Monaco that he visited once or twice a year. Although registered in Panama, AMEP had no offices or employees there. Its incorporation papers reflected as nominee officers and directors the names of Panamanian citizens who, in fact, had nothing to do with running AMEP's business. But when AMEP had initially registered in Panama in 1982, the incorporation papers identified Abdelnour as company president and two other officers: Ephraim "Fred" Nadler as Treasurer and Enrico Nadler as Secretary.

Fred Nadler was Sevan's best friend, and they had known each other since the early 1990s. Sevan was friendly as well with all of Fred's family, including two of Fred's brothers—Enrico and Emmanuel. Fred's sister was Leia Boutros-Ghali, the wife of then former Secretary-General Boutros-Ghali.

Fred Nadler spent much of his time in New York City, where he had an apartment a few blocks from the UN, but he also traveled extensively to Switzerland and Egypt. While Sevan headed up OIP, he and Nadler spoke with or visited each other very frequently. Available phone records from 1998 to 2001 reflect well over six hundred calls between their telephone numbers, and Sevan's official calendar reveals dozens of meetings or contacts between them.

Despite their friendship and having spoken so often with Fred Nadler, Sevan subsequently professed astonishing ignorance about him when interviewed by IIC investigators. When asked what Nadler did for a profession, Sevan claimed that he did not know.

Similarly, Sevan also claimed not to have known until recently of a relationship between Nadler and Abdelnour, the president of AMEP. In fact, phone records show more than two hundred telephone calls between the telephone numbers for Nadler and Abdelnour from 1998 to 2001. In several instances, the calling patterns suggested that Nadler was a coordinator or middleman for communications between Sevan and Abdelnour. Many of the calls between Nadler and Abdelnour occurred within minutes of, or immediately preceded or followed, calls between Nadler and Sevan.

Sevan, of course, had no legitimate reason to mention AMEP for an oil contract from Iraq. It was never Sevan's job to help Iraq decide to whom it should sell its oil. It certainly was not Sevan's job to recommend his friends for oil contracts with Iraq under the program. Nor would it have been remotely proper for Sevan to seek or receive any kind of financial benefit from Iraq.

In response to Sevan's request for oil, an Iraqi official told Sevan to have "his guy" Abdelnour call SOMO directly. In early August 1998, within just a few weeks of Sevan's trip to Baghdad, SOMO's Executive Director wrote to Oil Minister Rashid advising him that AMEP had made a request to purchase oil and that this was the same company that came recommended by Sevan. Rashid made a note on the letter recording the approval of Vice President Ramadan for the sale to AMEP of 1.8 million barrels of oil. SOMO's

Executive Director sent a telex to AMEP president Abdelnour inviting him in mid-August 1998 to visit Baghdad "to discuss matters
related to crude oil supply."

In the meantime, after Sevan returned to New York from Iraq in
July 1998, he renewed his support for the oil spare parts program.
(He was not alone in pressing for the oil spare parts program,
which was supported by members of the Security Council.) His report of the trip noted that both Rashid and Ramadan stressed that
he and the Secretary-General should "spare no effort in ensuring
the approval of the contracts for essential spare parts concerning
the oil industry as well as for other sectors, which had been delayed
far too long."

Although Sevan does not appear to have promised any specific
benefit to Iraq in return for his requested oil allocation, Iraqi officials hoped that granting Sevan's request would redound to the
benefit of Iraq. As Rashid explained it to IIC investigators, oil allocations were granted to individuals who had been "good to us, people of influence," and Sevan "was a man of influence." Another
Iraqi official who was involved in the process explained that Iraq
hoped for Sevan's assistance in expediting the 661 Committee's approval of oil spare parts contracts.

On September 24, 1998, Abdelnour went to SOMO's office in
Baghdad to sign AMEP's contract for 1.8 million barrels of oil.
SOMO's Executive Director confirmed again with the Iraqi mission
in New York that AMEP was the company that had been "recommended by Mr. Sevan." After Abdelnour signed the contract and
returned from Baghdad to Geneva, Sevan's best friend, Fred Nadler,
called AMEP's office early in the morning on September 28, 1998.
Approximately half an hour later, Abdelnour sent a telex to SOMO
to thank its officials for meeting with him in Baghdad. Then, about
ninety minutes later, Nadler called Sevan. According to Sevan's appointment book, he met Nadler for breakfast the next morning.

By the end of September, Abdelnour arranged to have AMEP register through the government of Panama as a qualified buyer of oil under the program, and the UN's oil overseers then approved the AMEP contract for 1.8 million barrels of oil. In contrast to SOMO's internal records, none of the materials transmitted to the UN for approval of AMEP's oil contracts disclosed the involvement of Sevan.

Like most companies contracting for Iraqi oil during the program, AMEP did not "lift" or take physical possession of the oil. Instead, it promptly sold rights to the oil to two other oil companies for which it received nearly $300,000 more than it had paid to Iraq for the oil. It was risk-free profit that cost AMEP little more than the trouble of Abdelnour's trip to Baghdad to sign a contract with SOMO.

This would be the start of AMEP's purchase of more than $144 million of oil from allocations that SOMO placed in Sevan's name. In some instances, Iraqi oil allocation tables did not even reflect the name of AMEP at all, but only that of Sevan.

Sevan requested a second allocation for AMEP. But Iraqi officials decided to reduce his allocation to only 1 million barrels, because they did not believe that Sevan—despite their repeated requests for assistance—had been helpful enough in lifting "holds" that were placed by the United States or Britain on the approval of many contracts by the 661 Committee. These holds were commonly placed on contracts that the United States or Britain suspected involved dual-use goods with potential military applications.

The reduction did not please Sevan or Abdelnour. In late March 1999, Sevan traveled to the annual OPEC conference in Vienna, where he saw Abdelnour and also met with Oil Minister Rashid. According to Rashid, Sevan quietly raised the subject of an oil allocation with him while they met at the Vienna conference and during a subsequent trip to Iraq. Iraq, however, ultimately declined to increase the allocation amount, and AMEP in turn decided not to go through with the transaction.

Because AMEP did not follow through on the deal, Iraq initially declined to allocate more oil for Sevan during the next phase of the program. But Sevan's prospects soon changed after he paid another visit to Rashid in Baghdad. According to his travel authorization request, Sevan wrote: "I had a call from the Minister for Oil yesterday urging me to go to Baghdad very soon, to discuss the requirements for the oil industry and how to increase production capacity and export." Sevan spent three weeks in Iraq from mid-June to early July 1999.

Immediately following this trip, Sevan's name surfaced again in SOMO's oil allocation records—this time for 2 million barrels of oil. Abdelnour journeyed back to Baghdad to sign a contract, and SOMO quickly secured final approval from Rashid, referencing Sevan's name side by side with AMEP in its request to Rashid. As before, AMEP did not lift or take physical possession of the oil. Instead, AMEP sold its rights to Shell International Trading and Shipping Company, Ltd., and Shell lifted the oil in October and November of that year. Shell paid AMEP about $500,000 more than AMEP itself paid for the oil from Iraq.

Back at the UN, Sevan urged expansion of the oil spare parts program. He briefed the Security Council during informal consultations about his recent trip to Iraq, and he supported Iraq's request for a doubling of funding for oil spare parts to $600 million per program phase. He assured the Council that the recommendation was made "purely on technical grounds," and he urged approval of the oil spare parts contracts without further delay. During the Security Council's informal consultations with Sevan, members of the Council acknowledged general support for the requested increase in funding but voiced concern about Iraq's recent low rate of contract submissions for parts and equipment. Sevan responded that the fact that Iraq was slow in contracting "should not minimalize the additional funds required."

During the next phase of the program, Iraq approved yet another 1.5 million barrel allocation for Sevan. SOMO's oil allocation table—which was personally approved by Saddam—included an allocation of 1.5 million barrels of oil in the name of "Mr. Sevan" and did not even reference AMEP. But Abdelnour again signed a contract on behalf of AMEP with SOMO for this fresh allocation of oil, and he again sold AMEP's rights to the oil to Shell, receiving about $300,000 more than AMEP had paid for the oil.

Within this same time frame, Sevan renewed his efforts to persuade the 661 Committee to release the large number of holds that had been placed on approvals for goods and spare parts contracts. Sevan told the 661 Committee that "my colleagues and I have never failed to raise the issue of holds on every occasion available; and if there was no occasion, we have created one." Sevan also told the Security Council on February 7, 2000, that the Iraqi oil industry was in a "lamentable state," and he appealed to all Council members to address the issue "urgently." One week later, he met with Iraq's UN ambassador, and they discussed the prospects for approval of Iraq's request to expand the oil spare parts program.

The following month, Sevan met with Rashid again at an OPEC conference in Vienna. At the end of March 2000, the Security Council approved an expansion of the oil spare parts program to $600 million per program phase.

For the next phase of the program during the latter half of 2000, Iraq dispensed another oil allocation in the name of "Mr. Sevan" for 1.5 million barrels of oil. A Ministry of Oil record reflects that this allocation was on a list that was personally approved by Saddam:

The Executive Director of the Marketing Company,

The oral approval of Mr. President, the leader—may God Protect him—was obtained and the oral notification of the Vice President of the Republic was communicated at the meeting of the Council of ministers on the morning of 25/6/2000.

Take the necessary action for execution.

Iraq continued its efforts to reduce the number of contracts that were held up by the 661 Committee. In late June 2000, Rashid complained to the Secretary-General about the number of contracts in limbo. Sevan met with the Iraqi ambassador to the UN and stated that he "fully share[d] the frustrations of the distinguished Minister of Oil," and he promised to "continue our efforts to further reduce the number of holds."

Sometimes Sevan's contacts with AMEP and the Iraqi government seemed to cross paths. On July 19, 2000, Sevan sent an e-mail to Iraq's UN ambassador to update him on a recent development in the Security Council on an expedited approval process for oil spare parts and equipment, and he also told the ambassador he had notified Rashid about the matter. On the same day, UN phone records reflect a call from Sevan's office to a cell phone number for Abdelnour. Indeed, Abdelnour's telephone number appears in Sevan's electronic organizer. The call lasted six minutes. According to UN phone records, Sevan called Rashid's office the next day.

Two weeks later, Sevan returned to Iraq for the first half of August 2000. His visit coincided with a trip by Abdelnour to Baghdad to sign another contract for AMEP for the 1.5 million barrels that had been allocated in the name of "Mr. Sevan" in late June.

About a month after Sevan returned to New York, he spoke before the Security Council on September 21, 2000, to complain about the large numbers of holds placed on contracts, including for oil spare parts:

I am sure some of you will now tell me: "Benon, come on, not again, you sound like a broken record!" Well, so be it. As the Executive Director of the Iraq Programme, I feel duty bound to draw the attention of the Council to the unacceptably high level of holds placed on applications. Just as playing a broken record hurts the ear, every hold placed on an application for an essential supply affects the implementation of the programme, or to put it another way, it hurts the Iraqi people.

In the meantime, AMEP again sold its rights to the 1.5 million barrels of oil to Shell. In late November 2000, Shell lifted the first 1 million barrels of this oil and paid AMEP about $180,000 more for the oil than AMEP paid to the UN escrow account.

Shell, however, did not lift the remaining 500,000 barrels because, as of December 1, 2000, Iraq required a payment of a 50-cent surcharge per barrel. Internal e-mail between Shell and AMEP reveals that this was the reason that Shell refused to lift the last installment of the oil. Phone records also suggest that Sevan, his friend Nadler, and AMEP president Abdelnour also discussed the new Iraqi surcharge demands. On the same day that SOMO advised AMEP of its demand for a surcharge of 50 cents per barrel, a flurry of phone calls ensued between telephone numbers used by Abdelnour and Nadler, mixed with phone calls between numbers used by Nadler and Sevan.

8:19 A.M. Sevan to Nadler
11:06 A.M. Nadler to Abdelnour
11:10 A.M. Nadler to Sevan
11:44 A.M. Nadler to Sevan
12:10 P.M. Nadler to Abdelnour

As discussed in the prior chapter, the Iraqi surcharge policy—which depended on a substantially lower oil price than the oil overseers would allow—resulted in a breakdown in oil price negotiations and a complete shutdown of Iraqi oil exports during the first half of December 2000. Sevan explained in a note to the Deputy Secretary-General that SOMO sought a lower price "to allow the necessary margin for the buyers to pay Iraq 50 cents per barrel, with payments made into an account outside the control of the United

Nations." In his address to the Security Council on December 4, 2000, Sevan complained that the program's implementation had become "politicized more than ever," and that "it is essential to adopt a Cartesian approach and find a pragmatic solution in order to ensure the resumption of oil exports for the sake of the Iraqi people." Within a few days, an agreement on price was reached, but at a lower level than the oil overseers had previously proposed.

Presumably, Sevan was also well aware from Abdelnour or Nadler that Iraq was in fact requiring the payment of illegal surcharges as a condition to lifting any oil. On March 7, 2001, he wrote to Iqbal Riza, the chef de cabinet of the Secretary-General, that Iraq was indeed imposing surcharges on oil purchases.

But not even Iraq's pursuit of illegal surcharges deterred Sevan from contacting Abdelnour or the sale of his oil allocations. The next month, Sevan was in Geneva on official business. His cell phone records show that he placed two more calls to Abdelnour during this Geneva trip.

In August 2001, SOMO allocated another 1 million barrels of oil for Sevan. Abdelnour signed a contract for the oil and then sold its rights to Shell again, for about $380,000 more than AMEP had paid for the oil. Because Iraq was continuing to demand payment of surcharges, Abdelnour signed an agreement to pay surcharges on this and his previous SOMO oil contract. Two months later Abdelnour paid about $160,000 of the surcharges due under this agreement. To conceal the illegal payment, he routed the money through another company that he owned.

This would be AMEP's last oil deal with Iraq. In later phases of the program, SOMO allocated more than 5 million barrels of oil for Sevan, but there is no evidence that he requested these allocations or used them. The onset of Iraq's surcharge policy, combined with the imposition of retroactive pricing by the United States and Britain, made it far less predictable and profitable to deal in Iraqi oil.

Although Sevan took many positions that were favorable to Iraq, his administration of the program sometimes irritated Iraqi officials, who often took vituperatively extreme positions on how the program should be run. On one such instance in 2002, when Sevan supported a UN request that the Iraqi Ministry of Oil allocate certain funds to another ministry, Rashid angrily exclaimed, "He forgot all of our favors?"

When questioned by IIC investigators, Sevan generally denied that he sought oil allocations from Iraq but admitted that he had initially taken a call from someone at AMEP and advised the company about how it could get oil imports under the program. He was equivocal when interviewed and even conceded at some points a likelihood of mentioning AMEP to Rashid and seeking an increase from Rashid in AMEP's allocation during their meeting in March 1999 at the OPEC conference. Sevan was asked "Did you ever tell the Iraq Oil Minister that this is a company that wanted to lift oil?" He replied: "I might have mentioned [it], I don't know." Then when asked about any request he may have made to Rashid at the OPEC meeting in 1999 for an increase in AMEP's oil allocation, he replied that he said to Rashid, "'the guy [Abdelnour] wants more,'" and "I might have said [that], yeah."

Sevan suggested at first to IIC investigators that he had met and spoken with Abdelnour only once and by chance: at the March 1999 OPEC meeting. He had no convincing explanation for why Abdelnour's name and telephone numbers appeared on three different versions of a contact list that he personally maintained in his electronic organizer. Nor could he explain why he kept two business cards for Abdelnour in his UN office or why his phone records showed calls to Abdelnour in 2000, 2001, and 2004.

Indeed, Sevan's description of his past contacts with Abdelnour colorfully evolved during the course of just a single interview with IIC investigators. At first, it was just a chance and one-time-only meeting at the OPEC conference in Vienna. Then, there was a second chance meeting at a restaurant in Geneva. Next, there was an acquaintanceship with Abdelnour lasting over several years. And finally—upon being shown telephone records of his repeated attempts to call Abdelnour in early 2004 (after reports of program abuses were brought to the UN's attention)—Sevan volunteered that he had become friendly with Abdelnour and looked him up when he passed through Geneva. "I came to like the guy," said Sevan. "He is an interesting character you know, he's been around the world."

In all, AMEP lifted 7.3 million barrels of oil allocated in Sevan's name. It sold this oil for about $1.5 million more than was paid by AMEP to the UN escrow account and to Iraq as an oil surcharge.

Did Sevan financially benefit from all these oil transactions? Despite a convoluted money trail and Sevan's steadfast denial of any benefit, a combination of banking records, phone records, and travel records strongly indicated Sevan's receipt of tens of thousands of dollars in cash payoffs from the AMEP oil deals.

Before Sevan first solicited an oil allocation from Rashid in June 1998, his personal finances were stretched exceedingly thin. Bank records for accounts used by Sevan and his wife, Micheline Sevan, who was also a UN employee, showed that they frequently spent more than they earned and that their accounts went into overdraft status almost two hundred times. But just after AMEP's first oil sale at the end of 1998, all of this changed: a mysterious chain of cash deposits emerged, as reflected in their bank statements. Both Sevan and his wife regularly deposited thousands of dollars of cash— usually in the form of one-hundred-dollar U.S. banknotes—to their New York bank accounts at the UN Federal Credit Union and Chase Manhattan Bank. Just as significant, soon after AMEP's last sale of oil in 2001, the number and amount of cash deposits by the Sevans sharply decreased. This pattern is illustrated in the chart on the facing page.

The evident source for these cash deposits was Sevan's best

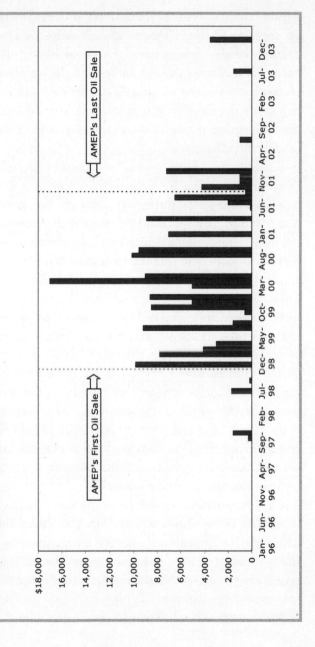

Benon and Micheline Sevan's Cash Deposits by Month, January 1996 to December 2003

friend—Fred Nadler, the business partner of Abdelnour and apparent treasurer of AMEP. After each sale of Iraqi oil by AMEP, Abdelnour wired a commission of 5 cents or 10 cents per barrel to a Swiss bank account in the name of Caisor Services, Inc. Fred Nadler controlled this account. Like AMEP, Caisor Services was inexplicably registered in Panama. Caisor Services did not conduct any independent business activity. It was, in essence, just a bank account for Nadler to use.

For one more layer of concealment, Nadler had a Geneva-based money management firm—Genevalor, Benbassat & Cie—handle transactions that went through the account. This meant that money sent to the account was routed through a clearinghouse account of the money management firm before being forwarded to the Caisor Services account. The wire transfers from AMEP would reveal that Genevalor, not Caisor Services, was the intended destination of the funds.

Nadler frequently traveled to Geneva, where he often withdrew cash from the Caisor Services account in varying amounts, from several thousand dollars to tens of thousands of dollars at a time. Nadler confided to one of the officials at the money management firm that the Caisor Services account was used to receive commissions from oil sales. During the time period covered by the AMEP transactions from late 1998 to late 2001, AMEP wired almost $580,000 to the Caisor Services account. Of this amount, more than $430,000 in cash was withdrawn from the Caisor Services account during the same time period.

Cash transactions leave little in the way of a paper trail, and there is no way to know for certain what Nadler did with all the cash withdrawn from the Caisor Services account. Sevan denied to IIC investigators that he received any cash, loans, or other items of significant value from Nadler. For his part, Nadler refused even to respond to efforts of the IIC's investigators to interview him. Nevertheless, bank and travel records reflect that more than $250,000 of the cash withdrawals from the Caisor Services account occurred on dates when either Nadler or Sevan, if not both, was in Geneva and soon returned to New York. It is these cash withdrawals that almost certainly funded the mysterious cash deposits by the Sevans to their bank accounts in New York. The money trail is illustrated in the chart below.

The flow of funds involved scores of transactions that are too complex to describe them all in detail here. A few examples, however, most convincingly reveal the link between AMEP's sale of oil and the cash deposits to the Sevan accounts in New York, which occurred shortly after cash withdrawals from the Caisor Services account in Geneva and the return of Sevan or Nadler from Geneva.

The first example occurred in February 1999, after two cash withdrawals totaling $9,500 were made that month from the

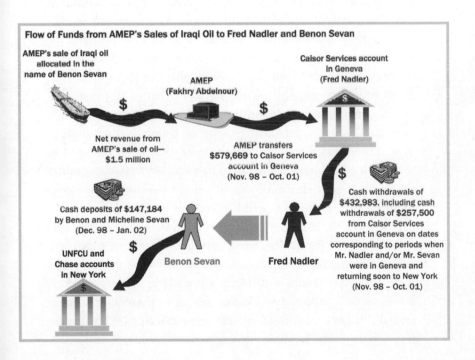

Flow of Funds from AMEP's Sales of Iraqi Oil to Fred Nadler and Benon Sevan

AMEP's sale of Iraqi oil allocated in the name of Benon Sevan

AMEP (Fakhry Abdelnour)

Caisor Services account in Geneva (Fred Nadler)

Net revenue from AMEP's sale of oil— $1.5 million

AMEP transfers $579,669 to Caisor Services account in Geneva (Nov. 98 – Oct. 01)

Cash withdrawals of $432,983, including cash withdrawals of $257,500 from Caisor Services account in Geneva on dates corresponding to periods when Mr. Nadler and/or Mr. Sevan were in Geneva and returning soon to New York (Nov. 98 – Oct. 01)

Cash deposits of $147,184 by Benon and Micheline Sevan (Dec. 98 – Jan. 02)

UNFCU and Chase accounts in New York

Benon Sevan

Fred Nadler

Caisor Services account while Fred Nadler was in Geneva. On February 17, the day after the second withdrawal, Nadler returned to New York, arriving at about 3:00 P.M. That night two calls were placed from his mother's apartment in New York to Sevan's apartment and office. Two days later, a call was placed at 7:47 A.M. from Sevan's to Nadler's apartment, and then at 12:07 P.M. from Nadler's apartment to Sevan's office. Within two hours, Sevan deposited $1,800—eighteen one-hundred-dollar bills—into his UN Federal Credit Union account at 1:27 P.M., and then $6,000—sixty one-hundred-dollar bills—into his Chase account at 1:42 P.M. Two weeks later, Sevan deposited an additional $1,700 (seventeen one-hundred-dollar bills) into his credit union account, for a total of $9,500.

Another instance occurred in March 1999, just after Sevan saw Abdelnour at the OPEC conference in Vienna and asked Rashid for an increase in AMEP's oil allocation. Phone records show two calls from Nadler's apartment in New York to Sevan's cell phone in the early evening of March 23, while Sevan was still in Vienna. The next day, Sevan left Vienna for Geneva where he had several days of UN-related meetings. Bank records show that on this same day, $6,000 in cash was withdrawn from the Caisor Services account in Geneva. At some point during this time frame, Nadler went to Geneva, and travel records show that he and Sevan returned to New York on the same flight on March 28, 1999. Two days after his return, Sevan deposited $2,400 in cash—twenty-four one-hundred-dollar bills—to one of his accounts in New York.

A few months later in mid-1999, when Sevan went to Baghdad at the request of Rashid, his name appeared in Iraqi records as the recipient of another oil allocation. On his way back from Iraq, he made a five-day stopover in Geneva beginning on July 9, 1999. Travel records reflect that Nadler was also present in Geneva around this same time. Bank records show that $11,000 was withdrawn from Nadler's Caisor Services account on July 9, and an ad-

ditional $4,000 was withdrawn on July 12. AMEP had previously
wired nearly $90,000 to the account. On July 14, Sevan left Geneva
and arrived back in New York. Just two days after his return from
Geneva, Sevan deposited $6,200 in cash to his UN Federal Credit
Union account. Three days later, on July 19, he deposited another
$3,000 in cash to his Chase account.

On July 22, 1999, Nadler called both Sevan and Abdelnour.
One week later, Abdelnour was back in Baghdad to sign another
contract for AMEP. The following day, starting just after 8:00 A.M.,
successive phone calls were placed first from Nadler's home to
Sevan's apartment, then from Nadler's home to Abdelnour's cell
phone and, finally, from Sevan's apartment to Nadler's home—all
within half an hour of one another.

Three months later, Abdelnour wired $100,000 in oil sales pro-
ceeds from the AMEP bank account to Nadler's Caisor Services account in Geneva. This amount was equivalent to 10 cents per barrel
for the initial 1 million barrels of oil that was lifted by Shell for one
of AMEP's contracts. Within five days, Nadler was back in Geneva,
where he withdrew $9,000 in cash from his Caisor Services account.
Nadler returned the next day to New York, and he called Sevan's
home and office several times. Two days later, on November 5, 1999,
Nadler called Abdelnour's cell phone, and then just twenty minutes
later, he called Sevan. Later that day, Sevan deposited $6,000 in one-
hundred-dollar bills to one of his bank accounts. Five days later,
Sevan deposited $2,500 in one-hundred-dollar bills to another bank
account.

More cash withdrawals and deposits took place in spring 2000,
when Sevan returned to Europe to attend another OPEC conference
attended by Rashid. On March 24, 2000, the day before leaving
New York, Sevan deposited $5,000 in one-hundred-dollar bills to
one of his New York bank accounts. During that day and the next
day, several calls were made between Sevan and Nadler and between
Nadler and Abdelnour. Then, after a few days at the OPEC confer-

ence in Vienna, Sevan stopped off in Geneva on the morning of March 29. On that same day, bank records reflect that someone withdrew $18,000 in cash from Nadler's Caisor Services account.

Two days later, Sevan returned to New York on April 1, 2000 and within days placed an order with his stock broker to buy about $20,000 of common stock. At the time he placed the order, he did not have enough money in his bank accounts to buy the stock. But funds soon materialized with two large cash deposits to his Chase bank account—a deposit of $9,000 on April 7 and another deposit of $8,000 on April 11. Had Sevan chosen to deposit this cash all at one time, this would have triggered a legal requirement for the bank to file a currency transaction report with the U.S. Department of the Treasury.

Months after Iraq began collecting surcharges on its oil purchases and the same month that Abdelnour signed an agreement to pay surcharges on contracts for two separate oil allocations under Sevan's name, cash proceeds continued to flow out of Nadler's Caisor Services account. While Sevan was back in Geneva in mid-August 2001, another $40,000 in cash was withdrawn from the account. Sevan returned to New York on August 21, 2001, and the next day he deposited $6,400 to his New York bank accounts. Over the next three months, the Sevans deposited more than $5,000 in cash to their bank accounts.

The description above includes only some of the cash deposits made by Sevan and his wife to their New York accounts. All in all, the Sevans deposited more than $147,000 in cash to their accounts from late 1998 to late 2001. This figure is a conservative estimate of the Sevans' cash deposits, because it does not include more than $35,000 in deposits that appear on bank statements as large, round-number deposits but for which it was not possible to obtain from Sevan's bank a deposit slip definitively confirming that the deposit was cash.

When interviewed by IIC investigators, Sevan acknowledged large cash deposits but claimed that the cash came from his aunt,

Berdjouchi Zeytountzian, who lived in Cyprus and who periodically came to New York for extended stays with Sevan. Unfortunately, the IIC could not verify this claim with Sevan's aunt. She reportedly fell down a narrow elevator shaft at her apartment building in Cyprus and died in June 2004.[1]

Nevertheless, other circumstances cast severe doubt on Sevan's claim of cash gifts from his retired aunt. She had earned a modest salary as a government photographer in Cyprus, was living on small pension payments, and lacked a significant balance in her bank account in Cyprus. Although she made periodic visits to the United States, the dates of her visits had little correlation to the dates of the Sevans' many cash deposits. Less than one-fourth of the Sevans' cash deposits were made on dates when she was in the United States. More than half of the Sevans' cash deposits occurred during a single fifteen-month period (from August 1999 to October 2000) when she was *not* in the United States. If Sevan's aunt had brought large amounts of cash to the United States, then she would have been required to declare this cash on forms filed with the U.S. Customs Service. No declarations were filed.

Sevan was placed on administrative leave from his UN duties pending the IIC's investigation. Before the IIC's final report of his activities, he left New York to return to his home country of Cyprus, where he apparently remains today. Although the United States has an extradition treaty with Cyprus, it is not clear whether or under what circumstances Cyprus authorities would honor a request to produce Sevan for prosecution.

THE FAILURE OF SEVAN AND OIP TO ACT AGAINST KICKBACKS

Beyond the fact that Sevan was corruptly receiving benefits from the Iraqi regime, he also mismanaged OIP in a manner that contributed to Iraq's ability to exploit the program for pecuniary gain.

The most disturbing aspects of mismanagement involved the repeated reluctance and reticence of Sevan and other senior OIP managers who worked for him to inform the 661 Committee and Security Council of the mounting evidence of illicit payments and smuggling. Sevan failed to address reports of humanitarian kickbacks and to keep the 661 Committee and Security Council apprised of the detailed information about the kickback scheme that was known to OIP. Despite the clear acknowledgement by both senior OIP and UN officials of OIP's responsibility to inform the 661 Committee and the Security Council, the general "party line" at OIP under Sevan was to downplay reports of Iraq's receipt of kickbacks and to limit the information provided to the 661 Committee.

The examples of evidence of illicit payments that were brought to the attention of OIP officials are numerous. Some of these instances reflect most clearly Sevan's unwillingness to address the Iraqi regime's accumulation of illegal funds.

In the summer of 2000, during the early phase of Iraq's kickback policy, a Swedish company, Scania CV AB, contacted J. Christer Elfverson, head of OIP's Programme Management Division, to complain that Iraq was seeking a 15 percent kickback on a program contract. Elfverson told Sevan about the complaint and wanted to report it to the 661 Committee. Sevan shot back that the matter was none of Elfverson's business. Sevan did not believe OIP should take any action in the absence of documented proof, and he told Elfverson to have Scania pursue the issue with the Swedish mission to the UN.

Other OIP staff also recalled learning from various suppliers of the kickback demands from late 1999 through 2000. But, according to Sevan, OIP had no authority or responsibility to address the matter. As Elfverson recalled, Sevan's "line" was always that his mandate was to get food and medication to the Iraqi people and that it was not his job to report the kickbacks, which he saw simply as part of the Iraqi culture.

Sevan's position and instructions to OIP staff flew in the face of the sanctions-enforcement obligations placed upon the UN Secretariat and OIP under Security Council Resolutions 661 and 986, the MOU, and 661 Committee procedures. The scope of OIP's responsibilities included responsibility for sanctions monitoring and not just humanitarian relief. UN and OIP senior officials interviewed by the IIC also confirmed that OIP had an obligation to investigate allegations of sanctions violations and to report them to the Security Council or the 661 Committee.

Sevan refused to be questioned by IIC investigators about the Secretariat's administration of the program and his involvement as Executive Director of OIP. But in a public statement during the program he acknowledged that the Secretariat had a duty to bring "irregularities" in the program to the attention of the 661 Committee, that the Secretariat's duties included "rigorously and automatically examining all credible reports of abuses," and that the Secretariat should comply with requests for investigation made by the 661 Committee. In fact, he failed to do these things when it mattered the most.

With complaints to OIP about the kickbacks increasing, Elfverson wrote a lengthy memo to Sevan on December 5, 2000 about the emerging pattern of kickback demands, urging Sevan to take action. According to the memo, one government and two companies had approached Elfverson in just the past twenty-four hours about Iraq's kickback demands. The memo stated Elfverson's view that "OIP has a clear mandate to bring any irregularity to the immediate attention" of the 661 Committee and that the kickback demands violated "both the letter and spirit of resolution 986 . . . which permits Iraq no access to the use of funds except under UN control." In prophetically dire terms, Elfverson warned that questions could be raised about the UN Secretariat's management of the program if the kickback "practices . . . [went] unreported, unchallenged and unchecked" by OIP.

Sevan was not persuaded. He declined to pursue the matter with the 661 Committee. Instead, he suggested to Elfverson that "whenever we receive information on such matters the suppliers concerned should be advised that they should bring the matter to the attention of their governments," who may in turn decide whether to tell the 661 Committee. Sevan also claimed that OIP did not deal with companies directly, but only with their respective permanent missions, and that it should not act on the basis of telephone conversations alone.

In fact, there was no rule requiring suppliers to raise sanctions violations complaints only with their home country missions, and OIP routinely dealt directly with companies on a wide range of contract matters, often by telephone. More significant, the oil overseers and OIP routinely gathered and relied upon informal sources of information—conversations with oil purchasers, industry publications, and media articles—in connection with monitoring and reporting oil surcharges. And the information that OIP officials had collected about the kickbacks included accounts from suppliers that had dealt directly with Iraqi officials.

Throughout 2001, OIP received a steady stream of evidence from suppliers that the Iraqi regime was demanding kickbacks on its contracts. With each report by a supplier or a UN member state mission, some of which included powerful documentary evidence, the program-wide nature of the kickback scheme became increasingly difficult to ignore.

By the fall of 2001, OIP's chief customs expert, Felicity Johnston, was convinced that the kickback payments were pervasive and occurring "left, right and center." She habitually forwarded information received from suppliers to her direct supervisor, Farid Zarif, frequently with a note or memorandum, and she discussed the incidents with Sevan as well. Like Elfverson, Johnston advocated raising this issue with the 661 Committee.

On October 22, 2001, Johnston prepared a lengthy memorandum itemizing and summarizing many specific allegations from both companies and missions about kickbacks on humanitarian contracts. For several of the incidents she described, OIP had received actual copies of illegal side agreements between contractors and the Iraqi regime. This was the "hard proof" Sevan had told the 661 Committee that OIP lacked. One company from India even furnished specific information about the bank account to which Iraq wanted the kickback paid. Some of the companies made clear that the kickbacks were not isolated occurrences but that Iraq was requiring payment of kickbacks by all companies seeking contracts under the program.

One of the companies mentioned in Johnston's memo was Belhasa Motors, which—apparently by inadvertence—had sent the UN a copy of a secret side agreement it had signed to pay a kickback of about $11,500 in connection with one of its program contracts. Belhasa Motors and its sister companies were among the program's largest contractors and would eventually pay the Iraqi regime more than $45 million in kickbacks.

Johnston's detailed memo went to Zarif and Sevan, but Sevan still refused to pursue the issue with the 661 Committee. The UN's records reflect that drafts of letters were prepared for Sevan to send to the government of Iraq and to Fréchette about the information set forth in Johnston's memo. Apparently, the letters were never sent.

The records of 661 Committee meetings suggest not only that OIP failed to press the committee to act against kickbacks but also that it misleadingly downplayed the evidence known to OIP about kickbacks. For example, at one time or another, the Secretariat received written complaints and information about illicit payments to the Iraqi regime from numerous UN permanent missions, including the missions of Algeria, Austria, Belgium, Canada, Denmark, India, Japan, Spain, Switzerland, and the United Arab Emirates. The 661 Committee was never told of the numerous kickback reports received at OIP from suppliers and various UN missions.

In early 2001, members of the 661 Committee began making specific requests for information from OIP on illicit payments to Iraq. But despite these pointed requests, OIP officials maintained what some of them later admitted was a misleading "company line" about the absence of specific information. For example, in February 2001, Farid Zarif was questioned by the U.S. representative to the 661 Committee about what information OIP had regarding the allegations that Iraq was demanding a 10 percent commission in connection with the award of humanitarian contracts. Zarif evasively responded that "OIP had received no *formal* complaints from any permanent or observer mission in that regard." When questioned by IIC investigators, Zarif admitted telling the 661 Committee that there were no formal complaints but claimed that he told the committee of informal complaints. Yet no mention of informal complaints was found in the meeting notes of the 661 Committee.

In another meeting, a 661 Committee member reiterated his interest in the subject, and he requested that OIP prepare a paper "providing *any information* it might have regarding allegations that Iraq was asking potential suppliers to pay a 10 per cent commission prior to being awarded contracts under the programme." Sevan's chief of staff, Stephani Scheer, agreed that "OIP would look into providing what very little information existed on the 'commission question.'" But OIP did not prepare a report on the kickback scheme as requested during the 661 Committee meeting.

Sevan also took a similar tack with the Secretary-General in late February and early March 2001, just as meetings were held between the Secretary-General and Iraqi officials and as the *New York Times* published its report about Iraq extracting kickback payments from program suppliers. At the time, reports to OIP regarding Iraqi kickback demands were increasing, as was the interest of the 661 Committee. Sevan supplied a briefing paper for the Secretary-General describing "allegations" of kickback demands and stating that the Secretariat "has no formal/official information on this, though some companies have called ... to complain about it." Sevan's advisory memo to Riza about the *New York Times* article repeated the briefing paper and stated that Sevan had told the 661 Committee that OIP did not have any "hard proof to corroborate the allegations." In his interview with IIC investigators, Zarif observed that in light of what OIP knew about the kickbacks, Sevan's comments were "an expanded version of the company response."

The Secretary-General was required to file quarterly reports updating the Security Council on the status of activities under the program. These reports were drafted in the first instance by staff at OIP, before being reviewed by both Sevan and Fréchette, and then by the Secretary-General. This transmittal of information was in keeping with OIP's basic duty to ensure that significant information it acquired from its operations in the field and its review of program contracts flowed to the 661 Committee. From 2000 and afterwards, as kickback complaints accumulated at OIP, the required quarterly reports to the Security Council never flagged the kickback issue, despite mounting evidence of a widespread scheme.

When interviewed by IIC investigators, the Secretary-General stated that he had conversations on the general subject of kickbacks with Sevan, Fréchette, and members of the Security Council during 2001, but the conversations were not detailed. There was no evidence that the Secretary-General received a copy of the Johnston memo or a similar detailed summary of the evidence of kickback demands and payments. The Secretary-General acknowledged that this kind of detailed information should have been included in reports to the 661 Committee and Security Council.

As with the reports of humanitarian kickbacks, Sevan generally gave short shrift to reports of oil surcharges and oil smuggling, disavowing to the 661 Committee any duty on the part of OIP to redress these issues. Although the Security Council did not press Sevan to take more enforcement-oriented action, his position was at odds with the dual role of OIP to carry out on the Secretariat's behalf the administration of the sanctions under Resolution 661 as well as the Oil-for-Food Program under Resolution 986.

During the last three years of the program, Iraq's largest source of illicit income was oil that it smuggled through its newly rehabilitated pipeline to Syria. When media reports of the pipeline's use emerged in late 2000, Sevan refused the request of some members of the 661 Committee to have OIP investigate and report on whether the pipeline was in fact being used. He made no secret of OIP's lack of engagement on this issue, reporting in a memo to Fréchette and Riza that "on the issue of the Syrian/Iraqi pipeline . . . you will note that I categorically objected to the request for an investigation by the Secretariat of the operational status of this pipeline, in the absence of a mandate from the Security Council."

Sevan also falsely advised the 661 Committee that he had no "sources of information" concerning the use of the pipeline. Sevan did not inform the Committee that the UN's own oil inspector—Saybolt—had e-mailed him to advise about the resumption of the pipeline and its transport of 150,000 barrels of oil per day. Nor is there any indication that Sevan disclosed a meeting he had in November 2000 with Syria's UN ambassador at which the ambassador discussed reopening the pipeline, and Sevan quite matter-of-factly suggested that Syria had a "choice" whether to comply with the sanctions or not to comply.

Some of the most remarkable and disconcerting behavior of OIP officials regarding their knowledge of these program abuses occurred after Saddam was removed from power and the U.S.-led Coalition Provisional Authority (CPA) uncovered evidence from Iraqi officials and government files of the widespread kickback payments and side agreements under the program. But OIP still downplayed its knowledge of these schemes. When OIP officials Zarif and Darko Mocibob traveled to Iraq in June 2003, they told CPA officials that, although OIP had heard rumors of kickbacks, the rumors were unconfirmed and that OIP was unaware of the scope of the kickback scheme. The next month, the Secretary-General, Riza, Sevan, and others met with the members of the new Iraqi Governing Council. In defense of the UN, Sevan told the Council that the "CPA had only recently made the UN aware of the 10% after sales fee." This claim was completely contradicted by the accumulation of detailed evidence within OIP and Sevan's own reports.

Similar representations were made to U.S. Congressional investigators. In a briefing to U.S. Congress staff members on March 26, 2004, the Secretariat advanced a slightly revised position regarding the kickback allegations. During that meeting the Secretariat maintained that it "had heard rumors and had seen media articles in late 2000" regarding 10 percent kickbacks but never had any hard evidence of such payments. Further, the Congressional staffers were told that while a handful of companies had informally approached OIP about kickbacks, the companies did not want to put the allegations into writing and OIP had advised them to go to their home country's missions. These statements from the briefing understated and conflicted with the substantial documentary and other evidence accumulated by the OIP customs experts during the program.

MORE OIP MANAGEMENT WEAKNESS

Problems also pervaded the operations of all three major divisions of OIP—the Contracts Processing Management Division (the Contracts Division), the Programme Management Division, and the United Nations Office for the Humanitarian Coordinator in Iraq (UN-Iraq). At the Contracts Division, a major weakness was lack of reviewers with appropriate expertise to review contracts for overpricing—the telltale sign of an illegal kickback. This deficiency was conceded by the Secretary-General when interviewed by IIC investigators: "Given what we know now, we probably should have had many more customs people, people checking prices and other things to be able to advise and support the 661 Committee much more effectively."

During the course of the program, the volume and complexity of contracts increased significantly, as did the diversity of goods and services. While the number of customs experts increased, their range of expertise was generally inadequate to conduct a thorough review of the proposed pricing. These concerns came to the fore in March 2001, after media allegations of kickback-inflated prices for program contracts. Sevan told the UN's contract processing section that it should tighten its contract review procedures. In response, Zarif wrote to Sevan that "evaluating the price of goods is a somewhat difficult task, and although this is one of the main duties of the customs evaluations, the Customs Experts are not actually experts in international commodities markets."

This was an astounding concession. Commodities such as wheat and rice were the most common products sold to Iraq under the program. For example, as discussed in chapter 5, two principal commodity suppliers—AWB and Chaiyaporn—collectively sold Iraq more than $2.5 billion of wheat and rice. These two companies paid more than $250 million in kickbacks to the Iraqi regime. Their kickbacks were financed by the inclusion of inflated prices in contracts that were approved for payment from the UN escrow account.

In response to Zarif's e-mail, Sevan suggested hiring only "one or two" commodities experts. Even this modest measure never happened. And there was no instance in which any of the contracts of AWB or Chaiyaporn were placed on hold because of concerns about overpricing.

The problem was not simply lack of qualified customs experts but also the absence of a rigorous price review process and necessary research resources. For each humanitarian contract, a customs expert completed a customs report, including the customs expert's opinion of the contract price. Unlike the oil overseers, customs experts had no access to commodity price reporting services, and they continued to find the pricing tools and resources at their disposal insufficient. As of 2000, pricing was still evaluated by comparison to previous contract applications and Internet research.

Even in the rare instance when a UN customs expert concluded a contract price was too high, very few customs reports included any quantitative or qualitative assessment beyond a generic notation that pricing seemed high or was higher than in previous applications for similar goods. A customs expert would ask for clarification from a supplier, and if the response provided "sounded credible" (e.g., "steel prices have been high"), it was accepted. The customs expert would not seek to corroborate the explanation (e.g., by checking whether steel prices actually had increased).

Even if OIP customs experts detected excessively high prices, they perceived that they lacked the authority under the program to reject the contract. Instead, the customs report would simply note the high price when OIP forwarded the contract application package to the 661 Committee for consideration (with any explanation received from a supplier). Very few contracts during the whole program were ever put on hold because of a concern about high pricing.

A simple comparison of market and program prices for some of the commodities purchased under the program would have revealed the stunningly high prices paid on many of the contracts. The IIC's forensic staff compared the program prices of three key commodities with corresponding market prices over the life of the program. The results of the analysis with respect to one commodity are illustrated in the chart on page 213, which plots the actual market price of the commodity (the lowest line), the "expected" program price, calculated by adding the costs of actual sea freight to market prices charged in the program (the middle line), and the actual price paid for the commodity in program contracts.

As reflected in the chart, for the first few years of the program until mid-1999 (Phases 1 to 5), the actual program prices were generally aligned with the expected program prices. The price difference that existed between these two values in all likelihood reflected the cost of doing business in a high-risk and uncertain legal and political environment. Then, beginning in the latter half of 1999 (Phase 6), around the time Iraq began imposing inland transport fees, the difference between expected program prices and actual program prices increased significantly. In the summer of 2000 (Phase 8), when after-sales service fees were imposed, these two prices diverged markedly, easily providing a supplier with the ability to pay a substantial kickback to Iraqi authorities, as had been reported in that period.

By early 2003 (Phase 13), the difference between expected and actual program prices was nearly three times greater. The sheer size of the price differential exceeds that necessary to pay the after-sales service and transportation fees demanded at the time, suggesting the possibility of significant price gouging by a supplier.

As noted above, one of OIP's major operating divisions was the Programme Management Division, which was designed to furnish management oversight of the program's activities, especially of its field operations in Iraq. Initially and for the first several years of the program, the Multidisciplinary Observation Unit (MDOU), which was responsible for reviewing and evaluating the use and distribution of humanitarian aid by the Iraqi government, reported to the Programme Management Division, which in turn reported to OIP in New York. This allowed the Programme Management Division to assure the accuracy of the characterizations and information presented to the Security Council. In fact, the division often found discrepancies between what the MDOU reported and the information that appeared in reports to the Security Council. The direct reporting line between MDOU and the division also served to ensure that pressures and influence from the government of Iraq did not override the objectivity of reporting from the field.

But over the years, Sevan increasingly marginalized the Pro-

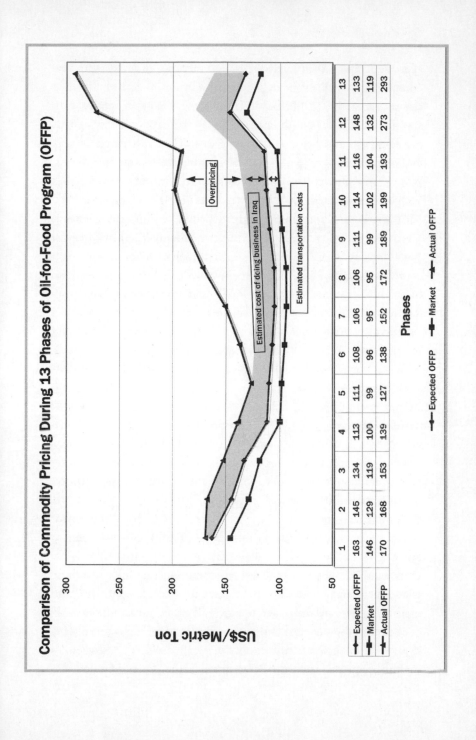

Comparison of Commodity Pricing During 13 Phases of Oil-for-Food Program (OFFP)

Phases	1	2	3	4	5	6	7	8	9	10	11	12	13
Expected OFFP	163	145	134	113	111	108	106	106	111	114	116	148	133
Market	146	129	119	100	99	96	95	95	99	102	104	132	119
Actual OFFP	170	168	153	139	127	138	152	172	189	199	193	273	293

US$/Metric Ton

Overpricing

Estimated cost of doing business in Iraq

Estimated transportation costs

Expected OFFP   Market   Actual OFFP

gramme Management Division, in part because of his personal in-compatibility with Elfverson, the hard-driving official who headed this division from 2000 to 2003. Elfverson sought to play a sub-stantial role in OIP's administration of the program through its headquarters and field-based operations. This threatened Sevan's authority and had the potential to complicate matters for Sevan, particularly since Elfverson was willing to confront thorny issues such as kickbacks and had his own access to Sevan's superiors.

Without the Programme Management Division's involvement, there was no other established, independent mechanism for New York's review of operations in Iraq. In a memo to Sevan, Elfverson contended that OIP's headquarters in New York needed to "exercise oversight over operations 'in the field'" and, in particular, that the di-vision needed latitude to carry out the oversight function, because a "supervisory body" such as Sevan and OIP's Executive Office should not delegate oversight of field operations to the field operation itself.

Sevan curtly rejected Elfverson's view, suggesting that the divi-sion "should be called the Program Division and not the Program Management Division," to make clear that it did not have true management responsibilities for operational aspects of the pro-gram. As a result of the division's diminished role, not only was UN-Iraq free from oversight by the division, but it stopped even re-porting its monitoring data to the division for use in its preparation of basic statistical reports.

Among steps taken to marginalize the Programme Management Division was the relocation in June 2000 of its offices to a different building from Sevan's Executive Office and the Contracts Division. Over time, Elfverson was driven to communicate only in writing with Sevan, and he was not provided the strategy, objectives, and plans for achieving the program's overall goals. Sevan routinely ig-nored Elfverson's correspondence and refused to engage in discus-sions with Elfverson about annual work plans, despite Elfverson's multiple requests. Thus, the Programme Management Division was divested not only of its role to oversee operations in Iraq but also of any ability to furnish strategic guidance for the program.

In short, Sevan mismanaged OIP in several ways, all consistent with his general failure to embrace OIP's responsibilities to maintain the integrity of the sanctions scheme as well as to carry out the humanitarian purposes of the program. He failed to ensure that the Contracts Division possessed adequate resources and expertise to scrutinize program-related contracts. He marginalized the Programme Management Division's oversight and management role. And he withheld from the 661 Committee significant evidence about Iraq's kickback demands, while also failing to confront Iraqi officials on the kickback issue and to demand that the kickbacks be stopped. He failed to properly resist and challenge the Iraqi regime's rampant sanctions violations, through which the regime diverted hundreds of millions of dollars away from the humanitarian effort. These failures were all the more troubling when considered against Sevan's corrupt receipt of oil allocations from the Iraqi regime.

Without a professional management oversight team, Sevan operated in essence as a "one-man band" to guide the program's activities. This meant that the program was ill-prepared to deal with the considerable challenges confronting UN-Iraq's field observation and monitoring operations in Iraq.

Iraq's hostility to internal monitoring activities under the program stemmed in part from its rocky relationship with the UN-SCOM weapons inspectors. The weapons inspectors were not required to obtain visas to enter the country, could travel freely within the country, and could visit any facility in the country without notice to Iraqi authorities. When Iraq negotiated its terms of participation in the Oil-for-Food Program, Iraqi negotiators categorically rejected any inspection, observation, or monitoring provisions that incorporated the weapons inspection model. Instead, the agreement between Iraq and the UN required UN inspection personnel to obtain visas and "coordinate with the competent Iraqi authorities." This latter condition became a tool for Iraq to require "ministry escorts" for UN-Iraq observers and to impede inspector efforts to conduct thorough observations.

The Iraqi regime strived to impede UN-Iraq from monitoring its activities. UN-Iraq personnel believed that they were subject to constant surveillance by Iraqi intelligence officials and faced the specter of expulsion at the whim of the Iraqi regime. As one senior UN-Iraq official observed, "it was commonly known that Iraq monitored the United Nations more than the United Nations monitored Iraq."

The Iraqi government regularly debriefed Iraqi employees for inside information about activities occurring at the UN compound in Baghdad. Similarly, because the heads of UN-Iraq and their Iraqi drivers spent considerable time together, the drivers were required to report every two to three weeks to Iraqi authorities. Iraqi citizens who worked with the UN field observers were required to present weekly reports to the Iraqi government of the observers' monitoring activities. Because of Iraq's "escort" requirement, UN observers were inhibited from asking questions or including information in their monitoring reports that might be disagreeable to the Iraqis. Several observers reported incidents in which interviewees indicated that they had more information to share but were reluctant to do so because of the presence of the escorts.

UN-Iraq personnel informed UN headquarters that observation units were threatened directly by Iraqi authorities and warned not to go into certain areas to perform their work. In the northern governorates, UN staff members were sometimes fired upon, and demining dogs were shot and killed.

As an additional intimidation tactic, the Iraqi regime commonly designated certain UN-Iraq and international staff as persona non grata—to force their removal from Iraq. To justify its expulsion efforts, Iraq often employed generalized accusations that the targeted staff members posed a threat to Iraq's security and national safety. Targeted staff members typically were required to leave Iraq within seventy-two hours; otherwise, Iraq ominously advised that it would refuse to ensure their safety.

THE THIRTY-EIGHTH FLOOR

For the UN, it was more than troubling that few safeguards existed to detect or prevent Sevan's misconduct and mismanagement. Sevan and his management of the program were subject to supervision from senior management officials on the top floor—The Thirty-Eighth Floor—of the UN headquarters building: Secretary-General Annan, Deputy Secretary-General Fréchette, and Iqbal Riza, the Secretary-General's chef de cabinet. Sevan spoke to Fréchette about the program nearly every day and routinely provided her with notes and memoranda concerning significant program-related issues. He also frequently met with or spoke to the Secretary-General and Riza about the program.

Although there is no evidence to suggest that the officers of The Thirty-Eighth Floor knew of Sevan's corrupt receipt of oil allocations or that they themselves were corrupt, they exercised little competent oversight of Sevan's activities. To explain his lack of attention, the Secretary-General told IIC investigators that it was the 661 Committee—not the UN Secretariat—that managed the program, and he went so far as to assert that Sevan "worked" for the 661 Committee. While clearly Sevan was the UN official who worked most closely at senior levels with the 661 Committee, these responsibilities did not dilute in any way the Secretary-General's own administrative and management responsibilities for Sevan. He was the one, after all, who both appointed and promoted Sevan. Moreover, it was the Secretary-General, not the 661 Committee, who had authority to remove Sevan and otherwise to supervise his management of the program.

More generally, Resolution 986 and successive authorizing resolutions charged the Secretary-General with making regular reports about implementation of the program. Beyond the administrative scope of OIP, the Secretary-General retained authority to ensure adequate auditing of the program by the UN's Office of Internal Inspection and Oversight Services.

The Secretary-General acknowledged that The Thirty-Eighth Floor had at least some role to play with respect to the program. In particular, he explained that the Deputy Secretary-General served as "an extra pair of eyes" for the Secretariat. The Secretary-General expected Fréchette to ensure that Sevan raised issues with the government of Iraq and that he reported program-related matters to the 661 Committee.

When interviewed by IIC investigators, Fréchette also minimized her true responsibility to oversee Sevan and his administration of the program. Although she maintained that she was not responsible for overseeing the program or supervising Sevan, this contention was contrary to the fact that the Secretary-General had formally delegated to her in March 1998 supervisory authority over Sevan and OIP.

According to Fréchette, because she did not receive complaints from member states about Sevan, she assumed that the program was "well run" and there was no reason for more proactive supervision of OIP. Yet she also knew of disputes within OIP, including Elfverson's concerns about Sevan's style of management. When interviewed, the Deputy Secretary-General ultimately conceded that, in hindsight, she should have asked more questions and played a greater role in ensuring that sanctions violations were addressed.

Although Riza similarly distanced himself from responsibility for OIP, he played a greater role than he was willing to state. He routinely received copies of significant documents and memoranda concerning the program, consistent with his role to screen for materials that warranted the Secretary-General's attention. His own handwritten notes on documents reveal that he closely reviewed the materials that Sevan forwarded and frequently met with the Secretary-General and Sevan to discuss major matters about the program. With far greater frequency than Fréchette, Riza also participated in meetings with Iraqi officials relating to the program.

To be sure, the Secretary-General and Fréchette were apparently not aware of the full scope of evidence that OIP had accumulated about kickbacks, and Sevan bears responsibility for withholding information. There is no indication, for example, that Sevan advised the Secretary-General or the Deputy Secretary-General of the detailed information concerning kickback payments that Elfverson accumulated in December 2000 and the even clearer evidence that Johnston documented in October 2001.

But the Secretary-General, Fréchette, and Riza were generally aware of the kickback scheme at least as early as February 2001. The Secretary-General discussed the kickback allegations and other sanctions violations with Sevan on numerous occasions. The Secretary-General told IIC investigators that detailed information concerning the Iraqi regime's receipt of kickbacks should have been conveyed to the 661 Committee and should have been discussed in his quarterly reports or even in a special report to the Security Council. Fréchette and Riza similarly acknowledged that such detailed information in the possession of OIP should have been transmitted to the 661 Committee. Despite mounting evidence of a widespread kickback scheme and The Thirty-Eighth Floor's own knowledge of it, the Secretary-General's reports to the Security Council never mentioned the problem.

Nor did the UN's senior officials raise their concerns with Iraq, even when it was suggested by staff to do so. For example, the Secretary-General met over the course of two days on February 26 and 27, 2001, with Mohammed Said Al-Sahaf, the Foreign Minister of Iraq, to discuss a wide range of issues. Although the Secretary-General's briefing materials suggested that he raise the surcharge and kickback issues with the Foreign Minister, the Secretary-General did not do so. When interviewed by the IIC, the Secretary-General stated these were "technical" matters that he would have expected Sevan to raise with the Iraqi delegation. Yet there is no evidence that Sevan did so. Nor is there evidence that at any other time during the program the Secretary-General, Fréchette, or Riza confronted Iraq about its illegal surcharge and kickback policies.

In short, there was little real oversight from The Thirty-Eighth Floor of Sevan's activities and, in particular, of his lack of response to reports of Iraqi abuses of the program to obtain illicit income from oil surcharges and humanitarian kickbacks. This is not to say that had The Thirty-Eighth Floor more aggressively supervised Sevan, the failures of OIP would have been eliminated. Nor is it to overlook the significant role and authority of the 661 Committee in guiding the program's affairs. But Sevan and OIP retained an important role in the day-to-day administration of the program and direct interaction with the government of Iraq. The Thirty-Eighth Floor had a critical role to play, but no meaningful control was exercised. The cumulative management performance of the Secretary-General and the Deputy Secretary-General fell short of the standards that the UN should strive to maintain.

THE UN-RELATED AGENCIES

Nine UN-related humanitarian agencies played key roles in carrying out the program, especially in northern Iraq, where they distributed humanitarian relief to the Kurdish people. These agencies were not formally part of the UN Secretariat. They acted in Iraq under terms that they negotiated with the UN Secretariat to govern how they would participate in the program, and their funding came through the UN Secretariat out of the approximately 2.2 percent of oil sales proceeds that were set aside for the UN's administration of the program.*

The size, structure, and nature of the program defied long-established patterns of the agencies' operations and lacked some of the more important incentives to implement projects efficiently and effectively that were present in more conventional funding arrangements. It was the largest humanitarian relief project many of the agencies ever had been involved with, and it was funded in ways that generally were novel to them. In most cases, when UN-related agencies plan an aid program, they must appeal to member states for funding. The agencies therefore have a strong incentive to implement programs effectively and efficiently. Their performance—as reflected in progress reports they must provide their donors—affects their ability to raise funds for future projects. By contrast, the agencies did not have to obtain their own funding to carry on activities for the Oil-for-Food Program. They were instead financed by income from the sale of oil by the government of Iraq, to whom the agencies were not directly responsible.

Despite operating under extremely challenging circumstances and prevailing uncertainty about how long the program would last, the agencies improved living conditions in northern Iraq by markedly reducing malnutrition and providing critical access to medical care. The agencies implemented a food distribution program, removed mines from the countryside, and increased access to electricity throughout the region. And they did so amid the kinds of Iraqi intimidation tactics and visa delays, which, as described above, were also employed against personnel of OIP and UN-Iraq.

Notwithstanding their successes, many of the agencies encountered problems when they extended their efforts to construction

---

*The discussion of UN-related agencies in this section is based on the Independent Inquiry Committee, *The Management of the Oil-for-Food Programme*, September 7, 2005, volume 4, chapter 1 ("The Cost of Administering the Programme") and chapter 4 ("The Performance of the UN-Related Agencies").

projects and rehabilitating infrastructure. These projects taxed the agencies beyond their core competencies, and they lacked the experience to execute projects they accepted. Their efforts fell victim to lack of management, coordination, and oversight by the agencies' headquarters and OIP. These failures were exacerbated by the difficult conditions faced by the agencies in Iraq.

For example, UNESCO undertook at the start of the program to build a chalk factory in Suleimaniyah governorate, ostensibly to meet the needs of school children throughout the northern governorates. It remains unclear why a chalk factory emerged as a worthy project during the first phase of what was meant to be an emergency humanitarian relief program. Nevertheless, the project advanced but was beset by delay, in large part as a result of UNESCO's decision to vest exclusive authority in a single consultant, who in turn hired a company that delivered faulty manufacturing equipment and for which there was no recourse because of the lack of warranties in the contract with the company. UNESCO violated its own procurement regulations by failing to use competitive bidding procedures to obtain this equipment. The chalk factory failed and was never fully operational.

The World Health Organization (WHO) was the lead agency for the program's health sector, and it assumed responsibility for constructing a four-hundred-bed hospital in Suleimaniyah, as well as fifteen more one-hundred-bed hospitals. After several years of planning and delays, WHO never built any of these hospitals. For the four-hundred-bed hospital, WHO spent more than $3.7 million in ultimately wasted development costs. A main reason for WHO's failure was lack of relevant experience and technical skills. Indeed, WHO's director in Iraq acknowledged that the last time WHO had built a hospital was approximately twenty to thirty years earlier, in Vietnam.

The Food and Agricultural Organization (FAO) completed several agro-industrial projects against the recommendation of OIP that it conduct advance feasibility studies to anticipate potential problems. At least four of FAO's projects—a renovation of a fruit processing plant, the construction of two dairy processing factories, and development of a sunflower oil processing factory—ended in failure because of problems such as lack of raw materials. These problems were revealed by feasibility studies that FAO commissioned only *after* the factories had been built.

A noteworthy example was the Darbandikhan Dairy Factory. Its location was selected without a thorough investigation of milk availability in the area, and FAO launched a feasibility study for the factory only after it had been built. The study found that "in Darbandikhan the milk supply is low and the demand does not exist; this district is too far away from milk producing zones and too far from the market." FAO ended up moving the plant nearer to Suleimaniyah, as recommended by the feasibility study, but at a cost of hundreds of thousands of dollars.

The United Nations Development Programme (UNDP) took primary responsibility for rehabilitating the electricity network in the three northern governorates. Its work slowed noticeably during the first two years of the program because of its decision to subcontract some of the fieldwork to the UN's Department of Economic and Social Affairs, which was essentially an advisory agency, not an implementing agency. "It was a crazy idea to take a headquarters agency previously responsible for organizing conferences and give them field contracts," noted Mark Malloch Brown, the former Executive Director of UNDP and now the UN's Deputy Secretary-General. As this and other troubles became apparent, UNDP assumed control of the electrification project's implementation in mid–1999 and far more effectively completed the rehabilitation work.

Apart from agencies taking on tasks exceeding their core competencies, some of the agencies had undefined lines of authority, poor communication among some of their departments or sections, and ineffective controls and oversight that contributed to the existence of a corruption-prone environment. Indeed, basic cash security was an issue.

Without any reliable banking system in the three northern governorates, the agencies resorted to transporting large amounts of cash from Baghdad or Amman, Jordan, and storing the cash in their offices. This created obvious targets for theft, leading to numerous investigations of incidents involving hundreds of thousands of dollars in cash that went missing from various agency offices.

The initial design and administration of the program did not give UN-Iraq sufficient authority to manage effectively the activities of the agencies. Neither Resolution 986 nor the MOU contained any guidelines for coordinating and managing the agencies. Instead, the terms of relationships were governed by ad hoc memoranda of understanding that were negotiated one by one between the UN Secretariat and each of the participating agencies. Although these various memoranda of understanding contemplated OIP's oversight of the implementation of humanitarian aid in the three northern governorates, they did not have mandatory language to require that the agencies be responsive to OIP and UN-Iraq. For reasons that are not clear, UN-Iraq did not resort to the proverbial "power of the purse"—its control over the program funds from which the agencies were being paid—to ensure better agency coordination. The agencies remained generally resistant to supervision from UN-Iraq.

Apart from these problems affecting the agencies' performance, UN accounting records revealed payments by the UN to the agencies for costs that lacked specific support or justification. First, throughout the program, the agencies were reimbursed from program funds for their *direct* costs of participating in the program. On top of this, however, the agencies also sought reimbursement for *indirect* costs known as "program support costs"—the overhead administrative costs incurred by their headquarters or other satellite offices outside of Iraq for supervision of activities in Iraq. Because these kinds of indirect costs are typically more difficult to quantify than direct support costs, they are usually reimbursed on the basis of a percentage of direct costs incurred.

The UN's Controller, Jean Pierre Halbwachs, resisted paying the agencies any program support costs, noting that the agencies were already receiving reimbursement for direct costs and that the UN Secretariat itself was not seeking reimbursement of program support costs. Halbwachs was also concerned that payments on the basis of mere estimates of overhead costs would not be consistent with the limitation of Resolution 986 that permitted use of escrow funds only for "actual expenses" incurred to administer the program. Nevertheless, under pressure from a U.S. ambassador and the Secretary-General to get the program moving, Halbwachs eventually relented and agreed in mid-1997 to allow reimbursement of the agencies for program support costs.

A continuing problem with the UN's decision to pay the agencies for their program support costs was double-counting—all of the agencies (except the World Food Programme) already included as direct costs their expenses for headquarters personnel who were assigned full-time to work on matters relating to the Oil-for-Food Program. But the calculation of program support costs did not take this into consideration; the payment formula assumed that headquarters costs were *not* subject to reimbursement as direct costs.

Nearly $102 million was paid out to the agencies from the UN's escrow account for program support costs, and this amount was about 20 percent of the $506 million expended by the agencies for direct support costs. Neither the UN nor the agencies furnished evidence that this large amount of program support costs was commensurate with the actual overhead costs that the agencies incurred to participate in the program.

More troubling was the UN's payment to agencies for expenses that they incurred in 2003 after the fall of Saddam and as the program was winding up its activities. In accordance with Security Council Resolution 1483, the UN tasked the agencies with prioritizing the outstanding program contracts and renegotiating certain terms of the contracts with suppliers. This task did not require the agencies to engage in any cost-intensive physical distribution of the goods. Rather than choosing as it had before to reimburse the agencies for direct costs and program support costs, the UN decided to pay the agencies a flat 1 percent of the value of each contract that they prioritized and renegotiated. This approach had the virtue of simplicity and easy administration. But in practice it resulted in an egregious overpayment to the agencies of nearly $50 million beyond their conceivable direct and indirect costs. After the IIC probed the UN and the agencies about this issue, the agencies promptly agreed to repay about $35 million to the Development Fund for Iraq.

ADEQUACY OF AUDITING AND INTERNAL INVESTIGATION

A significant focus of the IIC's investigation was the adequacy of auditing procedures and the degree to which more comprehensive and intensive audit procedures could have identified and redressed deficiencies in the UN's administration of the program. For the activities of the UN Secretariat, the Internal Audit Division of the Office of Internal Oversight Services (OIOS) had principal responsibility to conduct internal audits of UN operations. Two main external oversight bodies, the United Nations Board of Auditors and the Joint Inspection Unit, are in place to complement OIOS's internal oversight role.*

Admittedly, the program would have significantly challenged

---

*The discussion of program auditing and investigation activities in this section is based on the Independent Inquiry Committee, *Briefing Paper: Internal Audits of the United Nations Oil-for-Food Programme*, January 9, 2005; Independent Inquiry Committee, *Interim Report*, chapter 5; and Independent Inquiry Committee, *The Management of the Oil-for-Food Programme*, volume 3, chapter 2, 41–46 ("The Secretariat's Administration of the Programme from New York"), and volume 4, chapter 2 ("Assessment of Programme Oversight").

any internal audit department. Effective oversight required exceptional resources, firm organizational support, intensive interagency coordination, and compliance with "best practice" policies and procedures. But only five or six auditors were assigned to the program from the Internal Audit Division of OIOS. This was far fewer audit personnel in relation to the amount of expenditures than for other UN activities such as peacekeeping. Indeed, the Board of Auditors recommends twelve auditors per $1 billion of expenditures, and had this guidance been followed for the Oil-for-Food Program, then there should have been about 160 auditors for the program rather than merely five or six. Curiously, despite the significant staffing shortfalls, OIOS did not raise concerns about this issue with the UN.

Sevan's successful resistance to auditing oversight was yet another symptom of weakness in management of the program. In August 2000, the Internal Audit Division identified the program as a "high risk activity" and specifically proposed to audit the operations of the Programme Management Division. Sevan, however, derailed this initiative in May 2001, citing financial reasons and his view that the program's continuation was uncertain.

The Internal Audit Division renewed its efforts in early 2003 to audit both the Contracts and Programme Management Divisions. Sevan, however, declined to approve funding for an initial risk assessment of the Contracts Division, and the risk assessment and audit went forward only as to the Programme Management Division. The assessment detected significant risk factors relating to the program's communication and implementation procedures, and it also identified weak coordination by OIP and UN-Iraq of the UN-related agencies in Iraq and a lack of clear reporting lines.

An ensuing audit of the Programme Management Division highlighted the marginalization of that division's role to oversee the field operations of UN-Iraq and the lack of communication among Sevan, the division, and UN-Iraq. One of the auditors recalled that

Sevan was uncooperative and hostile toward the auditors to the point that his actions often "bordered on abusive."

When the audit report was ready for release in June 2003, Dileep Nair, the head of OIOS, suppressed its release because of concern that it would "hurt the United Nations" to make the criticism known. The three auditors who worked on the report could not recall any other instance in which an audit report had been suppressed from release.

Although OIOS routinely reported to the General Assembly, the utility of any audits by OIOS was impaired by the fact that OIOS could not report its findings directly to the Security Council. When OIOS sought permission in November 2000 to report to the Security Council on program-related audits, Sevan opposed it, and Fréchette then denied the request.

Because of its lean staffing, the internal auditors focused on the areas perceived as being of greatest risk: program activities in Iraq. This was to the exclusion of areas such as New York headquarters functions and the banking letter of credit processes. Of the fifty-five audits done by the Internal Audit Division, only four addressed UN headquarters functions.

Perhaps most significant of all, the Internal Audit Division did not attempt an audit of the program's contract approval process, citing concern that the activities of the 661 Committee were beyond its purview. But this abstention was erroneous, because staff of the UN Secretariat were also involved in the contract review process, including UN Secretariat employees such as the oil overseers and staff of OIP's contract processing section. Had the Internal Audit Division audited the contract review process, it may well have discovered and called attention to the lack of enforcement of the end-user provision in SOMO's contracts. Had it audited the humanitarian contract review process, it may well have raised questions about the lack of adequately trained personnel to review contracts and the lack of rigorous measures and resources to ensure the integrity of pricing reviews. Had it audited BNP's letter of credit operations, it may well have raised questions about the lack of transparency in BNP's handling of oil transactions. A thorough audit of these aspects could have uncovered or confirmed Iraq's various surcharge and kickback schemes.

Although Sevan resisted audits of his own operations, he was an advocate for external audits of the activities of the UN-related agencies in north Iraq. But plans by the Internal Audit Division to coordinate audits of these activities never materialized.

In any event, the internal audit units of individual agencies—though limited in funding and staffing and late to start—performed sixty-six audits of the agencies' program activities during the relevant years. These reports identified weaknesses in critical process areas and presented numerous recommendations for improvement. But the findings generally had little impact on strengthening the program's internal controls or improving its performance, because of deficiencies in timing, scope, funding, and reporting. Nor were the oversight activities coordinated across the program, limiting the ability of auditors and managers to identify the scale and seriousness of management issues confronting the program as a whole.

In contrast to the general auditing functions of the Internal Audit Division, the Investigations Division of OIOS is responsible for investigating reports of violations of UN regulations and assessing the potential within all program areas and UN offices worldwide for fraud and violations in high risk operations. But despite the fact that OIOS is supposed to be operationally independent from other entities in the UN, the Investigations Division must often seek funding from the relevant program manager whose program or staff it plans to investigate. During the seven years of the program, the Investigations Division received no additional budgetary or staffing resources to investigate complaints or to perform proactive assessments of fraud or corruption vulnerabilities relating to the program.

Indeed, in May 2001, Sevan quashed a request by the Investigations Division for funding to supply two investigators in Iraq. According to Sevan, the Iraqi government had complained about the large number of international staff in Iraq. It is far from surprising that of the thirty-nine program-related complaints received by the Investigations Division and for which an investigation file was opened, little investigation was actually undertaken.

The Board of Auditors was well positioned to scrutinize the program because of its complete budgetary independence. Although the size and complexity of the program increased and knowledge of its serious problems surfaced publicly, the Board of Auditors presented few serious concerns about the integrity and effectiveness of management and of the program's underlying activities.

For example, after 1999, the Board of Auditors substantially reduced its assessments of the pricing of oil and humanitarian goods contracts. Very large program areas, amounting to over $70 billion in transactions from 2000 onwards, were widely suspected of being manipulated by the Iraqi regime. When asked why it decreased its audit scope and testing of critical areas such as oil and humanitarian contracts, the Board of Auditors provided no definitive reason.

The Board of Auditors acknowledged that its audit procedures did not include testing for fraud or corruption. In the Board of Auditors' view, fraud and corruption were not relevant issues for its audits of the Iraq account. In fact, Board of Auditors officials stated that—even if they had been aware of fraudulently overpriced contracts, for example—their concern would not have been that contracts were fraudulent or overpriced. Rather, the Board of Auditors would have only addressed whether these contracts were recorded properly in the Iraq account at their full (albeit fraudulent) value and current status (i.e., whether liquidated or outstanding).

The Board of Auditors' strict emphasis on financial statement presentation appeared to conflict with the very auditing standards that it enforces. The estimated dollar amount of fraud and corruption from the program was almost $2 billion. Considering reports that the Iraqi government was extracting payments of 10 percent and higher on humanitarian contracts, the application of the Board of Auditors' materiality standards to the program would have resulted in material misrepresentations of the financial statements. Yet the Board of Auditors issued clean, unqualified opinions on all financial statements and sounded no alarms about the fraud that impugned the integrity of those finances.

Apart from the Board of Auditors, the other external audit body was the Joint Inspection Unit. It did not perform any reviews or investigations of the program.

The patchwork of auditing bodies was itself a sign of weakness in internal managerial controls. Currently there is no single coordinating mechanism within the UN organization for these various independent investigative units.

Just as some critical aspects of the program were not subject to audit, or audits were performed too late to have appropriate impact, for those parts of the program that were subject to audit, the UN did not react and take sufficient and timely corrective action. Apart from the instances cited of Sevan's noncooperation, these shortcomings were not generally caused by deliberate actions to frustrate or deny full oversight. Rather, they resulted from weaknesses in the structure, independence, professional standards, and resources of the oversight functions.

In sum, OIP management, the General Assembly, and the Security Council were not provided with audited financial statements and internal audit reports that comprehensively covered all aspects of the program and highlighted deficiencies affecting the program's effectiveness. Specifically, members of the 661 Committee themselves did not see completed audits. As with much of the UN's management of the program, the striving for secrecy signaled again a lack of transparency in UN operations and its pervasive culture of resistance to change.

APPENDIX A:

MAJOR CONCLUSIONS AND RECOMMENDATIONS

BY THE INDEPENDENT INQUIRY COMMITTEE

The following are the IIC's major conclusions and recommendations concerning the management of the Oil-for-Food Program, as reprinted from the Independent Inquiry Committee, *The Management of the United Nations Oil-for-Food Programme*, chapter 1, 63–66 (September 7, 2005).

GENERAL CONCLUSIONS

Broadly, the Committee's conclusions address the adequacy of political oversight and direction, the capacity of the Secretariat to administer its responsibilities under the Programme, the United Nations' ability to provide financial oversight and control to the Programme, and the question of persuading the entities in the United Nations' highly decentralized system to work effectively and efficiently together in an enterprise of this complexity and size.

The Committee's conclusions and recommendations are generally consonant with recommendations by others who have urged and are urging early action on United Nations reform. However the Committee cannot help but note that many of these recommendations, some of which are both detailed and holistic, have in large measure lain fallow for long periods of time, some for over a decade.

The Committee makes two contributions to the reform debate. First, the depth to which the Committee has analyzed the Programme leads uniquely to a detailed background from which the Committee's recommendations have come. Second, the Committee's analysis of the Programme confirms that reform is urgent. It suspects that the weaknesses in structure and ethic within the Programme may well be symptomatic of a wider malaise throughout the United Nations.

In short, this investigation leads to the firm belief that reform is necessary if the United Nations is to regain and retain the measure of respect among the international community that its work requires. As important, the Committee believes that action must be taken now. The urgency to pursue fundamental reform of the Organization is heightened by a sense that, in this volatile world, roughly analogous situations demanding sanctions, enforcement of sanctions, and/or humanitarian relief are more than likely to recur.

A. The Security Council Struggled

The Security Council struggled in clearly defining the broad purposes, policies, and administrative control of the Programme. Resolution 986 followed prior failed efforts to engage the Government of Iraq in an oil-for-food program. As a result, there appear to have been conflicting sentiments between treating Iraq with enough "flexibility" to get its agreement to a program and a concern to retain sufficient control that any program would not become a doorway to the clandestine reinvigoration of Iraq's ambitions for weapons of mass destruction. In the end, on one hand, far too much initiative and decision-making was left to the Iraqi regime while on the other, the Security Council took the extraordinary step of retaining, through its 661 Committee, substantial elements of administrative, and therefore operational, control. That turned out to be a recipe for the dilution of individual and institutional responsibility. When things went awry—and they did—when troublesome questions of conflict between political objectives and administrative effectiveness arose, decisions were delayed, bungled, or simply avoided—no one was in charge.

B. Administrative and Personnel Structure not Adequate

The Committee recognizes that the United Nations was faced with an extraordinary challenge, replete with conflicting political pressures, for which it was ill-equipped in terms of experience and administrative capacity.

Indeed, the Committee believes that "professional disciplines" at the United Nations are weak and eroded. As a consequence, the Secretariat, from its most senior levels, proved unable to deal effectively with the political pressures. There also appears to be a pervasive culture resistant to accountability and prone to escaping responsibility. The Secretariat was also hampered in effectively carrying out its functions under the Programme through an absence, at the time, of suitable administrative infrastructure for dealing with the sudden demands of this exceptionally large and complex "temporary" humanitarian program.

From what it has seen of the Programme's operations, the Committee considered whether the United Nations could reasonably limit operational responsibility to such areas as peacekeeping, where experience has led to the creation of some degree of permanent infrastructure. Ultimately, the Committee was convinced that, in a world where a myriad of considerations inform crises in a volatile and often violent environment, that approach would deprive the world of a needed resource.

If the United Nations is to fulfill that mission, the fault lines and flaws uncovered during the investigation clearly demand that the Organization's administrative capacity be strengthened. To this end, the Committee has made a series of recommendations, which are outlined elsewhere in this Report. The key point is that the Organization and its Secretary-General need a stronger structure at the top. A Secretary-General is, de facto, the Organization's chief political and diplomatic officer. In unsettled times, those responsibilities tend to be all consuming. The present Secretary-General, widely respected for precisely those very qualities, has regrettably been undercut by lapses in the administration of the Organization.

The United Nations Charter designates the Secretary-General as Chief Administrative Officer. But whatever the founders had in mind, the Secretary-General—any Secretary-General—has not been chosen for managerial or administrative skills, nor has he been provided with the instruments needed for strong executive control, most clearly in the area of personnel, where professional competence must compete with the political demands of member states.

A Secretary-General needs stronger support. That need has been recognized, in part, by the creation in 1998 of the new post of Deputy Secretary-General. However, the results of the investigation suggest that the role of Deputy Secretary-General as "Chief Operating Officer" must be strengthened and made more explicit. The Committee proposes that the Deputy Secretary-General be appointed by the General Assembly on the recommendation of the Security Council, as is the case with the Secretary-General. While ultimately responsible to the Secretary-General, the Chief Operating Officer should have direct authority for personnel, budgeting, and other key administrative functions with access to the Security Council and General Assembly as needed.

C. Lack of Effective Controls

Most notable among the administrative failures of the Programme was a grievous absence of effective controls and audits. In both areas, the Organization has in recent years worked to develop competence, but it has been from a standing start. The Oil-for-Food Programme exemplified the weakness of planning, the lack of adequate funding, and the paucity of manpower, even after the Programme went on and on. As important structurally was a palpable absence of authority and clear, if any, reporting lines, especially to the Secretariat's senior management. As a consequence, needed independence was lost. Line managers could and did divert auditing initiatives, and follow-up to critical findings was erratic at best.

D. Instances of Corruption Reflect Control Weaknesses

The instances of corruption detailed in the Committee Reports— corruption that reached to the top of the Programme management— are an important reflection of control weaknesses. The Committee's concern is that these influences are symptomatic of an absence of a strong institutional ethic—an ethic that should reflect the unique and crucial role of the United Nations system in exemplifying and encouraging the highest standards in which corrosive corruption— private and public—has been far too common. The General Assembly, Security Council, and Secretariat have been insufficiently conscious of the serious risks posed by not enforcing ethical standards, both to the Organization's credibility and to its internal morale.

E. Lack of Inter-Agency Coordination

The particular nature of the Oil-For-Food Programme placed in stark relief the difficulties of effective cooperation across the Agencies. There was and is no simple way accurately to track Programme expenditures across agency lines. The presumption of central budget authority was not matched by an ability to assess actual spending (much less the effectiveness of spending), or to insist on common accounting standards or treatment. Clearly, the demand for inter-agency action inherent in the Oil-for-Food Programme was exceptional. Arguably, such demands are unlikely to be repeated in so dramatic a fashion. But surely the difficulties perceived should not be tolerated in lesser programs.

MAJOR RECOMMENDATIONS

A. Create the Position of Chief Operating Officer

Create the position of Chief Operating Officer ("COO"). The COO would have authority over all aspects of administration and would be appointed by the General Assembly on the recommendation of the Security Council. The position would report to the Secretary-General, and the United Nations Charter should be amended as appropriate.

Creation of this position would serve to better insulate United Nations administrators from political pressures distorting management decisions. It would provide sufficient authority for effective management discipline and would free the Secretary-General of some of the duties inherent in the role of the chief administrative officer.

B. Strengthen Independence of Oversight and Auditing

Establish an Independent Oversight Board ("IOB") with a majority of independent members and an independent chairman. In discharging its mandate, the IOB should have functional responsibility for all audit, investigation, and evaluation activities, both internal and external, across the United Nations Secretariat and agencies substantially funded by the United Nations and whose leadership is appointed by the Secretary-General. The IOB should be particularly concerned with overseeing and monitoring:

1. Implementation of risk-based planning across the United Nations system;

2. Implementation of oversight, audit, and investigation best practices;

3. Implementation of a consistent framework for assessing findings and recommendations and bringing significant oversight issues to the attention of the Secretary-General/Director Generals and the General Assembly/Governing Bodies;

4. Investigations and improvements in the ethics and integrity of the Organization; and

5. The efficiency and effectiveness of the oversight function.

In the interests of transparency, there should be annual disclosure from the IOB to the General Assembly of the planned audit coverage and the actual results of oversight activity. IOB oversight reports should be publicly accessible. The IOB should consult with and coordinate as appropriate with all UN-related agencies.

C. Improve Coordination and the Oversight Framework for Cross-Agency Programs

The Programme demonstrated the need for significant improvements in the oversight of cross-agency programs, particularly regarding common principles, planning, transparent financials, and resources. The IOB should provide the needed coordination.

1. Establish high level coordinating bodies for all major cross-agency relief and emergency programs and provide them with real decision making ability, agreed to by all participating entities; these coordinating bodies should be empowered to set, implement, and enforce principles and policies;

2. Improve the following aspects of cross-agency programs by:
   - Promulgating, subject to audit, appropriate policies and procedures;
   - Documenting processes for rapid deployment and rapid response projects identifying areas of risk and applicable critical controls necessary to be in place to mitigate exposure; and
   - Developing standard audit plans for programs;

3. Ensure that each program has consolidated financial statements that are subject to external and internal audit; and

4. Make sufficient oversight resources available immediately and integrate them into the management and implementation of a new program. Mandate the creation of a rapid deployment audit program with investigatory presence ("rapid integrity") that allows oversight to begin at the inception of a new program.

D. Reform and Improve Management Performance

Strong and effective leadership and management is essential to the success of the United Nations' mission. There is a need for the United Nations to strengthen the quality of its management and management practices. To this end:

1. Improve the scope and quality of the internal management review processes by mandating periodic, high-level executive reviews against clear objectives of all major initiatives and activities;

2. Ensure that senior management and professional staff adhere to the highest standards of accountability and transparency in their performance, and remove those who do not meet these performance requirements;

3. Seek opportunities for peer review of management performance; and

4. Overhaul the management hiring, promotion, evaluation, and reward methodology basing each on key tasks, and agreed measures of performance.

E. Expand Conflict-of-Interest and Financial Disclosure Requirements

The financial disclosure requirement must extend well below the current Assistant Secretary-General level within the Organization and should also specifically include the Secretary-General and the Deputy Secretary-General. Financial disclosure requirements must include all United Nations staff who have any decision-making role in the disbursement or award of United Nations funds (e.g., Procurement Department, Office of the Controller).

A strong financial disclosure program is an integral part of creating an institutional culture that recognizes and understands actual, potential, and apparent conflicts of interest. The United Nations' conflict-of-interest rules and regulations need to be expanded and better defined so that they encompass actual, potential, and apparent conflicts of interest.

F. Cost Recovery

The Committee recognizes that fair compensation to third parties is necessary to enable the United Nations to complement its core resources with competent outside specialists, such as the Agencies. However, the United Nations should ensure that such compensation does not result in egregious profits. Agencies involved in the Programme should return up to $50 million in excess compensation secured as a result of work performed under Security Council Resolution 1483.

Appendix B:

About the Independent Inquiry Committee

As the Oil-for-Food Program was ending and after the fall of the regime of Saddam Hussein in early 2003, there arose substantial public allegations of corruption and mismanagement of the program. To address these questions, UN Secretary-General Kofi Annan created a three-person Independent Inquiry Committee (IIC) to conduct a thorough review of the program's administration and the allegations of corruption and maladministration. On April 21, 2004, the Security Council unanimously passed Resolution 1538, welcoming the Secretary-General's formation of the IIC and calling upon member states to assist in the inquiry.

The chairman of the IIC was Paul A. Volcker, former chairman of the U.S. Federal Reserve. A second member was Richard J. Goldstone, former justice of the South African Supreme Court and Chief Prosecutor of the UN International Criminal Tribunals for the former Yugoslavia and Rwanda. The third member was Mark Pieth, professor of Criminal Law and Criminology of the University of Basel in Switzerland, who is a leading expert in combating international corruption and chair of the Organization for Economic Cooperation and Development (OECD) Working Group on Bribery in International Business Transactions.

The IIC's investigative staff included more than seventy-five persons from twenty-eight countries, with a wide variety of professional backgrounds, including accountants, attorneys, and former law enforcement personnel. The staff was headquartered in New York and stationed at small offices in Paris and Baghdad.

The IIC's investigation was unprecedented. There has never been an investigation of similar breadth and intensity into the internal workings of the UN, the related activities of its member states, and the conduct of thousands of private company contractors that participated in the Oil-for-Food Program. All UN staff were compelled by the Secretary-General to cooperate fully with the IIC's investigation. More than 1,100 persons were interviewed in dozens of countries throughout Africa, Asia, Australia, Europe, North America, and South America. More than 13 million pages of documents were collected and reviewed. These documents came mostly from UN archives but also from scores of countries, banks, telephone companies, and program contractors all over the world. The IIC's investigators conducted numerous interviews in Iraq and also obtained extensive records from the government of Iraq, including records from the Ministry of Oil, the State Oil Marketing Organization (SOMO), and other Iraqi ministries that took part in the program's activities.

The IIC's investigation was independent. Its investigative methods, reports, and conclusions were not subject to the supervision of the UN, member states, or any third party. The IIC incurred investigation costs of approximately $36 million from April 2004 through the end of 2005. These costs were funded by unspent monies from the sale of Iraqi oil under the Oil-for-Food Program. (Subsequent reimbursement payments by UN-related agencies as a result of the IIC's investigation have substantially offset the IIC's cost of investigation.)

The IIC issued numerous reports and briefing papers throughout the tenure of its investigation. Except as otherwise noted, the facts recounted in this book are drawn from more than two thousand pages of narratives and tables set forth in the IIC's reports and briefing papers. Footnotes in each chapter reflect the portions of reports from which each chapter is derived. Readers who wish to know more about the events set forth in this book should refer to copies of the IIC's full reports, which may be obtained at the IIC's website: *http://www.iic-offp.org.*

Consistent with the IIC's reports, this book recounts and at times criticizes the conduct of certain UN officials, governments, and private parties that took part in the Oil-for-Food Program. Additional information on the conduct of these parties and many of their statements and responses to the IIC can be found in the IIC's full reports.

In offering this account of what went wrong with the Oil-for-Food Program, the authors do not call into question the general success of the program in furnishing vital relief to the people of Iraq during the UN sanctions regime. Moreover, a great many UN staff members, governments, and private parties performed their responsibilities with devotion and diligence amid considerable challenges posed by dealing with the former government of Iraq.

The Independent Inquiry Committee
and Staff List

The Committee

Paul A. Volcker, Chairman
Richard J. Goldstone, Member
Mark Pieth, Member

Senior Management

Reid Morden, Executive Director
Mark G. Califano, Chief Legal Counsel
Michael T. Cornacchia, Chief Investigative Counsel
Frank E. Hydoski, Chief of Forensics
Susan M. Ringler, Counsel to the Committee

Staff

Pauline Agumba, Administrative Assistant
Gemma Aiolfi, Special Assistant to Mark Pieth
Robert M. Allyn, Administrative Assistant

Ahmed Amer, Translator
Robert M. Appleton, Special Counsel
Zainab Aziz, Research Assistant
Hagop A. Baboujian, Investigator/Analyst
Maria A. Barton, Senior Counsel
Manisha Bharti, Senior Investigator
Philip A. Binder, Administrative Assistant
Emily S. Bolton, Investigator/Analyst
Nada Teresa Bouari, Investigator/Analyst
Bwalya Chilufya, Finance Associate
Carla J. Clark, Special Counsel
Kevin Curtis, Team Leader
Miranda Duncan, Deputy Counsel
John J. Durham, Deputy Counsel
Chris Eaton, Senior Investigator
Mary E. Eaton, Data Management Coordinator
Janet L. Engel, Senior Investigator
Jocelene D. Fouassier, Administrative Assistant, Paris Office
Harald Friedl, Analyst
John K. Gauthier, Senior Investigator
Beth I. Goldman, Research Analyst
Alistair Graham, Senior Investigator
Jeremy Griffiths, Forensic Accountant
Daniel E. Guerrini, Senior Investigator
Peter D. Hackshaw, Senior Investigator
Philippe Heinrichs, IT Manager
Barry A. Hogan, Senior Investigator
Nadim Houry, Deputy Counsel
Larry D. Kaiser, Senior Investigator
Andrew G. Kalashnik, Investigator/Analyst
Laurent Kasper-Ansermet, Head of Paris Office
Patrick J. Kelkar, Senior Analyst
W. Michael Kramer, Senior Investigator

Gabriele Lechenauer, Investigator/Analyst
Zora Ledergerber, Special Assistant to Mark Pieth
Andrew M. Levine, Deputy Counsel
Alasdair Macleod, Analyst
Marc Maisto, Senior Investigator
M. Shervin Majlessi, Deputy Counsel
Dean P. Manning, Senior Investigator
Bernard C. Marino, Senior Investigator
Michelle R. Meredith, Research Assistant
Jeffrey A. Meyer, Senior Counsel
Brian J. Mich, Senior Counsel
Richard P. Mika, Senior Investigator
Tshikaji Muleba-Sabwa, Finance Associate
Karen H. Naimer, Deputy Counsel
Eugenia Nalbatian, Senior Analyst
Momar Lissa Ndiaye, Senior Analyst
Genevieve Noundja-Noubissi, Controller
Hellen M. Nyabera, Data Management Officer
Bernard P. O'Donnell, Senior Investigator
Simeon Obidairo, Senior Analyst
Nadine Okla, Administrative Assistant
Monika Ora, Investigator/Analyst
Leanard Philip, Data Management Associate
Maya Prabhu, Deputy Counsel
Sandra A. Rutkowski, Executive Assistant to the Chairman
Shirin Sabri, Investigator/Analyst
Debbie L. Santalesa, Senior Analyst
Bridget M. Santiago, Administrative Assistant
Alan C. Schick, Senior Investigator
Wolf-Dieter Schlechthaupt, Senior Banking Expert, Europe
Gerard Sexton, Senior Investigator
Alan C. Schick, Senior Investigator
Aleksandr N. Shapovalov, Deputy Counsel

Gregory A. Shultz, Investigator/Analyst
Brett G. Simpson, Team Leader
Brian E. Spears, Senior Counsel
Thomas H. Steenvoorden, Senior Investigator
Jonathan M. Struggles, Deputy Counsel
Trevor C. Sutton, Investigator/Analyst
Philip Trewhitt, Head of Baghdad Office
Todd Trivett, Team Leader
Lodewijk A.P. Gualtherie van Weezel, Investigator/Analyst
Khaled Zaid, Translator
Stephen S. Zimmermann, Interim Chief-of-Staff

UNITED NATIONS STAFF ON LOAN

Dara Lysaght, Administrative Management Officer
Constance Samuel, Associate Administrative Officer
Kagure Karanu, Administrative Assistant

ADVISORS TO THE COMMITTEE

John M. Hennessey, Special Advisor
Walter McCormack, Special Advisor
Richard W. Murphy, Special Advisor

SECONDMENT FROM THE FEDERAL RESERVE BANK OF NY

Sean M. O'Malley, Senior Investigative Officer

INTERNS

Ross Banon
Lauren E. Baer
Patrick J. Dooley
Jane Okpala
Ari Simon
Alisa Valderama

CONSULTANTS

Deloitte Financial Advisory Services LLP

Mary Jane Schirber, Partner
Samir Hans, Senior Manager
Anthony DeSantis, Manager
Michael Wudke, Manager
Eric Baca, Manager
Michael Rossen, Manager
Justin Gallagher, Senior Consultant
Todd Swint, Senior Consultant
Bob Dillen, Senior Consultant
Tae S. Choe, Senior Consultant
Jared Crafton, Senior Consultant
Mahdi Bseiso, Associate Consultant

Dispute Analytics LLC

Jean-Michel Ferat, Senior Manager
Todd Nelson, Senior Manager
Natalie Taplin-Hall, Manager

Emily Kim, Senior Associate
Marni Wills, Associate

Glasgow Forensic Group LLC

David Wolfe, Managing Director
Deidra DenDanto, Director
Meena Marwaha, Senior Consultant
Viren Patel, Senior Consultant

About the Authors

PAUL A. VOLCKER, who wrote the Introduction to this book, served as Chairman of the Independent Inquiry Committee into the United Nations Oil-for-Food Programme. Among his many prior positions in public service, he was Chairman of the Board of Governors of the United States Federal Reserve System from 1979 to 1987. He also led an international committee established to investigate the Swiss bank accounts of victims of the Nazi holocaust. Until recently, he served as Chairman of the Board of Trustees of the International Accounting Standards Committee, overseeing a renewed effort to develop consistent, high-quality accounting standards acceptable in all countries. He is a graduate of Princeton University, Harvard University, and the London School of Economics. He lives in New York City.

JEFFREY A. MEYER (*jeffreyameyer@gmail.com*) served as Senior Counsel to the Independent Inquiry Committee into the Oil-for-Food Programme and chief editor of the Committee's reports. He previously served for nine years as a federal criminal prosecutor with the U.S. Department of Justice, where he specialized in the prosecution of financial fraud, environmental, and civil rights crimes, as well as in criminal and civil appellate practice. He is a graduate of Yale College and Yale Law School. He is currently an Associate Professor of Law at Quinnipiac University School of Law in Connecticut.

MARK G. CALIFANO (*markcalifano@gmail.com*) served as the Chief Legal Counsel of the Independent Inquiry Committee into the Oil-for-Food Programme. He was responsible for supervision of the Committee staff and led many of the major aspects of the Committee's investigation. He previously served for twelve years as a federal criminal prosecutor for the U.S. Department of Justice, where he specialized in complex financial fraud, corruption, and international criminal investigations and prosecutions. He is a graduate of Princeton University and Duke University School of Law. He lives in Connecticut with his family.

ACKNOWLEDGMENTS

The narrative of this book is drawn from a series of reports issued last year by the Independent Inquiry Committee (IIC). The reports were the product of the extraordinary efforts of an extremely dedicated staff of more than seventy professionals, investigators, accountants, analysts and experts, drawn from around the world to work together for a period of just over eighteen months. The IIC staff went to great lengths to find and interview witnesses and recover records and documents, at times putting themselves at great physical risk. They diligently assembled, edited, reviewed, and verified complex information that comprises the reports issued by the IIC. They worked well together over long hours, despite months without a break, assembling the final reports in September and October 2005.

None of the IIC's work would have been possible without the dedication and leadership of the three Committee members, Chairman Paul A. Volcker, Justice Richard J. Goldstone, and Professor Mark Pieth, as well as Executive Director Reid Morden. Each of them unflaggingly directed and supported the efforts of the staff to go wherever necessary in the UN, its agencies, and in the dozens of jurisdictions where evidence was sought. At various times each of them supported the efforts of the staff to continue the investigation even in the face of roadblocks from some governments, companies, and other individuals who were subject to investigation.

Several former staff of the Committee read all or parts of the manuscript for this book, including Committee Counsel Susan Ringler, Chief Forensic Accountant Frank Hydoski (now with Deloitte & Touche), Deloitte & Touche Partner Mary Jane Schirber, Special Counsel Robert Appleton, Senior Counsel Brian Spears, Deputy Counsel Andrew M. Levine, Deputy Counsel Karen Naimer, and Investigator/Analyst Trevor C. Sutton. We are especially grateful to Frank Hydoski, Andrew Levine, and Susan Ringler for their detailed and thoughtful advice, comments, and suggestions.

Tony Miodonka, a law student at Quinnipiac University Law School, performed invaluable cite checking and verification services. Sandra Rutkowski coordinated meetings and graciously collected and assembled additional reports for our work on the manuscript.

We were very fortunate to have the advice and assistance of Peter Osnos, Susan Weinberg, and Clive Priddle at PublicAffairs, who were kind enough to take this project on and help us through its initial stages and an expedited publication. Clive Priddle patiently and carefully reviewed our manuscript and offered invaluable guidance. We also appreciate the diligent copyedit work of Beth Wright and the production editing of Melissa Raymond.

We owe special thanks to our families for the sacrifice of their time and effort that allowed us to prepare this book. Our wives, Linda Meyer and Margery Feinzig, have full-time careers of their own and patiently tolerated yet more months of late nights and tables covered with dog-eared copies of IIC reports as we prepared this book. Our children, Cara and Zane Meyer, and Olivia and Nicholas Califano, would have rather played with us than watch us typing away on our home computers. And we thank our parents, who raised us to believe in the value of public service and hard work.

The authors have agreed that all royalties owing to the authors from the publication and sale of this book (except for reimbursement to the authors of the direct, out-of-pocket expenses incurred by them in connection with this book) will be donated to Relief International (*www.ri.org*) for the benefit of humanitarian assistance to the people of Iraq.

Jeffrey A. Meyer and Mark G. Califano

NOTES

Chapter 1: Destined for Corruption

1. "The Iraqi Invasion; 'One Who Confronts,'" *New York Times*, August 4, 1990; Iraq Foundation, "Biography of Saddam Hussein of Tikrit," http://www.iraqfoundation.org/research/bio.html; "Saddam Hussein al-Tikriti Biography," IraqiNews.com, http://www.iraqinews.com/people_saddam.shtml.
2. Michael R. Gordon, "Army Invades Capital of Kuwait in Fierce Fighting," *New York Times*, August 2, 1990; R. W. Apple Jr., "Invading Iraqis Seize Kuwait and Its Oil," *New York Times*, August 3, 1990.

Chapter 2: Politics and Perfidy in Procurement

1. "Former U.N. Procurement Officer Pleads Guilty to Federal Charges Arising from his Receipt of Hundreds of Thousands of Dollars from Foreign Companies Doing Business with the U.N.," Press Release, United States Attorney's Office for the Southern District of New York, August 8, 2005; Warren Hoge, "U.N. Looking at Charges of Fraud in Procurement," *New York Times*, January 24, 2006.
2. Lloyd's activities in Aqaba are described in a report of the Independent Inquiry Committee, *The Management of the Oil-for-Food Programme*, vol. 2, September 7, 2005, 204–6.

Chapter 3: Son of the Secretary-General

1. William Hall and Jimmy Burns, "SGS Quits Group Linked to Bhutto," *Financial Times*, October 4, 1997, 3.
2. John F. Burns, "House of Graft: Tracing the Bhutto Millions—A Spe-

cial Report: Bhutto Clan Leaves Trail of Corruption," *New York Times*, January 9, 1998, A1.

3. Jimmy Burns and Frances Williams, "Swiss Judge to Indict Benazir Bhutto," *Financial Times*, June 4, 1998. Notwithstanding the newspaper's use of the term "indictment," the matter against Robert Massey was the initiation of a formal investigation and prosecution inquest of Robert Massey, but without the filing of a formal accusatory charge. Accordingly, the authors refer to the proceedings against Robert Massey as an investigation.

4. Downes-Thomas's refusal is confirmed from an IIC investigator who spoke with him to request contact information.

5. It is not known if there were more calls than reflected in Kojo's cell phone records. The IIC did not have records from the UN of calls placed from the procurement department during the fall of 1998. A one-minute call from Kojo's cell phone could, in theory, have been followed by a call back from the UN. Nor did the IIC have records from any other phones used by Kojo during the fall of 1998 or phone records of other persons (such as Dias, Mills-Aryee, Wilson, and the Masseys) of telephone calls placed by them during the bidding process.

6. "Annan's Son to Repay Duty on Mercedes," CNN.com, January 25, 2006, http://www.cnn.com/2006/WORLD/africa/01/24/annan.car/index.html.

Chapter 4: Saddam's Slush Fund

1. Russian News and Information Agency Novosti, "Flamboyant Party Leader Zhirinovsky to Turn 60 with Kremlin Bash," April 25, 2006.

2. Daily Press Briefing of Office of Spokesman for Secretary-General, February 16, 1999.

3. Lally Weymouth, "The Saddam Lobby," *The Washington Post*, May 8, 1994, C7 (stating that, according to United States intelligence sources, Pasqua was "coaching the Iraqis behind the scenes" about ending sanctions).

4. Al-Chalabi's role as a nominee for Galloway is identified through the interview of Tariq Aziz by investigators from the U.S. Senate Permanent Subcommittee on Investigations, and in a review of SOMO allocation tables. *Report Concerning the Testimony of George Galloway Before the Permanent Subcommittee on Investigations: Majority Staff*

Report, October 25, 2005, 10 (citing interview of Tariq Aziz on July 7, 2005), and 21 (citing SOMO Allocation Table of January 6, 2000).

5. The figures and descriptions of payments and transfers of oil proceeds from the IIC report have been augmented with the review of bank records conducted by the staff of the U.S. Senate Permanent Subcommittee on Investigations. *Report Concerning the Testimony of George Galloway*, October 25, 2005, 25–36 (reviewing commissions received by Zureikat from Taurus and payments of oil sales proceeds made from various accounts used by Zureikat to the Mariam Appeal).

6. The amounts received in accounts in Dr. Abu Zayyad's name include over $120,000 received from Delta in the first half of 2000 and a transfer of about $150,000 from Zureikat's Citibank account on August 3, 2000. On that same date Zureikat transferred $340,000 to the Mariam Appeal account at Lloyds TSB and $15,666 to an account in Ron McKay's name. *Report Concerning the Testimony of George Galloway*, October 25, 2005, 30. In response to the U.S. Congressional interrogatories, Dr. Abu Zayyad stated that she had never solicited or received from anyone any proceeds of any oil deals, either for herself or her former husband. Ibid., 28.

7. Hari Kumar, "Indian Minister Stripped of Post Amid Charges of Kickbacks," *New York Times*, November 8, 2005; "Minister in Oil-for-Food Scandal Quits," *New York Times*, December 7, 2005; Murali Krisman, "Oil-for-Food Scam: No Progress in Pathak Probe," *Hindustan Times*, April 25, 2006.

8. Statement of Mikhail Kamynin, Spokesman for Russia Ministry of Foreign Affairs, April 6, 2006, available on website of Permanent Mission of Russia to the United Nations, http://www.un.int/russia/runews/060406/060406.htm#en-apr.

9. Julia Preston and Simon Romero, "Oilman Charged with Kickbacks to Iraqi Regime," *New York Times*, October 22, 2005 (describing charges against Oscar Wyatt); Julia Preston and Judith Miller, "Texan Is Indicted in Iraqi Oil Sales by Hussein Aides," *New York Times*, April 15, 2005 (describing charges against Chalmers).

10. Julia Preston, "U.S. Company Admits Oil-for-Food Bribes," *New York Times*, October 21, 2005.

Chapter 5: Kickbacks-for-Contracts

1. Raymond Bonner, "Australian Panel Focuses on Possible Government Role in Bribes and Kickbacks in Iraq," *New York Times*, February 3, 2006; Raymond Bonner, "Australian Testifies on Wheat Company's Payments to Hussein," *New York Times*, February 4, 2006; "AWB Chief Quits Over Iraq Probe," *BBC News*, February 9, 2006; Raymond Bonner, "Australian Chief Denies Seeing Cables on Payoffs," *New York Times*, April 14, 2006.

Chapter 6: Stumbling in the Security Council

1. James Norman, "Petrodollars," *Platts Oilgram News*, November 17, 1998.
2. Adam Zagorin, "Our Man In Baghdad: Saddam's Demise Could Actually Hurt his Oil-Producing Neighbors," *Time International*, November 30, 1998.
3. Robert Corzine and Paul Solmon, "The Iraqi Crisis—Doubt Cast on Oil-for-Food Programme," *Financial Times*, December 18, 1998, 3.
4. U.S. Senate Permanent Subcommittee on Investigations Minority Staff, *Report on Illegal Surcharges on Oil-for-Food Contracts and Illegal Oil Shipments from Khor al-Amaya*, May 17, 2005, 55 (quoting February 20, 2003, 12:38 p.m. e-mail from Tsakos Hellas to Petrian Shipbrokers and Odin Marine).
5. A few days later, Boks e-mailed OIP Executive Director Benon Sevan and told Sevan that the *Argosea* had just loaded at Khor al-Amaya and that a number of other tankers were to lift oil from the terminal as well. Ibid., 52 (quoting February 18, 2003, 5:37 p.m. e-mail from Peter Boks to Benon Sevan).
6. Ibid., 53 (citing February 20, 2003, 12:38 p.m. e-mail from Tsakos Hellas [owner of *Argosea*] to Petrian Shipbrokers and Odin Marine, and February 24, 2003, 5:51 p.m. e-mail from Odin Marine to Jamil Sayegh, Shaheen Business Investment Group Holdings).
7. Alix M. Freedman and Bhusan Bahree, "Iraq is Shipping Large Cargoes of Crude, Violating UN Rules," *The Wall Street Journal*, February 21, 2003, A1.
8. U.S. Senate Permanent Subcommittee on Investigations Minority Staff, *Report on Illegal Surcharges on Oil-for-Food Contracts and Il-*

legal Oil Shipments from Khor al-Amaya, May 17, 2005, 54 (citing a transcript of a U.S. State Department briefing by spokesperson Richard Boucher, US Fed News, January 13, 2005).

9. Ibid., 59 (quoting February 25, 2003, 2:11 p.m. e-mail from Millennium to Michael Richards, Odin Marine).

10. Ibid. (quoting March 3, 2003, Note to File by David Young, Odin Marine).

11. Ibid., 56–58 (quoting February 21, 2003, 3:56 p.m. e-mail from Odin Marine to Petrian Shipbrokers [forwarding Millennium messages]).

12. Ibid. (quoting February 28, 2003, 7:58 p.m. e-mail from Odin Marine to Silver Line, Ltd. [forwarding Millennium message]).

13. Ibid., 63–68.

14. Ibid., 57 (quoting March 4, 2003, 3:55 p.m. e-mail from Odin Marine General Counsel Howard Jaffe to Michael Richards).

15. "Iraq and Syria Agree to Reopen Oil Pipeline in November," *Middle East Economic Survey*, November 6, 2000 (noting that the article was "text of the MEES News Flash released on 31 October"); Axel Busch, "Iraq Said To Have Started Filling Line To Syria," *Energy Intelligence Briefing*, November 20, 2000; "Iraq starts illegal oil sales to Syria," *Reuters News*, November 21, 2000; "UK urges Syria to make Iraq oil purchases legal," *Reuters News*, November 21, 2000.

16. Barbara Crossette, "Iraq is Running Payoff Racket, U.N. Aides Say," *New York Times*, March 7, 2001, A1.

17. Edith M. Lederer, "Iraq Reported to Demand Illegal Kickbacks on Humanitarian Goods," *Associated Press*, March 7, 2001; William M. Reilly, "U.S.: No Surprise Report Iraqis Seek Payoffs," *United Press International*, March 7, 2001; United States Mission to the United Nations, "Transcript of Remarks by Ambassador James B. Cunningham, Acting U.S. Permanent Representative to the United Nations, on the Oil-for-Food Program, at the Security Council Stake-Out, March 8, 2001," http://www.un.int/usa/01_034.htm; Associated Press, "Iraq is Demanding Illegal Payoffs on Humanitarian Goods, U.N. Says—'No Hard Evidence' That Firms Are Paying Surcharges to Iraqi Government," *Wall Street Journal Europe*, March 8, 2001, p. 2.

Chapter 7: "The Story Will Quickly Turn Negative"

1. William M. Reilly, "Inquiry Critical on UN & Oil for Food," *United*

Press International, February 3, 2005; Claudia Rosett, "I Am Not Running Away: Meet Benon Sevan, the Man at the Center of the Oil for Food Scandal," *WSJ.com Opinion Journal*, April 1, 2006, http://www.opinionjournal.com/editorial/feature.html?id=110008172.

INDEX